Buying & Selling Antiques and Collectibles on eBay®

Pamela Y. Wiggins

THOMSON

COURSE TECHNOLOGY™

Professional ■ Trade ■ Reference

ISBN: 1-59200-499-7
Library of Congress Catalog Card Number: 2004106454
Printed in the United States of America
04 05 06 07 08 BH 10 9 8 7 6 5 4 3 2 1

THOMSON

COURSE TECHNOLOGY
Professional ■ Trade ■ Reference

Thomson Course Technology PTR,
a division of Thomson Course Technology
25 Thomson Place
Boston, MA 02210
http://www.courseptr.com

SVP, Thomson Course Technology PTR:
Andy Shafran

Publisher:
Stacy L. Hiquet

Senior Marketing Manager:
Sarah O'Donnell

Marketing Manager:
Heather Hurley

Manager of Editorial Services:
Heather Talbot

Associate Acquisitions Editor:
Megan Belanger

Senior Editor:
Mark Garvey

Associate Marketing Managers:
Kristin Eisenzopf and
Sarah Dubois

Developmental Editor:
Kate Shoup Welsh

Technical Reviewer:
Judith Katz-Schwartz

Thomson Course Technology PTR Market Coordinator:
Amanda Weaver

Interior Layout Tech:
Shawn Morningstar

Cover Designers:
Joel Sadagursky and
Mike Tanamachi

Indexer:
Kelly Talbot

Proofreader:
Kim Benbow

*To my loving husband, Bob,
and my inspiring mother, Eva Paschal*

Acknowledgments

I've often said that writing this book has been an arduous albeit rewarding process, and every word of that statement is true. I've leaned on more than a few people for support along the way, and they've all come through for me with more encouragement than I could have ever hoped for. From my husband, Bob, who taught me the Internet ropes so many years ago and encouraged me to write in the first place, to my friends and other family members who spurred me on with their excitement for the project and, most importantly, with their love and friendship. This includes my mother, Eva Paschal, who let me tag along with her going to flea markets and garage sales when I was a just a wide-eyed kid, teaching me so much about buying and selling antiques along the way.

I couldn't have asked for a better crew to work with than the folks at Thomson Course Technology either. Kate Shoup Welsh, editor extraordinaire, pointed me in the right direction over and over again to produce a great book to share with other antiquers, and Judith Katz-Schwartz shared her time and expertise on the topic of eBay and the antiques business as my technical editor to make my work even stronger. A big thanks to Megan Belanger, too, for being a great cheerleader as well as the superb acquisitions editor who approached me about putting this book together in the first place.

And lastly, but certainly not least, a big thanks to Barb Doyen, my agent, for helping me to navigate uncharted waters as a first-time author and providing words of encouragement when I really needed them.

About the Author

PAMELA Y. WIGGINS has been a collector since childhood when she first learned about antiques and collectibles in her mother's shop. Her personal collections include vintage costume jewelry, Depression glass, vintage Barbie dolls, vintage Halloween and Santa postcards, Texas Centennial collectibles, and a host of other interesting odds and ends.

As the antiques guide for About.com, Pamela has shared her knowledge of the Internet and collecting with her users since 1999. Her feature articles and columns on antiques-related topics have appeared in magazines and newspapers nationwide, including *Antiques & Collecting Magazine*. Pamela has also been seen and heard on a number of radio and television broadcasts as an antiques expert. She has completed the International Society of Appraisers core courses in appraisal studies, and holds a bachelor's degree in journalism with magazine specialization from the University of Texas at Austin.

Pamela sells antiques and collectibles at the Austin Antique Mall in Austin, Texas, on her Web site Chic Antiques (http://www.chicantiques.com) established in 1995, and on eBay as www.chicantiques since 1996. She has also been known to set up at shows when time permits, including the legendary City Wide Garage Sale in Austin.

In her "free" time, when she's not surfing eBay, maintaining Web sites, writing about antiques, or doing public-relations work for a non-profit organization (her day job), Pamela coordinates the Austin Vintage Jewelry Club for area collectors. She also participates in VFCJ, a national organization for costume jewelry collectors, and encourages others to hook up with similar organizations relating to their personal collecting interests.

Originally from Houston, Pamela now resides in Round Rock, Texas, with her husband, Bob, and one very spoiled dog named Robin who keeps her company while she's writing.

Contents at a Glance

Contents

Chapter 9 Titles, Descriptions, Photos, and More 189

Chapter 10 Setting Your Starting Price, Understanding eBay's Fees, and Creating a Basic Listing 209

Chapter 11 Managing and Completing the Sale 251

Introduction

You know what they say: "Necessity is the mother of invention." That explains why when Pierre Omidyar and his girlfriend needed to sell her Pez collection, Pierre invented an auction program to enable them to unload the dispensers online. Legend has it, from those humble beginnings, auction giant eBay was born.

Incredibly, in the mid-1990s, my husband, who works as a software engineer, also built an auction program to sell—of all things—Pez dispensers. A friend of ours had found a big box of 1960s footless dispensers in her attic the previous year, and we all figured we could turn a tidy profit for her by selling them online. We lured customers to our auction site through advertisements in news-groups (Usenet was the in thing for online collectors back then); once they started using our online auction device, they were hooked.

Unfortunately, my husband and I didn't have the foresight to continue work-ing on our auction software. Who knows? Maybe we could have given eBay a run for its money. Over the years, though, I *have* continued to sell collectibles—and antiques—online. In fact, I've been buying and selling on eBay since 1996, an eternity in Internet years. And through it all, I've learned a thing or two, which is why I wrote this book.

I know what you're thinking: There are loads of eBay books out there. How is this one different? I'll tell you: In addition to the step-by-step information you'll need to get started buying and selling on eBay, you'll also find lots of information on antiques and collectibles that just don't crop up in other eBay guides. I've gathered the tidbits I share in this book over a lifetime of collecting; indeed, my career as an antiques and collectibles enthusiast began when I was about eight years old. I used to tag along with my mother to flea markets and garage sales, looking for old stuff she could sell in *her* antiques shop. As we nosed around, I asked lots of questions, and she answered them.

I was able to parlay this knowledge I gleaned from my mother—and from my own studies of antiques and collectibles—into a career writing about buying and selling antiques and collectibles. I've written magazine features on various collecting topics, and even a weekly newspaper column, "Collection Connection," that ran in a number of Central Texas newspapers for four years. Eventually, I signed on as the antiques guide at About.com, and I've been answering people's questions about antiques and collectibles—and about buying and selling them online—ever since. In short, I know what types of questions people have about using eBay, and I know how to answer them.

After you finish reading this book, you will too.

What You'll Find in This Book

Learning to register, buy, and sell on eBay is easy with the step-by-step instructions included in this guide. But getting into the details that really make your eBay experience more enjoyable or more profitable can help everyone, from the neophyte collector to eBay users who've been online for years. By reading this guide you'll learn to do the following:

- Research antiques and collectibles more effectively.
- Use photographs to evaluate online buys and represent your wares in the best light.
- Gauge important condition issues before bidding on or putting an antique or collectible up for auction.
- Use keywords to effectively search as a buyer, and to attract more buyers than ever as a seller.
- Evaluate item titles and descriptions to make wise buys and initiate more sales.
- Keep an online antiques and collectibles business alive and thriving.

Who This Book Is For

This book is for anyone interested in buying and selling antiques and collectibles on eBay, whether they've successfully used the site for years or are entirely new to the venue. Seasoned pros are sure to find a few tips and tricks to broaden their skill sets; if you're in an online rut, this book can jolt you out.

Likewise, new users will appreciate the step-by-step information this book provides on setting up their eBay account, locating goodies on eBay, and listing items for sale. Whether you already run an antiques business that you want to take online or just have a few dusty pieces in the attic you'd like to unload, you'll find in this book everything you need to get started.

How This Book Is Organized

For both buyers and sellers, Part I, "An Introduction to eBay for Buyers and Sellers," offers a getting-started overview and valuable research tips useful to anyone interested in antiques and collectibles. Buyers get the nuts and bolts they need to be smarter eBay consumers in Part II, "Buying Antiques and Collectibles on eBay." And in Part III, "Selling Antiques and Collectibles on eBay," sellers will find lots of useful information to help them achieve their goals for online auction success.

part I

An Introduction to eBay for Buyers and Sellers

chapter 1

Getting Started

Let's face it: Americans, as collectors, love our junk. Indeed, this passion for collecting fuels our relentless searches for Bakelite bangles, antique firearms, Limoges porcelain, Civil War memorabilia, Chippendale chairs, Hummel figurines, Fiestaware, Wedgwood—the list is virtually endless. In the old days, pre-eBay that is, collectors were limited to scouring flea markets near and far, combing through neighborhoods for garage and estate sales, or traveling to antique malls in the hope of finding a steal. Not anymore.

Life before eBay

In the mid 1990s, a new venue for buying and selling antiques and collectibles arrived: the Internet. Those of us selling online in those days created our own static Web sites to display our wares, which we advertised on Usenet newsgroups, and conducted transactions by phone or e-mail. As buyers began to discover the Internet as a resource for adding to their collections, the handful of us with cyber storefronts enjoyed reaching more customers than had ever been possible. And people like me, who buy as well as sell, found another resource for shopping. Suddenly, a World Wide Web of opportunity opened up to us, and it was nothing short of amazing.

Around that time, some of us branched off to join e-mail listservs on special topics; in my case, these topics included Depression glass, Barbie dolls, and vintage costume jewelry. The groups offered a great way to exchange information, enjoy camaraderie with other collectors, and reach even more online customers.

Some of these listservs still exist today; TIAS.com hosts a number of them. Dedicated Web sites, clubs, and groups, like those on Yahoo.com (see Figure 1.1) have replaced others.

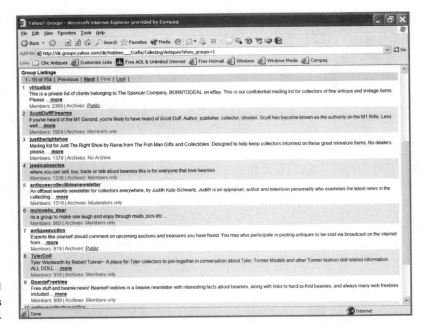

Figure 1.1

More than 700 collectors groups exist on Yahoo.com.

Even with the newsgroups and listservs at our disposal, however, we were limited in the number of potential customers we could reach in cyberspace. After all, in the mid 1990s, the Internet hadn't yet completely caught on; only a relative few buyers and sellers were online. By and large, most antiquers and collectors were still shopping in large brick-and-mortar malls and visiting shows to find quality pieces, pretty much oblivious to the changes brewing on the horizon.

At that time, in addition to selling my wares online, I also worked in a large antique mall situated on a busy Interstate highway in central Texas. On weekends, people filed into the mall, literally in droves. Sometimes, the lines were three and four people deep, with everyone attempting to pay for their antiques-mall finds at once; minor scuffles occasionally erupted over who was next in line. It's safe to say things were pretty darned good at the antique mall back then, as far as sales went anyway.

In 1996, though, all that changed. You see, that was the year eBay was born.

On eBay, buyers discovered that antiques and collectibles they previously thought of as scarce were actually plentiful, and the prices were sometimes better too. Rare items they'd never dreamed of finding in their antiquing adventures were available to them with the click of a mouse. As for me, I was in the right place at the right time the year eBay was born. I could buy things in the mall that were selling well on eBay, and buy things on eBay that were selling better at the mall, and turn a profit. (I still do that, actually, as often as I can.)

As more and more people discovered eBay, things began to change. Before long, in every antique mall, flea market, and shop, it seemed as though all you heard as you wandered the aisles was "eBay," "eBay," "eBay." "She said she could buy that piece cheaper on eBay," one dealer would say to another. Or, "He told me eBay has a better selection of glassware than any mall in town." As mall and show sellers heard about more and more successes on eBay, many jumped on the proverbial bandwagon to avoid missing the proverbial boat. Others, however, grumbled about the new development, and began blaming eBay for dismal sales in shops (even though high prices and less-than-desirable inventory were probably at fault). These sellers refused, and still do in many cases, to price their wares to compete with eBay, and that's a big mistake. After all, it's the tried-and-true bargain hunter who plays the antiques and collectibles game. The only people who seem to throw caution to the wind when the pocketbook is concerned are those spending other people's money to achieve a certain "look"—that is, decorators, stylists, and set designers.

As for me, I could see both sides of the equation. I hated to see merchants in the malls losing business. Many of them were my colleagues, my co-workers, and even my friends. Everyone was making such a fuss over the Internet antiques business, it was almost enough for me to boycott eBay altogether. But then again, being the opportunist that I am, I couldn't help thinking that eBay was pretty great. After all, I could now shop for antiques day and night without ever leaving home. It was an antiquer's dream come true. And, at that time, I could sell almost anything online. eBay wasn't yet flooded with common items in the early days, so things that weren't selling in the mall might find eager buyers waiting for them online.

Besides, even back then, I knew that any fight against eBay was a losing battle. I sensed there was no turning back. More and more people were finding their way online as each week passed. Buyers loved the selection and convenience, and sellers were more than pleased with their sales. I knew that if *I* enjoyed eBay, thousands of others did as well. I exchanged information with many of them regularly via the listservs I subscribed to, and the topic of eBay came up frequently. While no one could fully predict the eBay phenomenon, there was no denying that the potential for growth was beyond great.

eBay Today

Still, those of us who signed on to eBay in its early days never fully anticipated what the site might become. I had an idea that the advent of eBay might revolutionize the way many people, including those of us engaged in the antiques and collectibles trade, do business, but never in my wildest dreams did I imagine that eBay would become a global marketplace boasting tens of millions of registered users. I never dreamed that on an average day, millions of items would be listed on eBay, with many of them being antiques and collectibles. And I certainly never guessed that I personally would find customers with such ease in distant lands like Japan, France, and Italy, and would buy from sellers as far away as Australia. It would have taken a considerable amount of effort to be able to reach these buyers and sellers without eBay bridging our deals.

But what about the future? Is it safe to assume that eBay will continue to support global commerce in this way? If history is any indication, then the answer is a resounding "Yes!" In this climate of economic uncertainty, eBay, itself a publicly traded corporation, has consistently proven to be a company with staying power, which is particularly important considering that anyone who conducts business on the site must provide personal information to the company. That is, thanks to eBay's consistent performance, you need not worry that the personal information you provide will be sold by the company in a desperate effort to stay afloat. Even more importantly, if you're building a business on eBay, or have come to rely on the site as a supplier, you need not worry about the company biting the dust—and your profits along with it. Financially speaking, eBay appears sound, having experienced a pattern of growth and earnings during the past few years that exceeded expectations. (If you're interested in finding out the monetary value of eBay stock, plug the ticker symbol EBAY into your favorite financial Web page to get the latest quote.) In addition to being great news for shareholders, that's also a strong indicator that the rest of us can look forward to using eBay as a buying and selling tool for many years to come.

Live versus eBay

If you've ever been to a live auction, you probably realize that they offer buyers an opportunity to get some great bargains on *sleepers*, or pieces that aren't recognized by sellers as valuable items. This is one reason the venue has remained popular for so long. You'll be happy to learn this is the case on eBay as well. There are a number of other remarkable similarities between auctions on eBay and their live counterparts, and just as many differences.

Here are some similarities:

- Most eBay auctions allow you to bid on or sell lots, one by one, just the way many live auctions do.

- Sometimes, people interested in purchasing an item being auctioned on eBay get caught up in bidding wars similar to those seen in live auctions, driving up prices far beyond the usual market value and thoroughly delighting the seller.

- In both venues, once a bid is made, the seller expects it to be honored.

- Bidders online and at live auctions have a tendency to scoff at high starting bids on most items. This is true in most cases on eBay, but there are exceptions, such as high-priced items that everyone acknowledges are valuable. For example, you wouldn't start the bidding on a car at $10.

- Both online and in person, a bidder can swoop in with a high bid at the last minute. This is commonly called *sniping* on eBay.

On the other hand, online auctions can be quite different from their live counterparts. Here's how:

- Unlike with live auctions, you can't physically inspect an item for damage before bidding on eBay.

- With online auctions, the seller doesn't have the opportunity to verbally hawk merchandise to get bids going the way a live auctioneer does.

- When operating online, you can't size up the seller in person to decide whether you trust him or her. That makes it tough to assess whether you think the description of the item is accurate, and even tougher to send your money out into the void in the hopes you'll actually receive your merchandise. In turn, it's hard for sellers to trust that buyers aren't crooks in disguise trying to pass off hot checks and stolen credit cards.

■ If you buy on eBay or another online auction site, you don't get the immediate gratification of picking up your purchase the day of the sale. Worse, you have to pay to ship the goods home. Sellers, on the other hand, have to worry about packing and safely shipping the merchandise sold through online auctions. In contrast, in a live auction environment, after the bidder wins an auction, the goods are his or hers to deal with—which includes packing them up for the ride home.

■ When the item you bought online reaches your home, it may be possible to return it if it's not what you expected. In live auctions, however, all sales are generally final. Sellers, in turn, have to deal with bothersome return issues from time to time when selling online that don't generally crop up with live auctions.

■ Live auctions provide sellers with a way to clear large amounts of merchandise quickly and efficiently. Auctioneers at live auctions typically sell items on consignment or are liquidating an estate on behalf of an executor. On eBay, however, sellers typically hand-pick their lots and it takes much more time to sell an equal number of items online. However, online sellers have the potential to reach a much broader audience than most live auctions offer.

After you learn the ins and outs of online auctions and how to handle any discrepancies that crop up (and believe me, you will), you'll find that eBay offers a fun and profitable alternative to live auctions that can be enjoyed right from home.

Registering with eBay

Before you can get started buying and selling on eBay, you must register with the site. Registering with eBay is actually quite easy, but I'll walk you through it here to make sure each step is clear.

1. eBay's main page, shown in Figure 1.2, offers two quick links to the site's Registration pages. One link, labeled "register," appears at the very top of the page. The other, a button labeled "register now," is located below the search box near the top of the page in the Welcome New Users area. Click on either of these to open the first of eBay's Registration pages.

Figure 1.2

eBay's home page is located at http://www.ebay.com.

2. Enter your name, address, telephone number, and e-mail address (see Figure 1.3).

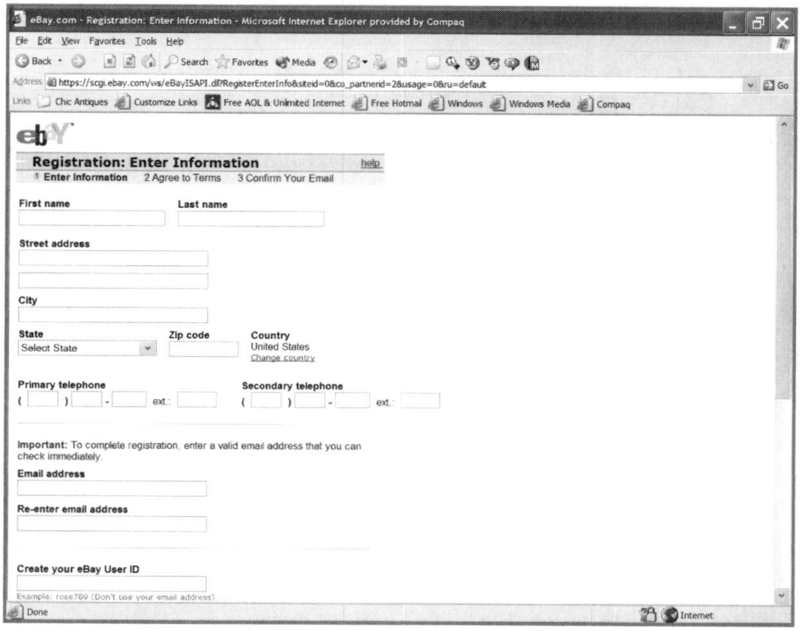

Figure 1.3

To begin your eBay registration process, fill in the contact information shown.

3. Scroll down to fill in your e-mail address (if you use an account obtained through a free e-mail service, such as Yahoo! or Hotmail, eBay requires a credit card to register to help eliminate fraudulent accounts). Then choose a user ID, password, and secret question (this will be used to give you a hint about your password in the event you ever forget it). Enter your birth date, and, when you're satisfied, click on the Continue button at the bottom of the page (see Figure 1.4).

Caution

Never share your password with anyone. Otherwise, you run the risk of someone fraudulently using your account.

Tip

Your user ID must be something other than your e-mail address, so consider selecting something fun or expressive. For example, if your primary hobby is collecting pistols, a user name like PistolPirate might be good. Feel free to have fun with it!

Figure 1.4

Continue your registration process by scrolling down to fill in the rest of the required information.

4. The next screen you'll see contains eBay's user agreement and privacy policy (see Figure 1.5). Don't panic; this is standard procedure when you sign on to a big commercial site for the first time. Take a few minutes to review the material here, being sure to scroll down in both windows in order to read both agreements in full.

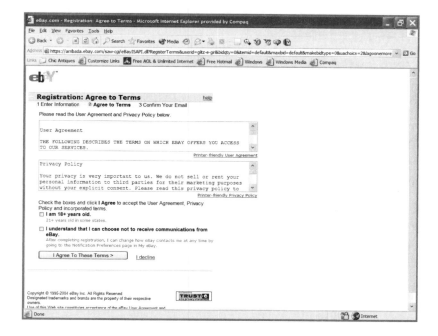

Figure 1.5

After you've reviewed eBay's policies, click on the I Agree to These Terms button at the bottom of the screen.

5. When you're finished, click the I am 18+ years old and the I understand that I can choose not to receive communications from eBay check boxes to select them. Then click the I Agree to These Terms button.

6. After you've agreed to eBay's terms, eBay will send you an e-mail message that will enable you to complete your registration and activate the user ID you just set up. This is done as a security measure so eBay accounts can only be set up with valid e-mail addresses. Simply log in to the e-mail account you used for registration purposes and open up the message. In it, you'll find a Complete eBay Registration button; clicking it completes the registration process and returns you to eBay's Web site.

Answering the additional questions in the box that pops up at the end of the registration process is optional. You're officially an eBay user now. You can bid on items at any time. Before you do, though, I recommend that you read Part II, "Buying Antiques and Collectibles on eBay"; doing so will make you a smarter eBayer right off the bat. If you're interesting in selling on eBay as well as buying, check out Part III, "Selling Antiques and Collectibles on eBay," for the specifics on setting up a seller's account.

Setting Up a PayPal Account

Now that you've registered with eBay, consider setting up an account with PayPal, which is a Web site that enables you to quickly and easily send and receive money online. Although doing so is not mandatory for buying and selling on eBay, utilizing PayPal enables you to pay for your auction purchases by using a credit card, by transferring cash directly from your bank account, or by applying the existing balance in your PayPal account—plus, using PayPal to pay for goods purchased on eBay is free for buyers.

Sellers, in turn, like the fact that they usually get instant credit to their own PayPal accounts, which allows them to mail out a customer's merchandise more quickly than waiting for a money order to arrive or a check to clear the bank. For many sellers, the convenience of receiving payments in a timely manner far outweighs the fees associated with using the service. Indeed, especially for Buy It Now auctions (you'll learn about these later), more and more sellers are limiting their buyers' payment options to PayPal *only*, although I personally don't like to limit my buyers' options in this way.

Tip

PayPal can be used for more than simply paying for your auctions. In fact, you can use PayPal for a host of other purposes like sending money to your kid at college, paying for merchandise on other Web sites, or making charitable contributions.

Because eBay now owns PayPal, you can reasonably hope that information sharing is in the works to make the registration process more convenient. For now, however, you do have to provide personal information once again to set up a PayPal account. In addition to providing your contact information, you must also provide more sensitive data: a credit-card number, a bank-account number, or both.

Tip

Although you can set up your PayPal account to carry a balance of funds, transferring the money from your bank account to your PayPal account, you might prefer to instruct PayPal to pay a seller directly from your bank account and/or credit card instead. That way, instead of gathering dust in your PayPal account, your money remains in the bank—hopefully earning a little interest in the process. Also, it's not a bad idea to link to your bank account *and* to a credit card to give yourself maximum flexibility when it comes to paying for goodies you buy on eBay. Plus, some sellers don't accept credit-card payments through PayPal because of higher fees.

If providing that sort of information is more than you're willing to deal with right now, you can always mail in checks or money orders to auction sellers who accept them. But if you are ready to dive in with a PayPal account (and I hope you are for convenience's sake), follow these easy steps, and you'll be good to go in no time:

1. Steer your Web browser to http://www.paypal.com.

2. In the upper-right corner of the site's main page, click the Sign Up button (see Figure 1.6).

Figure 1.6

Access PayPal's home page at http://www.paypal.com.

3. PayPal prompts you to choose an account type. As shown in Figure 1.7, you have two options:

   ■ **Personal.** If you plan to buy online, but don't intend to sell much, go with a Personal account. It provides all the features you need to pay for your eBay purchases, and even allows you to accept payments from PayPal account balances or bank accounts free of charge. (If you wish to be able to accept credit-card payments, you'll have the option of upgrading to a Personal Premier account, which enables you to accept these types of payments for a fee, in step 7.)

   ■ **Business.** If you plan to do some serious selling on eBay, you'll probably want to go with a Business account. A Business account will provide you with all the payment-related features you need to set up your business on eBay, including the capacity to accept credit cards. You'll also be subject to a sliding fee structure that goes down incrementally as your eBay sales volume increases, and receive exemption from the spending and receiving limits imposed on Personal accounts.

   Review PayPal's policies on both types of accounts to help you decide which type you need. To do so, click on the Sign up for your FREE PayPal account link on PayPal's home page. Then click the Account Types link (see Figure 1.7) to view a pop-up explanation of the different account types. (Note that I've chosen to create a Personal account here. If you opt for a Business account, the steps you'll follow to set up the account will differ slightly from the ones shown.)

4. After you click the option button next to the type of account you want to create, open the pull-down menu next to your choice to select your country of residence.

5. Click the Continue button.

6. In the Account Sign Up screen, shown in Figure 1.8, simply type your name, address, and phone number in the spaces provided. When you're finished, scroll down to continue.

7. Fill in your e-mail address and password, and answer your security questions, as shown in Figure 1.9.

8. Scroll down a little more and click the Yes or No option button to specify whether you want to set up a Premier account, as shown in Figure 1.10. (Note that I've chosen Yes.)

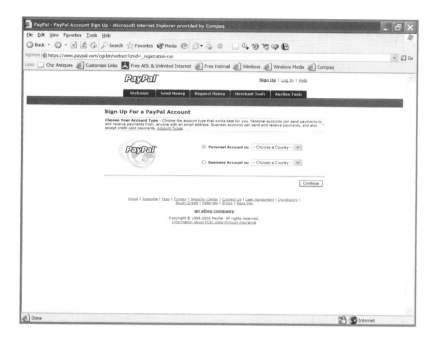

Figure 1.7

To get started, choose the type of account you want to set up and your country of residence.

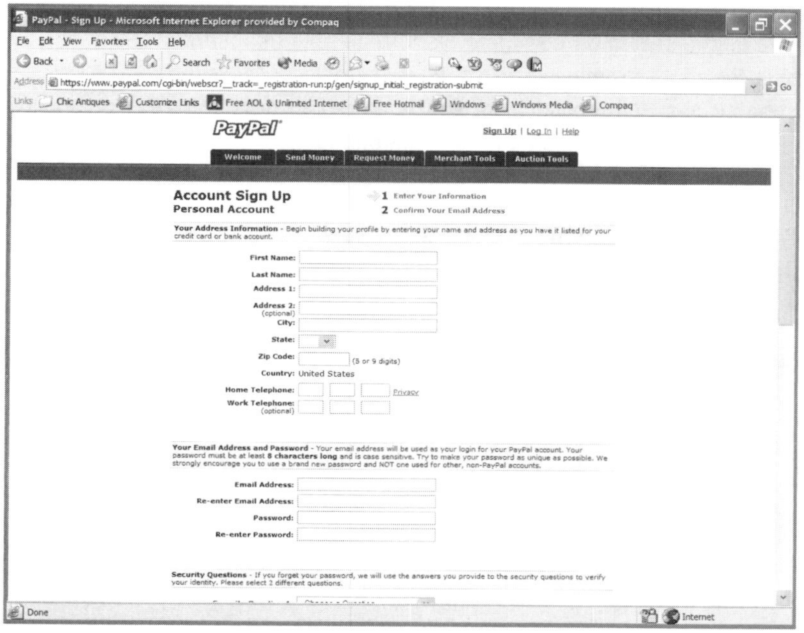

Figure 1.8

Fill in your basic contact information and scroll down to continue.

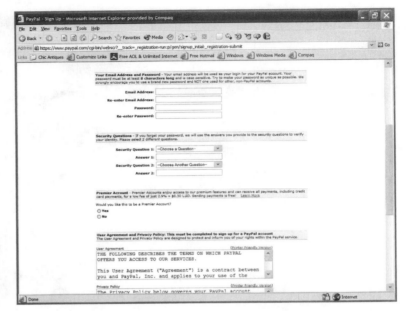

Figure 1.9

Fill in your e-mail address and password and answer the security questions before scrolling down again.

Tip

If you plan to do a little selling on eBay and want to be able to accept credit-card payments, opt for a Personal Premier account. If you're not sure whether you need this option, it's probably best to sign up for a simple Personal account. You can always upgrade to a Personal Premier account later if you need to.

9. Review the user agreement and privacy policy. If you agree to the terms, click the Yes option button.

10. As shown in Figure 1.11, you'll be required to input a series of letters and numbers. This is done to keep online robots, also known as *spiders*, from logging in to set up fake accounts.

11. After you type the series of letters and numbers, click the Sign Up button to complete this part of the registration process.

12. As you did with your eBay registration, you'll confirm the creation of your PayPal account through e-mail, as shown in Figure 1.12. To do so, simply access the e-mail account whose address you typed in step 6 and open the message you just received from PayPal. Click on the "Click here to activate your account" link to return to the PayPal site.

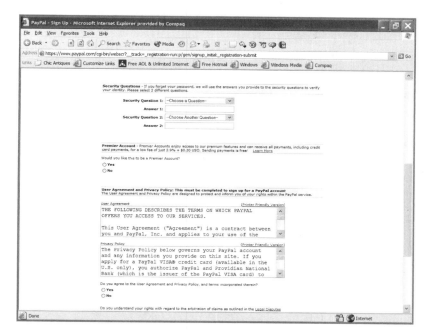

Figure 1.10

Specify whether you want to upgrade to a Premier account and review the user agreement and privacy policies.

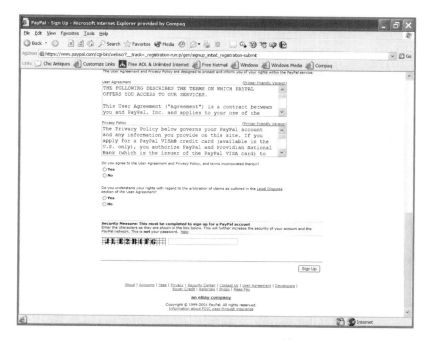

Figure 1.11

Fill in the series of letters and numbers as shown in the grid provided, then click on Sign Up.

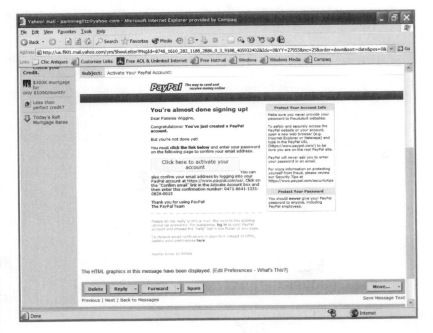

Figure 1.12

Through the e-mail you receive from PayPal, click on the "Click here to activate your account" link to return to the PayPal site.

13. Enter your PayPal password to confirm your e-mail address and click Confirm.

14. You now have the option of adding bank-account information through a pop-up screen. Because you can receive payments from other PayPal users and spend the balance in your account without associating it with credit card or providing bank-account information, however, I'll skip that step here. You can always go back into your PayPal account to add that info some other time (see below). Instead, click the Skip button.

Now that you've finished setting up your account, PayPal displays an Account Overview screen, as shown in Figure 1.13. Because you've just set up your account, your balance will be zero, and no transactions will be displayed. You can initiate payments to sellers and send PayPal invoices to buyers from this screen. As you begin to use your account, however, the information in this screen will be updated to reflect payments coming in to and going out of your account.

On the left side of the screen, you'll also notice links that you can click to add a bank account or credit card to your account. Depending on how you'll be

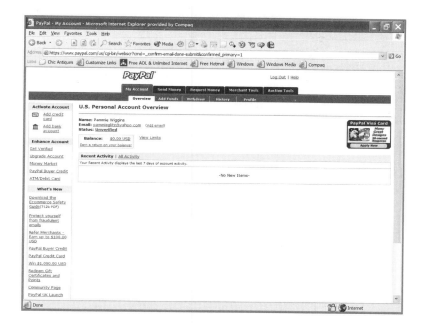

Figure 1.13

Your account overview screen shows a balance of zero, because you just set up the account.

using your account, you'll want to consider these options. If you add a bank account, you can also transfer funds from that account to increase your PayPal balance. You can explore these options now, or come back to this section to learn more about them as you begin buying and selling on eBay.

Adding a Credit or Debit Card to Your PayPal Account

To add a credit or debit card to your PayPal account, do the following:

1. Log in to PayPal using the user ID and password you set up (refer to Figure 1.6).

2. At the top of the left-hand column, click on the Add credit card link (refer to Figure 1.13).

3. Fill in your name, credit-card information, and billing address (if different than the primary address associated with your PayPal account), and click on the Add Card button as shown in Figure 1.14 to complete the process.

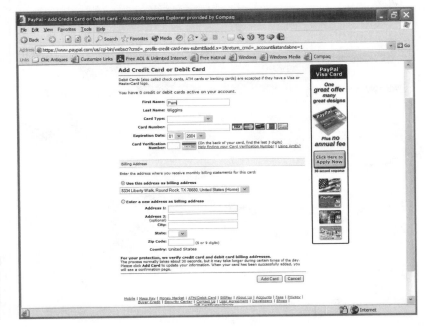

Figure 1.14

Fill in your name, credit-card information, and billing address, and click Add Card to complete the process.

You will now be able to pay for eBay auctions you win using your credit card through PayPal.

Associating a Bank Account with Your PayPal Account

To associate a bank account with your PayPal account, do the following:

1. Log in to PayPal using the user ID and password you set up (refer to Figure 1.6).

2. At the top of the left-hand column, click on the Add bank account link (refer to Figure 1.13).

3. Fill in your bank-account information as shown in Figure 1.15, and click on the Add Bank Account button to complete the process.

You can now transfer money you receive for sales made on eBay directly from your PayPal account into your bank account.

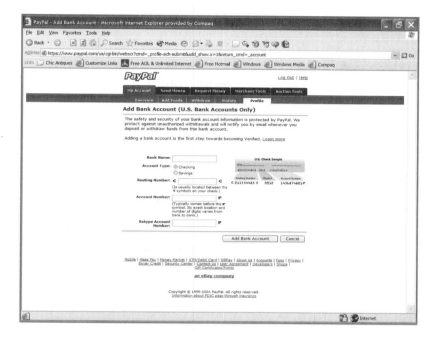

Figure 1.15

Fill in your bank account information and click on the Add Bank Account button.

Note

You can also pay for eBay auctions you win directly from your bank account through ACH (a banking term that stands for *Automated Clearing House*) debit transactions.

Transferring Funds to Your PayPal Account

It's probably smarter to keep your money in your own bank account rather than transferring it to PayPal to run a balance there (in case PayPal has an outage, and to, hopefully, draw interest), but increasing your PayPal balance by transferring funds from your account is now an option. To increase your PayPal balance by transferring funds from your bank account, do the following

1. Log in to PayPal using the user ID and password you set up (refer to Figure 1.6).

2. Click the Add Funds button in the blue shaded area at the top of the screen (refer to Figure 1.13).

3. Under Options, click the Transfer Funds from a Bank Account link, as shown in Figure 1.16.

4. Select a bank account (if you have more than one on file with PayPal), and fill in the dollar amount you're transferring to your PayPal account, as shown in Figure 1.17.

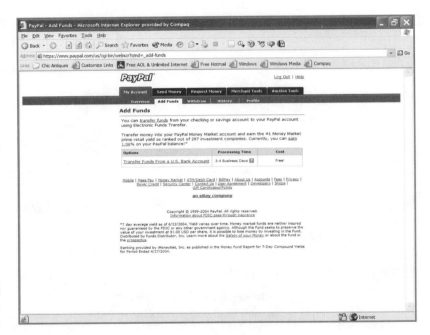

Figure 1.16

Under Options, click the Transfer Funds from a Bank Account link.

5. Click the Continue button.

6. Confirm that the bank account selected and dollar amount entered are correct, as shown in Figure 1.18, and click the Submit button to complete the process.

Figure 1.17

Select a bank account and fill in the dollar amount you're transferring to your PayPal account.

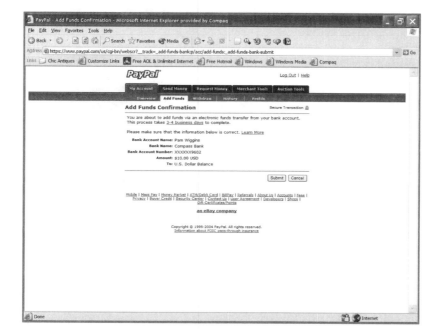

Figure 1.18

Confirm that the bank account selected and dollar amount entered are correct and click the Submit button.

The Spoof: Not as Fun as it Sounds

In the category of "Things You Need to Be Aware of Now That You've Signed on with eBay," there's a troubling trend on the Internet: spoofing. *Spoofing,* sometimes referred to as *phishing,* is when unsavory characters send mass e-mails that attempt to trick unsuspecting users into providing personal financial information, such as credit-card or bank-account numbers, or the user names and passwords required to access financial records, as shown in Figure 1.15. Typically, these spoof messages are designed such that they *appear* to have been sent by eBay, PayPal, or some well-known bank such as Citibank, and more often than not they try to convince you that your account will be suspended if you don't reply with the requested information. Sometimes they make it seem as if your account has *already* been suspended.

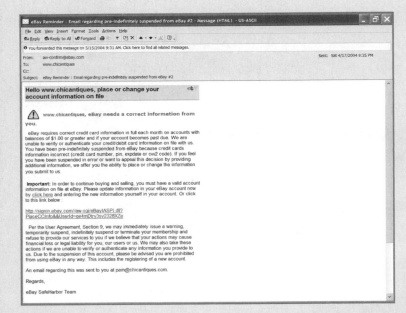

Figure 1.20

Keep an eye on your inbox for an eBay spoof e-mail similar to this.

Do not be fooled. For one thing, no respectable business will *ever* request that you send such sensitive information via e-mail. The problem is, many of these fraudulent messages offer a clickable link that takes you to a page where you're asked to enter some very personal information, similar to one you would see on eBay or PayPal, which is meant to "reassure" you that your information will remain private. In that case, you'll need some way of assessing whether the request is legitimate.

First, if the message says your eBay or Paypal account has been suspended, open your Web browser and log in to your account by going directly to either *www.ebay.com* or *www.paypal.com*. (Be sure you actually open your browser and type the URL by hand rather than clicking on links provided within the e-mail you're questioning; that way, you know you're at the actual site and not a dummy site designed to rob you of your personal data.) If you can still access your account by going directly to one of these Web pages, then it makes sense that the e-mail you received was meant to deceive you.

Another way you can tell that these e-mail messages are not in fact from eBay, PayPal, or a bank with which you have an account is that they usually greet you in a general way. That is, they never address you by name. Instead, "Dear User," "Dear eBay Customer," or something similar is used. Generic greetings are telltale signs of unspecific mass mailings. If eBay, PayPal, or your bank wanted to get in touch with you, you can bet they'd have the good sense to address you by name, which they have on file. And even if the message greets you using your e-mail address, remain suspicious. Any message failing to greet you using your first and last name may be fraudulent.

Check, too, to see whether the message is professionally worded. Many spoof e-mails are characterized by broken grammar, less-than-professional language, and even misspelled words. The presence of any of these is a good sign that something about the communication is fishy—or maybe I should say *phishy*.

The wise thing to do when you receive one of these e-mails is to ignore it. Do not reply to it, and if it contains any links, do not click on them. Instead, if the message appears to be from eBay or PayPal, immediately forward it to spoof@ebay.com or spoof@paypal.com respectively for evaluation. You'll then receive a reply stating whether the message you forwarded was indeed a spoof (the majority of the time they are). If you get a questionable e-mail from your bank, check out the institution's real Web site for fraud information or call the bank's customer-service line to verify the message's authenticity. Messages from financial institutions where you don't even have an account should be promptly deleted.

chapter 2

Research: Don't Buy or Sell Without It

No matter where you are in your eBay career—whether you're a seasoned veteran or a novice user—when it comes to research, you probably know more than you think you do, but not as much as you need to. There's always something you can learn to make your online buying and selling experiences more fruitful and enjoyable, and that's where research comes in.

Tip

If you feel overwhelmed by what you don't know or are afraid that your lack of knowledge may translate into mistakes made while buying and selling antiques and collectibles on eBay, try not to become paralyzed. Otherwise, you'll never make any headway in improving your buying and selling skills. Besides, my mother always told me that the mistakes we make in the antiques business "pay for our education." Sure, you'll be faced with a faux pas here and there, but if you learn something in the process, it's never for nothing. Don't beat yourself up about it. Instead, move on to something bigger and better, knowing that's how we all learn in this game.

What Exactly Is an Antique?

In the old days, anything that was more than 100 years old was considered an antique. That rule came about in the 1930s, when the United States Custom Office needed a way to define old objects so that duty could be appropriately assessed on imports. Nonetheless, when I was growing up, people referred to Depression glass as antique. It wasn't 100 years old then; indeed, even today, 30-something years later, it still isn't. But sometimes it just doesn't seem right to exclude an item from antique status just because it's a few years shy of 100 years old. Besides, I can't help but wonder why we would let the U.S. Customs Office dictate our terms to us. What made sense back then might not be appropriate today. The rule is so old, it's practically, er, an antique! So maybe the definition of "antique" found on Dictionary.com is more appropriate: "belonging to, made in, or typical of an earlier period."

Wait…the early 1970s qualifies as an earlier period, but most of my colleagues in the business wouldn't categorize a rotary dial "donut" phone as an antique—although it most certainly is collectible. In fact, I sold the one shown in Figure 2.1 on eBay for $95 a couple years ago. So perhaps we can tap into another widely used definition that refers to an antique as "an older object valued because of its aesthetic or historical significance." I've found similar definitions far and wide, but that particular wording is used on the *Antiques Roadshow*'s Web site (http://www.pbs.org/wgbh/pages/roadshow/).

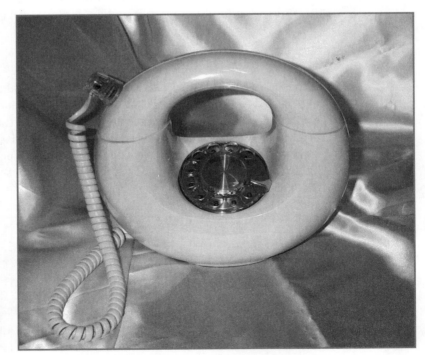

Figure 2.1

This rotary dial Bell telephone from the early 1970s that I purchased at a garage sale for $8 isn't an antique, but because it's very collectible, it sold on eBay for $95.

Fueling the Fire with *Antiques Roadshow*

With amazing stories, living history, and incredible values, the *Antiques Roadshow* television series on PBS has captured the hearts and imaginations of millions of Americans. Although it no longer generates quite the buzz of years past, thousands of hopeful people still flock to locations throughout the country to have antiques and older collectibles examined by the *Roadshow's* resident experts.

The dawning of this appraisal craze has become a two-edged sword for antiquers and dealers. On the plus side is the fact that a new generation of collectors was born based on the stories told on the *Antiques Roadshow*. Everyone wanted to garner a treasure of their own, whether by haunting flea markets each weekend or cleaning out grandma's attic. People who had never expressed an interest in antiques suddenly perked up and paid attention. The down side was that over-inflated values broadcast on the show made less knowledgeable viewers believe everything they owned was worth a fortune. Some older pieces are quite valuable, but as you'll discover buying and selling on eBay, most of them aren't.

As for me, I consider an antique to be any object that's older than 75 years of age, give or take a few years. I know, it's arbitrary, but it just seems like some things are just too old to be a stickler over a couple of years. The way I see it, if they've survived wear, tear, and peril for 80 years, they deserve to be called antiques. My point is, though, that the definition of "antique" is a bit fluid. In fact, these days, whether something is considered to be an antique often has more to do with the age of the person doing the assessing than the age of the object being assessed. A teenager might think anything older than she is is an antique. (No wonder I feel so old.) It's ultimately going to be up to you to decide what does—and doesn't—make the cut. When selling, you'll need to do this in order to place your items in the appropriate categories on eBay so that interested buyers can find your listing. There are also tools available to you that ease the listing process when you choose the correct category. (I'll talk more about categories and their importance in Chapter 9, "Titles, Descriptions, Photos, and More.") And when buying, you'll want to have a definition of the word "antiques" in mind so you can search eBay more effectively and can assess the believability of item descriptions. Sellers who use the term "antique" inappropriately give themselves away as amateurs, and offer educated buyers the opportunity to profit from their oversights and errors.

How Does an Antique Differ from a Collectible?

Using my definition of "antique"—that is, objects older than 75 years of age—most things made during the 1930s and earlier qualify. Pieces from the 1940s onward, then, are collectibles. The fact is, just about anything can become a collectible: bobby pin cards, razor blade packages, cereal boxes, baking powder tins, Matchbox cars, you name it. The problem is determining how old the item must be to qualify. For example, if you found a package of toilet paper from the 1940s that was completely intact, it would absolutely be considered a collectible. But the package you bought last week at the store? Not so much. Confusing the matter is the fact that the definition of a collectible is always changing. For instance, disco attire from the 1970s is popular with collectors now, but a few short years ago it was simply seen as used clothing with little value.

You may have your own opinion about where the age split between antiques and collectibles occurs, and that's fine, lots of people do. My main concern here is simply that you sellers out there make sure you describe and categorize your items properly on eBay so that shoppers with big bucks to spend can find your wares, and that you buyers know what's what so you can make an educated decision before placing a bid. But please, don't refer to a Madame Alexander doll from the 1950s, or any other item in that age range, as an antique. To people who know better, it's just a collectible. Frankly, placing the word "antique" in its item description—or categorizing it as an antique—will seem pretty silly. You'll either come off as an amateur or, worse, as a seller who tries to inflate the importance of your wares. That can be a big turnoff for knowledgeable buyers.

Note

Some collectibles manufacturers have been around for a very long time. Take Hummel, which makes collectible figurines, and Bing and Grondahl, which makes plates, as examples. These companies are still successfully producing collectibles today, but the older versions will be our focus here. Indeed, most of the collectibles referred to in this book are older pieces you won't find every day, even if they're not quite antiques yet.

Where Do Limited-Edition Collectibles Fit In?

Limited-edition collectibles are basically new items made in a more limited quantity than the usual pieces issued by a collectibles manufacturer. For instance, a doll crafted specifically for collectors may have a production run of 1,000,000 items, while a limited-edition doll might have a production run of 100,000. Depending on demand, the one produced in the lower quantity might end up being harder to find and more valuable on the secondary market, at least in the short term. Oodles of different plates and dolls and figurines can be purchased as limited-edition collectibles, and some have been wildly popular. Sometimes they're sold through magazine advertising and direct marketing, while others are available in gift shops around the country.

Although people do make collections out of these items—massive collections in some cases—they aren't generally collectible from a scarcity standpoint. If you like them, they're simply fun to own. I have a few of them myself. But from an investment standpoint, they may never be worth any more than you paid for them, and sometimes they lose value over time. Why? Demand may be high when limited editions first come on the market and they're relatively hard to find through retailers. However, as collectors lose interest in those pieces in the short term—which was the case with a host of limited editions introduced in 2000 to celebrate the new millennium—prices inevitably go down. It may take 10, 25, or even 50 years for collectors to begin seeking those items on the secondary market, causing prices to rise. (With regard to those millennium collectibles, because so many were made, they may never hold more than sentimental value. Time will tell.)

Making Informed Buying Decisions

Whether you're a collector buying a piece you can't live without or a seller purchasing a lot to stock your inventory, part of making informed buying decisions involves doing some research of your own before you start browsing the eBay listings. If you're interested in Hummel figurines, for instance, you'll want to know the difference between an old figurine and a new one.

If Hummels are your thing, then you're probably going to already know this, or have a reference guide on hand or a bookmarked Web site to which you can easily refer. But when you don't have a clue and you leave all the research to the seller, you can bet that he or she is going to know way more than you do about the piece being offered for auction. Worse, the seller might build the item up with lots of fluff, and you'll buy his or her spiel without knowing the difference.

In most cases, I know quite a bit about what I'm looking to buy online before I place a bid, and I suggest that you do the same.

The beauty of buying on eBay is that most decisions don't have to be made immediately. The vast majority of online auctions run for seven days. Unless you discover an item with two minutes left on the clock, you've usually got a little time to mull over the acquisition before you place a bid. You can bookmark an auction or put it on your watch list through your panel of eBay buyer's tools and do a little research to see if the seller is representing the item correctly. You can also evaluate the price at which similar items have sold by performing a completed listing search. I'll talk a little more about these tools and how to use them in Chapter 5, "Bidding Strategies."

Beyond the age of an item and the top price you should pay, you'll also want to consider these things:

- Has the seller described any marks on the piece, and what do those marks mean in terms of identification and value?

- Is this item authentic, or is it perhaps a reproduction?

- What is the condition of the piece, and how much should you pay for it in said condition based on rarity?

- Is this piece common in your area? Would it be sold less expensively locally in an antique shop?

- Is the price fair considering you'll be paying a shipping charge, and just how much is the shipping charge?

After you've researched the piece thoroughly enough to answer these questions—and any others you may come up with given an auction's parameters—you'll be ready to place a bid as an informed collector or dealer. And believe me, you'll want to consider these points earlier rather than later. There's nothing more disappointing than opening a package you've been anticipating, only to be hit with the sinking feeling that you've made a big mistake.

Don't Miss the Mark (Other Important Research Tips)

If you're feeling like you'll never get the hang of buying and selling antiques and collectibles on eBay because you're nowhere near being an expert in the field, think again. I'm not an expert on all antiques either, but I am good at research, and I'm getting better all the time. All you need to do is keep a few simple points in mind, starting with investing in a good magnifying glass and/or jeweler's loupe depending on your needs. Take a look at these suggestions for more ideas:

■ **Don't miss the mark.** Some readers will probably think it should go without saying that you should thoroughly examine all your eBay wares for an identifying mark before putting them up for auction. But if you knew the number of sleeper finds I've purchased on eBay that were clearly marked, but whose mark was either overlooked or misread, you'd be amazed. Every time you overlook a mark, you're taking money right out of your own wallet and putting it in someone else's—preferably mine. Use your magnifying glass or jeweler's loupe to thoroughly inspect each item you're considering selling on eBay, even if you don't see a mark with your naked eye. Some marks, like those on pottery and cut glass for example, can be very faint or even cryptic symbols. Using a guide such as *Kovels' New Dictionary of Marks Pottery and Porcelain 1850 To The Present*—or a specialty guide on silver, toys, jewelry, or what have you—will help you determine who made the piece and when the mark was used. Figure 2.2 shows an example of a mark used on a piece of vintage costume jewelry.

Note

You may be wondering why I'm sharing my secrets for exploiting sellers' mistakes to find bargains on eBay. After all, if sellers become better educated and stop making these mistakes, it may sharply reduce the number of bargains on eBay! But educated sellers offer wares I'm seeking more readily than uneducated sellers, and I'd rather have that as an online shopper. I generally don't have time to page through tons of listings trying to find a cup in my Depression glass pattern or a certain chintzware serving piece for my mother's birthday gift. I want to search a keyword and have what I'm looking for pop up with ease, and I'm not the only one who feels this way.

Figure 2.2

Marks, like this one on a piece of vintage costume jewelry, are key in determining age and value. This Eisenberg Originals mark was used during the 1930s.

As mentioned previously, if you're a buyer, you should evaluate any marks information described by a seller before placing a bid on an eBay item. If you suspect a piece has a mark but hasn't been identified, you can always ask the seller to take a closer look. But keep in mind that if you do so, the seller may be tipped off that they've made a mistake and revise the listing to reflect this oversight so other potential bidders have this information as well.

■ **Off the mark.** If the item you're researching is *not* marked, it doesn't mean it's not worth keeping for your collection. Likewise, the absence of a mark doesn't mean a buyer out there somewhere won't value a piece. That said, items that aren't marked certainly present more of a research challenge. But after you get a feel for different types of antiques, you'll recognize a piece of pottery as pottery, for example, instead of confusing it with porcelain. Once you can do that, you're one step closer to figuring out just what type of object you have on your hands. For example, you first can scour sites related to, say, American art pottery. If that doesn't work, switch to English pottery, and so on. You might eventually find that it's a valuable unmarked piece. Patience will be your greatest virtue in these situations. Of course, after a while, you may decide to go ahead and keep the piece, or list it on eBay and leave the intense research to its next owner. Writing a description to the best of your ability and moving on is perfectly acceptable in these situations.

■ **Bank on the books.** A good general guide like *Schroeder's Antiques Price Guide* or *Kovels' Antiques and Collectibles Price List* will go far in your reference library. You'll want to make sure you have a couple of good reference guides on your specialty areas as well. Study them cover-to-cover so you're familiar with the material and can easily refer to them when the need arises in the future. You may find that you wake up in the middle of the night with one of those *aha!* moments that cause you to get up and investigate something further. Knowing which book to reach for will get you back to bed a lot quicker.

■ **Phone a friend.** One of the best parts of participating in online collectors' groups, such as the listservs and Yahoo! groups I mentioned earlier, is easy access to others who may be able to help you when you have a question about one of your finds. If you haven't participated in one of these groups, you'll be surprised at how willing collectors and other dealers are to share information with you. Whether it's a point you just can't quite remember or a mark that's throwing you for a loop, chances are someone in the group will have an answer for you. You can also hit up your own dealer friends for information, especially those you've purchased from in the past. As long as you don't impose on them too often, they'll more than likely help you as much as they can.

■ **Go shopping.** By searching eBay itself for similar items, along with large online antique malls, you can find useful information very easily. In addition to seeing what the pieces are going for pricewise, many collectors or dealers selling on these sites will provide valuable details in their descriptions. Although this is always a great place to start your research, be sure to confirm what you learn because many inexperienced dealers have set up shop online. When searching these sites, you'll also want to narrow your focus as much as possible. Typing **blue willow** will get you hundreds of items to browse. By trying **blue willow pitcher**, however, you'll narrow the field to a manageable number of listings to cruise for information.

To sum it up, you basically start broad, narrow your focus as you go, and cover all your bases before reaching a conclusion or, finally, giving up. After you get the hang of researching your potential eBay wares, you'll probably enjoy the discovery part of the venture just as much as the shopping and selling.

Detecting Reproductions

Realizing that reproductions can crop up anywhere is an important aspect of research whether you're buying for a collection or buying to resell. The problem you run into with reproductions online is that you can't inspect an item to get a feel for whether it might be a new piece. For instance, some reproduction glass feels rather slick and clunky compared to old glassware, and the way the décor is applied to a piece of porcelain can provide subtle hints to age as well. All you've got to go with online is a photo, a description written by a marketer, and your ability to ask pertinent questions when a listing sends up a red flag that something may not be quite right.

Unfortunately, some people selling reproductions, reissues, and fantasy items on eBay don't make much of an effort to reveal that fact. I know of one dealer who sells recasts of expensive-looking vintage costume jewelry pieces that look good enough to fool an inexperienced buyer (and some experienced buyers as well).

This seller shows a photo of the front of the piece, and it looks pretty nice. The seller describes the piece, and it still sounds pretty good. But then, as if it's an afterthought, the seller adds the word "recast" in parentheses in tiny type at the very end of the description to denote its reproduction status. Not everyone knows that a recast is a new piece made from an original mold, even if they happen to notice the miniscule wording. That's tricky, if not downright misleading, from my vantage point. That's why it's important to read every line of an item description, and to read *between* the lines as well.

Note

Reproductions are exact copies of old pieces; some of them are made to deceive collectors into believing they are of an earlier vintage. *Reissues* are items made by an original maker using old molds. For instance, Homer Laughlin regularly reissues Fiestaware in new colors. *Fantasy items* are pieces made to look as if they came from an earlier era, but are not copies of items that existed in the past. They are newly designed items meant to fool collectors into believing they are old collectibles. Cola-Cola fantasy items, for example, are prolific in the secondary market. All these items can be sold in vague terms that will confuse neophyte collectors. Make sure you do your homework before bidding or buying for resale to avoid costly (and sometimes embarrassing) mistakes!

Some sellers also play dumb if they aren't certain about an antique's age. This is where those all-important questions you're going to ask a seller will make a big difference, so be sure and read more about that in Chapter 5. If you don't get an answer, or if the answer you get doesn't really address your concerns, it might be wise to move along to something else. If you still decide to take a chance and bid, be sure to ask about return policies beforehand. At the very least, you'll want to have that option open.

Of course, when you're buying pieces that are within your area of expertise, there's a good chance that you'll know more about the item being sold than the seller does. If you're an avid collector, you've probably experienced the same thing at shows on occasion. Using the same skills you employ when evaluating a piece in person, you can also evaluate pieces on eBay. If the photo isn't clear, ask for a better one. Ask clear, concise questions about the piece based on your vast knowledge. Don't assume the seller is trying to cheat people, however. Use the "do unto others" rule to guide you. If you do have to educate a seller, do it in a polite and respectful way, realizing that we all make mistakes from time to time.

Take the supposed piece of R.S. Prussia porcelain shown in Figure 2.3 as an example. The owner of this item bought it at a flea market, thinking it was the real thing. She purchased it from someone who usually knows her stuff and thought the mark, which is very similar to a genuine RSP mark, was the real deal. But because my mother has collected R.S. Prussia for about 25 years or so, I've learned a lot about it, and I could tell just by looking at this clunky bowl with modern-looking decaled décor that it was not an authentic piece. Authentic R.S. Prussia decals more closely mimic hand painting than those seen in reproduction pieces. It would have been easy for the seller to put it on eBay thinking she was offering a great piece to RSP collectors, but I could have spotted it as a reproduction a mile away because of my experience in this area. You'll be able to do this in your specialty areas too—with a little photo-analysis practice under your belt.

Figure 2.3

This piece was mistaken for genuine R.S. Prussia porcelain by an unsuspecting buyer shopping at a flea market. Even though the mark was close, the modern-looking decaled décor and thickness of the porcelain gave it away as a reproduction.

Note

Photo analysis on eBay allows you to assess many of the same elements you would look for when holding a piece you're considering purchasing in person. Look for photos of marks to evaluate age and authenticity, condition issues you know to be common problems, signs that might lead you to suspect the piece to be a reproduction, and characteristics of quality that would indicate a good buy. If you can't readily distinguish these elements from the photos provided by an eBay seller, either e-mail him or her to ask for additional pictures (and be specific about what you want to see) or move along to an item you feel more comfortable evaluating by photograph.

Condition Issues

What often makes an antique worth collecting is its condition. Because many of today's antiques are items that were originally designed to be used, such as dishes, glassware, and textiles, the people who owned them were less interested in saving and preserving them and more interested in, say, eating on, drinking from, and wearing them. And so, over time, dishes naturally were scratched, glassware was chipped and broken, and textiles were used and abused, which means it's difficult to find them in like-new condition today. When you do discover older objects in good to excellent condition, that pristine state is where a good bit of the value lies.

Some types of antiques are so rare and valuable—take Newcomb pottery as an example—that most any piece you find is a keeper. Even those with minor to moderate condition issues can be quite costly when you can find them. It's good to be familiar with those rarities, just in case you run across one (and you never know what you're going to discover out there). But most of the antiques and collectibles you find today should be in really good condition when you buy them so they'll hold their value over time.

Knowing whether it's acceptable to add a flawed piece to a collection depends on whether repairing the piece will diminish some of the item's value. For example, when I buy vintage costume jewelry, I'm willing to accept a few missing stones if I can easily replace them. I might even buy a piece that needs to have a pin back soldered on and have it expertly repaired. But pieces that have already been haphazardly repaired are more problematic. If it's a piece I know to be extremely rare, it might be worth buying it anyway. I may never find another piece like it within my budget, so I'm willing to do a little research to find out for sure. But when I'm buying Depression glass, for example, I look for items in excellent-to-mint condition with very few exceptions. Reading reference guides on specific topics and talking with other collectors will provide the input you need to make these types of buying decisions when condition issues arise.

Of course, discerning the actual condition of a piece can be as troublesome as assessing whether a piece is a reproduction. If you're shopping on eBay, you have to look at a photo, which can be misleading when it comes to detail; trust a seller to describe every flaw correctly; and ask all the questions you feel are warranted before bidding. Lips on pitchers and teapots are particularly prone to chipping. Gold trim can wear off on glassware and porcelain. Certain moving parts can degrade on old toys and mechanical banks. Sometimes you can't discern these details in auction photos, and in most instances, these issues will affect how much you should bid on a piece. If you're concerned, it makes good sense to ask the seller to be your hands and eyes. Query him or her about specific problem spots you're aware of on particular pieces if he or she hasn't already addressed these issues in the item description and through complete photo illustration.

On the selling end, this is another time when your loupe or magnifying glass will help you avoid overlooking a condition issue that could be important to a buyer. If you discover a crack, chip, or repair, research how much impact said damage has on the value of the item before listing it on eBay. And when you do, disclose those issues in an up-front manner in your description. Adding photos that appropriately highlight the damage will also help in this instance. If the damage truly is minor, an informed collector will be able to recognize that fact and bid accordingly.

Developing an Eye for Quality

Whether you're a buyer or a seller, one of the biggest favors you can do for yourself in the antiques business is to work on developing your eye for quality. If you know the attributes of the cream of the crop, then you'll more easily know how to categorize lesser antiques and collectibles. Don't get me wrong: The times you'll actually *find* a top-of-the-heap item at a bargain price are few and far between, but if you're not prepared when those opportunities do present themselves, you may well walk right past a very valuable antique, as oblivious as the owner and a million other people to its potential value. In addition, armed with your eye for quality, you'll also be more apt to distinguish reproductions from originals and spot valuable unmarked pieces. As time passes, you'll learn to recognize a quality antique or collectible without even looking for a mark.

For instance, I once heard about a Rhode Island antiques dealer who, several years ago, found a rare black pearl brooch tossed in a basket of cheap costume jewelry in a shop. He didn't know the piece's value, but recognized that it was a quality antique piece that would likely be worth quite a bit more than its $14 price tag, so he bought it. Long story short, the brooch turned out to be priceless. Indeed, it would tour the world before being auctioned in Asia, where pearls are highly prized. Had this dealer not developed an eye for quality, he may well have simply dug around looking for flashy rhinestones like the many other dealers who probably pawed through that basket before him.

Note

If you luck out and find a valuable piece for a song, you may decide that eBay is not the appropriate place to resell it. I urge you to do some research about appropriate venues before putting such a piece up for sale.

The easiest way to cultivate an eye for quality is to physically handle as many nice antique pieces as possible. Odds are these won't be the types of items you'll be buying or selling on eBay on a day-to-day basis, but they'll certainly be what you aspire to buy or sell when the opportunity strikes. Of course, you may not actually be able to *touch* pieces such as these—for example, if a piece is in a museum—but even viewing them in person can help you cultivate the eye for quality. In particular, you'll want to note the materials, craftsmanship, and the way in which such valuable items are decorated. One great way to see very valuable pieces in person is to take in a high-end antiques show, even if you don't hope to buy a thing while you're there. When you're not sure what makes a particular piece valuable, or if you see a piece attributed to a maker but it's not marked, ask the dealer for an explanation. As long as you're not interrupting a sale and ask for the information in a respectful way, he or she will usually be more than happy to show off a treasure, and will probably gush like a proud parent. Likewise, if you're watching an appraisal show on television or run across a very high-priced item on eBay that you've never heard of, be sure to jot down the name for further research. When you're reading about those pieces, pay particular attention to what the author or interviewed experts say about what makes the piece a unique find. Often, it's the quality of the workmanship and materials used in manufacture.

Online Resources for Researching Antiques

Whether you're looking for reproduction information, listings of marks, or just a general overview to beef up an auction description, there are many sites where you can research antiques and collectibles online. If you've been exploring the Web for a while, you probably have a few spots you frequent to learn about your collecting interests. I can't possibly list every good resource for researching antiques online here—there are just too many of them—but I would like to share a few of my favorites with you:

■ **A to Zee.** This site, http://www.atozee.com, is billed as a "Web guide and resource directory for collectors," which is pretty much accurate. You'll not only find articles on antiques and collectibles here, but other resources to put you in touch with dealers and collectors who might be able to aid you in your research.

■ **About.com.** I can honestly say that I use my own site at http://www.antiques.about.com (see Figure 2.4) as a starting point for research as much as any other. My articles there include historical information, dates, and descriptions of marks for many antiques and collectibles, and I know they're accurate. The links I've included to other sites offer everything from a variety of online price guides to silver marks. It truly is a great point of departure. That said, I'd be remiss if I didn't also mention my colleagues at About.com. My fellow guides for books, collectibles, dolls, stamps/coins, and toys, along with several others, all provide the same type of information as I do. You can find all our sites through the About.com home page in the Hobbies & Games channel.

Figure 2.4

My site on About.com offers articles and links on many antiques-related topics that can help you with research.

- **AskArt.com and artprice.com.** My knowledge of fine art is limited, so when I need to know about an artist, I check http://www.AskArt.com first. This site offers information about more than 25,000 artists working in a variety of media. The information contained there has helped me point many people in the right direction when it comes to finding out more about artists. http://www.artprice.com comes in handy when you're actually trying to find out how much an original work of art or art print has sold for in the past.

- **Collect.com.** Krause Publications puts out some well-researched books and magazines about antiques and collectibles, *Antique Trader* being one of them. The company also offers lots of information about collecting topics online through http://www.collect.com as well. Use the site's search engine to see if they've posted an article on a subject about which you're trying to find out more.

- **CollectingChannel.com.** http://www.CollectingChannel.com is another site I refer to time and again, especially for historical information. Most of the articles here provide pertinent information, and the variety of topics is vast. This site also includes links to related sites, appraisal services, shopping resources, and experts on specific topics.

- **eBay.** I use eBay's search feature to peruse completed listings—that is, listings for auctions that have already ended—more frequently than any other resource. By looking at completed listings, I can get recent pricing information, check out photos of pieces similar to my own, and read what others have found out about them in doing their own research. I rarely procure a piece for my collection or list an item on eBay without consulting the completed listings first. Only registered users are allowed to search for completed listings on eBay, so be prepared to enter your user ID and password.

- **Glass Encyclopedia and Glass Museum.** You'll find a host of glass-related articles at http://www.glassencyclopedia.com. From objects made of glass, like apothecary jars and beads, to specific manufacturers, from Baccarat to Westmoreland, this site is a true encyclopedia of glassware information. Another great resource for researching all types of glass can be found at http://www.glass.co.nz. This "museum," whose home page is shown in Figure 2.5, consists of a series of articles and other resources valuable to collectors and dealers alike.

Figure 2.5

The Glass Museum provides collectors with a great starting point for learning more about all types of antique and collectible glassware.

■ **Ruby Lane and TIAS.** When I want to check out an online antique mall to see how others are pricing or describing a particular item, I usually refer to http://www.rubylane.com or http://www.TIAS.com. These sites have so many shops, which are really individual Web sites, it's unusual not to find something related to what you're researching listed there for comparison.

■ **Yahoo! and Google.** When it comes to general search engines, I prefer http://www.yahoo.com. Quite simply, I seem to get more relevant results when I use Yahoo! than when I use other search engines for antiques research. Lots of people think "Googling" is the way to go these days, and I confess I do use http://www.google.com from time to time, too. Either way, I usually add the word(s) "information," "article," "story," "history," or "feature" to my searches to weed out some of the commercial listings and get to the point of my research.

part II

Buying Antiques and Collectibles on eBay

chapter 3

Finding Antiques and Collectibles on eBay

As with antiques-mall shopping, where every collector has his or her own tried-and-true strategies for sniffing out treasures, everyone seems to find the items they're looking for on eBay a little differently. For example, my favorite way to find what I seek on eBay is to use eBay's Search page. I simply type in a keyword or two in the Search text box, click the Search button, and voilá—auctions galore. Others prefer to *browse*. They'll park in their favorite category on eBay and sift through page after page of listings. Whether what interests them is Roseville pottery, Steiff bears, vintage powder compacts, or what have you, they want to see every item that's available so they don't miss a thing.

Whether you prefer browsing the categories that interest you or using eBay's search feature to comb the entire site, shopping eBay effectively takes a little trial and error. Just avoid getting in a rut when it comes to the tools you use to locate the items you want. Try a few new techniques from time to time and see where that leads you.

Browsing eBay by Category

If you're a fan of antiques malls or collectibles shows, you might be thinking you have all the training you need in "browsing." After all, that's your primary approach for finding the hidden gems you seek! But online, *browsing* refers to moving from one Web page to another. Essentially, when you browse eBay, you page through the listed auctions by category to see what you can turn up.

To browse on eBay, simply click on the Browse button near the top of the eBay home page to access the available categories as shown in Figure 3.1. Notice that many of the categories have numerous subcategories; for instance, when you click the Antiques category, you'll find everything from architectural items to textiles, and many of those subcategories have additional layers as well. Keep clicking deeper within a category to find the exact section you're looking for.

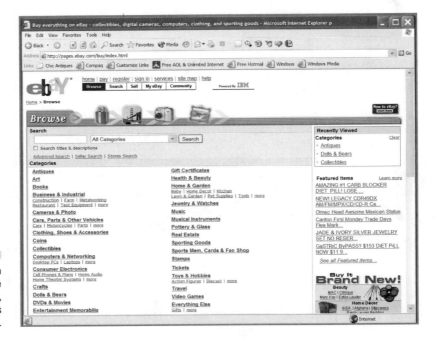

Figure 3.1

Click on the Browse button at the top of any eBay page to see the page shown here, which enables you to access deeper category pages.

Bookmarking Categories on eBay

After you find the exact subcategory—or auction—you're looking for, you can use your browser tools to bookmark that page. That way, in the future, you won't have to click your way through a gazillion subcategories to find the items you seek. Alternatively, you can use your My eBay page to keep track of your favorite categories (along with your favorite sellers and searches). Here's how:

1. Click the My eBay button at the top of any page on eBay.

2. Under the All Favorites heading, click the Categories link, as shown in Figure 3.2.

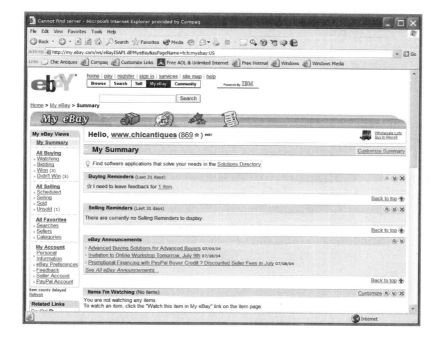

Figure 3.2

Your My eBay page enables
you to keep track of your
favorite eBay categories.

3. Review the information stored by eBay regarding your category preferences, as shown in Figure 3.3.

4. To delete any of the categories shown (which are stored by eBay based
   on your most frequent usage), click the check box before the category
   name and then click on the Delete button.

5. To add new categories to the list, click on the Add new Category link in
   the upper-right corner.

6. Click through the category names to pick your exact favorites, as shown
   in Figure 3.4. You can store up to four favorite categories in total.

Tip

To learn more about the My eBay page, see the section "Tracking Your Auctions with the
My eBay Page" in Chapter 5, "Bidding Strategies."

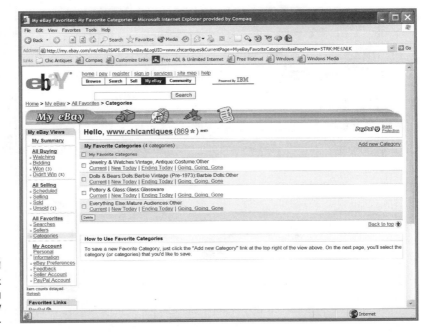

Figure 3.3

Click on the Categories link under the All Favorites heading to see your most frequently accessed categories.

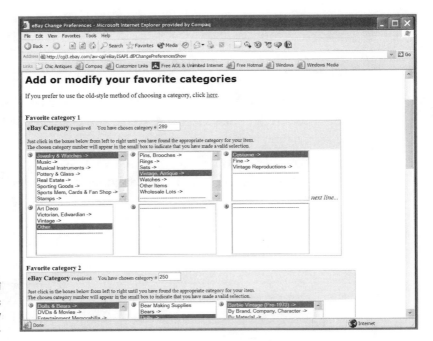

Figure 3.4

Add and delete categories to keep track of as many as four favorites.

Running a Category Search

When you consider that on any given day, you'll find more than 1,000 Steiff animals listed on eBay (see Figure 3.5), you'll realize that browsing through them all might be a little time consuming. In that case, you might want to think about performing a *category search* to narrow a broad field into a more limited number of items to browse. For instance, if you type **vintage** in the text box that appears at the top of pages of listings in the Steiff category, the field narrows from more than 20 pages to browse down to three or so (see Figure 3.6)—a much more manageable number if you want to actually view the available items.

Figure 3.5

Simply searching for "Steiff" on eBay will get you tons of results.

Browsing the New Today and Ending First Listings

Another effective method for browsing is to use the New Today and Ending First lists. New Today listings include auctions that have come up within the past 24 hours. In turn, Ending First listings are those auctions set to end in less than 24 hours. Some shoppers enjoy finding Buy It Now items—that is, items that can be purchased immediately at a fixed price—among new listings (I'll talk more about Buy It Now in Chapter 5). Others prefer to focus on items in the Ending First list so they can find some last-minute deals on auctions nearing their close.

Figure 3.6

Adding the word "vintage" to your search narrows the field to a more browse-friendly number.

To access these lists, click in the site map link just above the main toolbar on any eBay page. The site map page summarizes all of eBay's features. Because the list of features is long (see Figure 3.7), it might seem a bit overwhelming to digest; even so, when you're looking for answers quickly, it's the place to go. Once you're there, click either the New Today or Ending First link to view a list of categories containing items with new listings or with listings about to close, respectively; drill down through the categories as normal to find the items you want (see Figure 3.8).

Making the Most of eBay's Search Features

Although browsing has its uses, my favorite way to find what I'm looking for on eBay is to use the site's Search page, which opens when you click the Search button near the top of eBay's main page (next to the Browse button). In the Search page, I can type a word or two that is unique to what I'm trying to locate, called a *keyword*. For example, if I want to find all the Royal Winton chintz pieces in the Welbeck pattern, I'll type the keyword Welbeck, click the Search button, and scroll through the items that appear, as shown in Figure 3.9. Changing the keywords to vintage Welbeck narrows my result a bit.

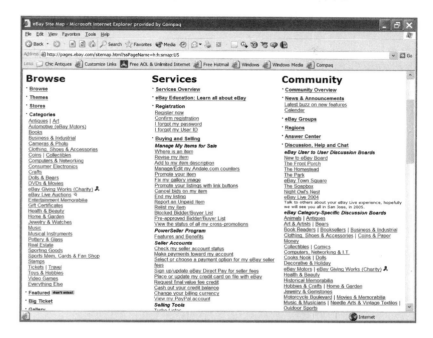

Figure 3.7

eBay's site map can be a little overwhelming, but there's a lot of good information there to explore.

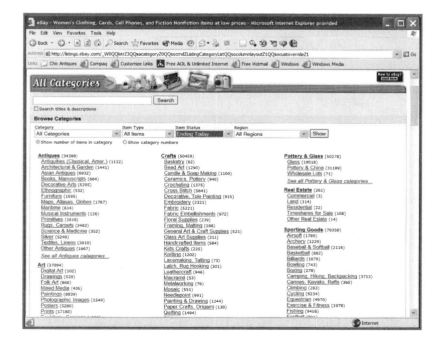

Figure 3.8

When you click on the Ending First (or New Today) link from the site map page, you'll be taken to a page where you can define a search to show all items ending first or go into specific categories to browse.

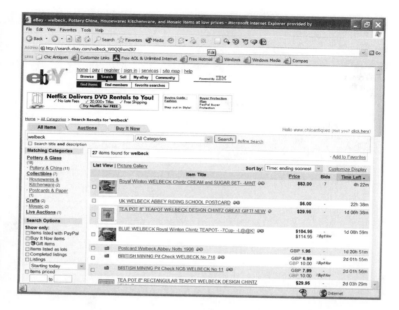

Figure 3.9

Using the Search page on eBay can be one of the most effective ways of finding what you seek.

Gaining proficiency using eBay's search features will save you time when shopping the site, and at the same time help you net many more attractive auctions.

Note

If you locate an auction item on eBay that looks interesting and you make a note of the item number, you can plug that number into the search feature to pull up the listing. Although it's probably easier to track interesting auctions using the watch list on your My eBay page (see Chapter 5), this search option does come in handy if, for example, a friend is interested in your opinion about a particular item and e-mails you the item number so you can view it.

eBay's Search Feature

Perhaps the easiest way to search for an item on eBay is to simply type a keyword in the Search field on the site's main page. However, eBay's Search page will give you many more options for narrowing your search. For example, if I'm looking for vintage Hollycraft jewelry marked 1952 on each piece (Hollycraft dated most of the jewelry it produced during the 1950s), I might decide to select the

Search title and description check box on the Search page. Why? Because sellers sometimes omit the dates from their listing titles, but include them in their descriptions, where they have more room to elaborate on details. This is just one option for refining searches.

Specifically, using eBay's Search page (see Figure 3.10) enables you to do the following:

- Search by keyword.
- Search both titles and descriptions.
- Search completed listings only.
- Search in all categories or specific categories.
- View all items meeting your search criteria, or just the items in the gallery.
- Sort by time—either by auctions ending soonest or by newly listed auctions.
- Sort by lowest price or highest price.
- Sort by distance, placing items that are nearest you geographically first.
- Select a list view, and decide whether or not to show item numbers in search results.

eBay's Additional Search Options

You can further refine your search by clicking the More search options link next to the Search button, which opens an expanded screen (see Figure 3.11). There, in addition to the abovementioned options, you can do the following:

- Exclude words that don't apply to your search.
- Search for items listed by specific sellers.
- Search within a price range.
- Search for only Buy It Now items.
- Search for items whose sellers accept PayPal.
- Search for items listed with a gift icon.
- Adjust the number of results per page.
- Sort items by zip code.

■ Search for items listed located in a particular country or items whose sellers accept a particular type of currency—for example, U.S. dollar, Canadian dollar, Pounds Sterling, and so on.

■ Locate items being sold by nonprofit organizations.

More on Those All-Important Keywords

Because all your searches are going to begin with a keyword or two, it pays to figure out what keywords will yield the best results. First and foremost, you'll want to make these keywords as specific as possible. For example, suppose you're searching for a Shawnee Smiley Pig cookie jar. If you type *cookie jar*, you'll be stuck paging through tons of listings, only some of which will be of interest. Changing the keyword to *Shawnee cookie jar* will narrow your results, but will still yield several listings that won't be of interest to you. Instead, try *Shawnee Smiley Pig cookie jar*. That way, you ensure that eBay returns only those listings that meet your criteria. It won't take long to learn exactly the words to use to get the best results for items you seek regularly on eBay. You'll also learn the words to exclude to bring your search results down to a handy number.

This is especially true when you're trying to weed out new items from your searches. For instance, suppose you are looking for vintage Chanel designer clothing on eBay. If you just plug in *Chanel*, you'll wind up sifting through listings containing everything under the sun, including perfume, jewelry, and handbags. Plus, you'll have old, new, and in-between items all jumbled in together. Why not change your search to *vintage Chanel*? That way, the majority of the items returned by eBay's Search feature will be older, even though you haven't completely narrowed the field yet. Trying *vintage Chanel suit* will result in even more applicable search results. (You can change *suit* to *blouse*, *dress*, or *skirt* to reshape the dynamic of your search.) The problem is, not all sellers use the designation "vintage" in their auction titles, even if the item they're selling is not new. For this reason, again using the search for an older Chanel suit as an example, try conducting a search for *Chanel suit* and excluding words like *new* or *nwt* (an abbreviation for "new with tags") to limit the search to older pieces.

As important as it is to hit on the right combination of keywords, there are times when it pays to think outside the normal realm when conducting eBay searches. For example, is one of your favorite collecting categories commonly misspelled? If so, think about ways you can capitalize on this type of mistake. Take our Steiff example again. "Steiff" is the correct spelling for this German manufacturer, but searching under "Stieff" might pay off as well when you're searching for the company's adorable mohair animals on eBay. As you'll quickly find, sellers aren't always as careful as they should be, which can lead to some great bargains for buyers who perform creative searches.

Figure 3.10

A look at eBay's Search screen.

Figure 3.11

A look at eBay's expanded Search screen.

Assessing eBay's Search Options

In truth, some of eBay's Search options seem a bit like overkill to me. For example, I've never searched specifically for items listed with a Gift icon because choosing the perfect gift for any given occasion is so subjective. Likewise, I usually prefer not to search both listing titles *and* descriptions for the keywords I've entered because listing titles typically contain the most important words relating to the item being sold. I've found that searching the listing descriptions as well as the titles skews my results most of the time, yielding a bunch of listings that may or may not relate to what I seek. Other features, however, do come in handy. For example, it's sometimes helpful to search by price in order to find listings within your budget. Sorting your results by highest or lowest price is also useful in that case. The following sections cover some of the more useful eBay Search features, some of which appear in the Search page, while others appear on the expanded Search page.

A Gallery of Choices

Because I really enjoy browsing photos whether I'm shopping on eBay or elsewhere online, I particularly like eBay's Gallery view, which displays the results of your search in thumbnail format, as shown in Figure 3.12. When sellers purchase the Gallery feature, their thumbnail photos show up automatically when the listing matches search criteria you enter, but they will be mixed in with listings that do not have gallery photos. If you prefer, you can view only Gallery listings by defining the view items option in either the Search or exanded Search page. I find that I am more likely to click to see an item's complete description if I get a little tease through the gallery photo first, so I scan the photos rather than reading every word of every item title when I'm in a hurry or browsing a category containing a gazillion listings. If you've never tried searching in this way, you might like it too.

That said, I don't always search using the Gallery view because, by definition, that view displays only those listings whose sellers paid extra to feature a Gallery photo—and not all sellers do. So if I'm conducting a search for some rare object I'm dying to own, choosing Gallery items only from the View results drop-down list won't cut it. The bargain hunter in me demands that I see each and every item that matches a given keyword search because the thought of over-looking something great because I took a shortcut in my search is almost

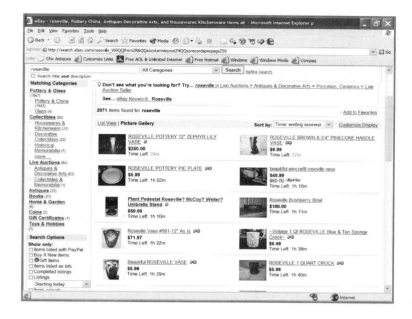

Figure 3.12

Another search option pulls up only auctions that display a gallery photo.

unbearable. You might be a little more casual with your searches and shopping, however, so consider a Gallery search if thumbnails appeal to you.

Sorting by Distance

With most *smalls*, a term dealers and auctioneers use to describe easily portable antiques and collectibles such as jewelry, glassware, and all types of knick-knacks, the seller's location doesn't make all that much difference to a buyer on eBay. As long as the item's shipping charges are reasonable, collectors will pay to have pieces mailed from coast to coast (or even internationally) without thinking twice. After all, part of eBay's appeal lies in being able to find things you can't readily locate in your area.

But when it comes to bidding on furniture, architectural antiques, and larger decorative items like, say, a grandfather clock, location can make or break a deal. When you're using eBay to find these cumbersome items, configuring eBay to sort your search results by location, placing those items that are nearest to you geographically first, can be a real benefit. To sort by location, simply choose Distance: nearest first from the Sort by drop-down list box. Bidding only on items in your area will enable you to arrange delivery more economically—or even allow you to pick up your purchases yourself.

Caution

eBay's Standard Protection Program (see Chapter 7, "Working Through the Bad Buy") doesn't cover items picked up directly from the seller. It's implied that you have the option to inspect items before taking them home, and work out any disputes with the seller personally should they arise during the money/merchandise exchange.

When You Just Need to Buy It Now

One attractive feature in the expanded Search toolkit is the ability to search only for items with a Buy It Now option (see Figure 3.13). As mentioned previously, Buy It Now offers buyers the ability to purchase an item at a fixed price—sometimes as an alternative to bidding, and other times as the *only* buying option for a listing.

Because not everyone listing items on eBay is knowledgeable, and because a host of others research only haphazardly, using eBay's Buy It Now feature can be a great way to get a bargain. If you see an item listed with Buy It Now at a price you know is reasonable, why risk bidding and paying a higher price, or losing out to another bidder altogether? Although you may not always want to choose Buy It Now, there are times when it makes sense to use this feature.

Figure 3.13

One of the expanded Search features allows you to pull up only Buy It Now items.

I also find that searching for Buy It Now items makes sense when you're under the gun to find a particular item—for example, if the item is a gift and the recipient's birthday is just a week away. By focusing on items with a Buy It Now option, you avoid having to wait for an auction's end date to buy, which means you get a jump on receiving the item.

Tip

If you're looking to buy a gift on eBay, take comfort in the fact that many sellers will ship directly to the recipient. Don't be shy about asking if this will make your life easier!

Buying Domestic

Paying via PayPal helps to alleviate some of the hoop-jumping that is often involved with international payments, but if you've opted to pay by check or money order, converting from U.S. dollars to the seller's currency can be a challenge. If that's just too much to deal with, you can eliminate many foreign listings from your searches altogether by changing the value in the expanded Search page's Currency drop-down list to U.S. Dollars. That way, you'll avoid having to view items listed abroad in the seller's non–U.S. dollar currency, while retaining listings by foreign-based sellers who do accept American greenbacks.

In addition, if you prefer to buy domestic, eBay enables you to excise *all* listings from abroad from your search results, even if the seller accepts U.S. currency. Simply click the Items located in option button and choose United States (or whatever your country of residence) from the corresponding drop-down list.

Searching by Seller, Searching by Bidder

Impeccable taste, an eye for great antiques, a penchant for reasonable starting bids with no reserves—sellers who embody these characteristics can be a bidder's dream. If you had a particularly stellar transaction with a certain seller, and you love everything that person puts up for auction, you'll appreciate the fact that you can search eBay by seller. Some sellers consistently list wares worthy of attention, some have low starting bids and reasonable shipping charges, and others give exceptional customer service. As you develop Internet relationships through eBay, you'll probably find the idea of doing business with some of the same sellers over again to be appealing. Searching by seller will help you to keep in touch with these worthy individuals through their auction listings.

Tip

Often, it's inexperienced sellers, or those dealing in lots of different types of items, who post *sleepers*—that is, items that are potential bargains because of the seller's lack of knowledge. When you find an exceptional item that isn't quite described correctly, making it a potentially major bargain, take a look at the other objects currently offered by the seller to see if there are any additional bargains in the making. You might even add that seller to your My eBay page's Favorite Sellers list in the hopes of capitalizing on his or her mistakes in the future, as well. To do so, open your My eBay page and, under the All Favorites heading, click the Sellers link. Then click the Add new Seller or Store link, and enter the seller's user ID on the page that appears.

To search for items on the block by a particular seller, do the following:

1. From either the Search or expanded Search page, click the Items By Seller link along the left side of the page.

2. On the Items By Seller page, enter the seller's ID. (Locating a seller's ID can be tricky; if you've purchased from the seller you're adding, check the end-of-auction e-mail notice you received from eBay during the transaction. The seller's user ID will be displayed there.

3. Click the Search button.

4. A complete list of items offered by the seller will come up for your review.

Tip

If you prefer browsing to searching and notice several items you like offered by the same seller, click one of the item listings to open it. Then click the View seller's other items link at the bottom of the seller information box.

In addition to searching by seller, you can also search by bidder—a technique known as *bid stalking*. I admit, when I notice that a particular bidder seems to have taste similar to my own, I've been known to search by bidder—that is, to pull up their active auction list, as shown in Figure 3.14—to see what else they've got their eye on. You see, bid stalking is actually a bidding strategy whether you do it on occasion like me, or on a regular basis. Some people despise bid stalkers, but it can be an effective way of finding the cream of the crop if you follow the right bidders.

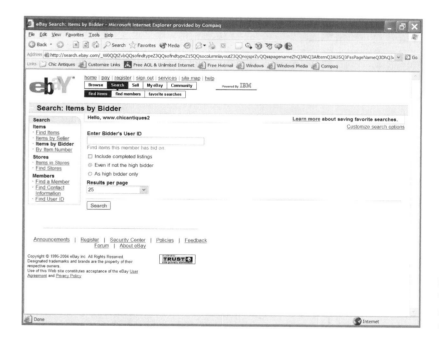

Figure 3.14

The bidder search screen is simple to navigate; the seller search screen looks very similar.

Searching by bidder is similar to searching by seller. Simply do the following:

1. From either the Search or expanded Search page, click the Items By Bidder link along the left side of the page.

2. On the Items By Bidder page, enter the bidder's ID, which you can obtain from an auction listing you've recently viewed.

3. Click the Search button.

4. A complete list of items on which the bidder is currently bidding is displayed for your review.

Saving a Search

Suppose you're always on the prowl for a vintage Mainbocher dress, but they don't pop up on eBay very often. Rather than checking the site daily to see if any Mainbochers have been posted, you can save your search criteria on eBay, and even have eBay e-mail you when items matching your criteria are listed. To save your search criteria, do the following:

1. Using either the Search or expanded Search page, enter the desired criteria and click the Search button.

2. Whether eBay displays a list of auctions that match your criteria or a page that notes that no matching items were found, you'll have the option of clicking an Add to Favorites link, which appears on the right-hand side of the screen. Click it.

3. Type an easy-to-remember name for the search in the Search Name field.

4. If you want eBay to e-mail you any time an item matching your search criteria is listed, click the Save Options check box.

5. From the drop-down list box, choose how long you want eBay to check for items that match your search.

6. Click the Save Search button. The search you saved will appear on your My eBay page, where you can access it by clicking the Searches link under the All Favorites heading.

Note

eBay enables you to save as many as four searches on your My eBay page.

chapter 4

Buyer Be Aware: What to Know Before You Bid

If eBay offered a "Power Buyer" designator, the way they do the "Power Seller" one, I would definitely qualify. Even after years of shopping the site, I still find antiques and collectibles I'm thrilled to have the opportunity to own—or resell. But before I buy anything on eBay, I make sure I learn as much as possible not only about the item I'm bidding on, but also about the person who's selling it. That way, I can determine whether the item is a good buy and assess the likelihood that the seller will deliver it as promised. This chapter covers the steps you should take before you consider placing a bid.

Do Your Research before You Bid

If you only skimmed through the information in Chapter 2, "Research: Don't Buy or Sell Without It," now's an excellent time to go back and read it in more detail—especially the section on making informed buying decisions. The more you know about the objects you're seeking on eBay, the better your odds of finding them—and ensuring that you don't get taken by an unscrupulous seller.

Pre-bidding research includes, but is not limited to, the following:

■ Getting a rough estimate of how much the antique or collectible you're contemplating buying usually sells for on eBay. Here's where conducting a completed listings search, as discussed later in this chapter, comes into play.

- Having an idea how much similar pieces sell for in other venues.

- Considering how condition issues mentioned in the auction listing's description affect the value of the piece.

- Asking specific questions about features you know to be of concern with regard to the item in question, such as chipped lips on glass pitchers or handles that are prone to crack at the base.

- Looking up any unfamiliar marks mentioned in the description.

- Identifying characteristics that might indicate that the piece is a reproduction.

- Asking any other questions you may have that would increase your comfort level in bidding.

You'll find detailed information on how to accomplish these tasks in Chapter 2. Once you become more knowledgeable about antiques and collectibles in general, you'll often know more than the seller about certain pieces in your areas of interest; as such, you'll inherently know what types of questions to ask and recognize red flags more easily. Until then, researching your items prior to bidding won't eliminate all the associated pitfalls, but it will help to minimize them in a big way.

Assessing a Listing

When, through the course of browsing or searching eBay, you hit upon a listing that interests you, you have two basic options with regard to assessing its value: the item's description and, ideally, one or more digital photos of the item.

Deciphering Listing Descriptions

Actually *reading* a seller's description is one of the most important steps you can take as an eBay bidder. All too often, people see an attractive photo and bid without really studying the description in detail because they're in a hurry or are overly excited about an item. How do I know? I've done it myself—more often than I'd care to admit—and when I received the eagerly awaited goods, I was sorely disappointed to discover the error of my ways.

If I had been smart on those occasions, I would have more thoroughly examined the item description with an eye toward all those critical points I'd discovered during my research prior to bidding. In particular, you'll want to look for the following tidbits in the item description:

- The date the piece was manufactured.

- Any marks on the piece. If none are noted, look at the item photos to see if any marks were overlooked or for characteristics that may help you discern whether an unmarked piece can be attributed to a specific maker.

- Condition issues that might affect the value of the piece such as chips, cracks, scratches, tears, holes, dents, wear to enamel or paint, stains, excessive soiling that may hide damage, or missing parts. Be sure your specific areas of concern are addressed.

- If the item has been cleaned or restored, make sure that it was done by a professional to ensure that the piece wasn't damaged in the process.

- If the object has been repaired, make sure it was done professionally. Also, determine whether the repairs are detectable to the naked eye.

- See if the item has been examined using a black light to detect glue used in repairs or telltale signs that the piece is a reproduction. (You'll want to read up on reproduction issues for the item you're considering as part of your pre-bidding research.)

If these issues—or any others—aren't addressed adequately in the item description you're evaluating, click the Ask seller a question link located in the item description and fire away with your concerns. Sellers should always be willing to answer your questions; if they aren't, don't hesitate to move along to another auction.

Most description omissions relate to condition issues. For example, sellers may fail to disclose condition information about a piece, or they'll be way too vague—stating simply that a piece is in "good" condition. You also need to be aware that sellers will sometimes bury important condition information among lots of fluff wording in the auction's description, especially if he or she is trying to deemphasize a piece's flaws. For instance, I once saw a listing that glowingly described a piece of pottery—a rare vase—including information about the history of the maker and how it came from the estate of a 90-year-old socialite in Chicago. The seller went on to describe the piece as "gorgeous," with no chips or crazing damage to the glaze, in fabulous condition overall, before noting, almost as an aside, that it had one tiny hairline crack down its back. Wait a minute…a tiny hairline crack? How can the piece be in fabulous condition if it has a crack in it? You have to wonder, is this seller counting on you to get excited and quit reading before you get to the part about the hairline crack? It seems that way. Is he or she trying to minimize the fact that much of the piece's value, unless it is very rare, is diminished by this tiny crack? I'd say yes. Is this a good way to do business? Not for me. And you might as well get used to the phrase "but this doesn't detract from the beauty of the piece." You'll see this, in one form or another, over and over again. It's up to you to determine whether the damage is major or minor and the extent to which it devalues the item (or its beauty) because, quite frankly, you can't always rely on a seller to do it for you. Sometimes the seller may not know; other times he or she may not want to tell you.

When I'm selling on eBay, I prefer to make both good qualities and bad qualities clear to the buyer, much like the seller whose auction is shown in Figure 4.1. I don't try to oversell the good points, and I don't diminish the bad points. I don't post a photo unless it's clear and bright, and I'll likely include a second or third photo to show any damage in detail. As a buyer, I appreciate it when sellers take the same care. It proves to me that they're attempting to be as honest as possible in making a deal. When they don't, I tend to view them as untrustworthy and avoid doing business with them—especially when so many other truthful individuals on eBay are vying for my bid.

Sometimes, though, you can read a description from top to bottom and still get burned. Whether they mean to or not, it's an unfortunate fact that sellers often fail to accurately describe the condition of their wares. Sometimes sellers are right on target in their descriptions—and occasionally, the item for sale may even be in better condition than described—but more often than not, sellers totally blow it when it comes to evaluating the condition of their items. For example, a seller might describe a piece as being in "mint" condition, implying that there are no flaws present, when that is not the case. Or a seller might say an item is in "excellent" condition, suggesting that any condition issues are minimal, when in fact the piece has a small crack or chip. Again, it's up to you to decide whether the seller's description is apt, either by studying the photo or asking loads of questions (see Figure 4.2).

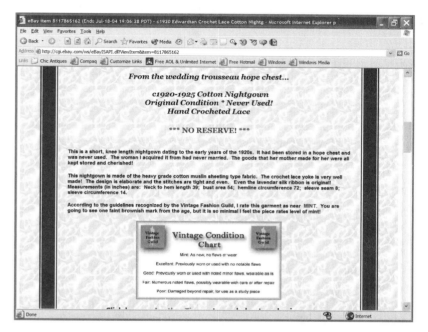

Figure 4.1

This seller (user ID boycetime on eBay) provided a basis for her condition rating system in the auction description. You won't always find this level of detail, however, so be prepared to ask questions of the seller if needed.

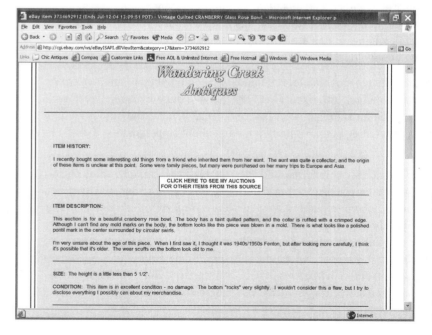

Figure 4.2

While the seller (user ID wanderingcreekantiques on eBay) has done a good job of explaining her assessment of age and condition on this piece concisely, you should still ask questions if you're not sure about the accuracy of the description before bidding.

Caution

I avoid auctions—or at least ask a few questions before bidding—that describe a piece as being in "good" condition. Unlike "excellent" or "mint," which have pretty standard meanings, "good" is just too subjective. After all, a piece could be in good enough condition to be considered useable, but might not be worth two bits with regard to collectible value. Be aware, too, that some sellers don't correctly use terms like "mint" (meaning "just like it came from the factory with no wear") and "excellent" (meaning "items showing very minimal wear with all parts intact"). If you have any reservations about condition, freely question the seller.

Candor about Shipping Charges

These days, it seems that more and more eBay sellers are overcharging for shipping. In some cases, the added expense is deliberate; sellers charge you for Priority Mail, but send the package first class and pocket the difference. Some sellers even sneak in "handling" fees, or charge for insurance that is never purchased. Other sellers overcharge out of ignorance. They just don't know how to handle the shipping issue, so they spit out a number that may or may not make sense (but that usually works to *their* advantage). Compounding the problem is that many sellers don't state their shipping rates up front in the item description, and instead inform you of the cost *after* you've won the item. That's fine when the fees are fair, but it can be aggravating when the price to ship the object renders the piece a rip-off.

To avoid getting burned by outrageous shipping fees, consider avoiding auctions that don't state the shipping charge up front to weed out surprises. That way, you'll know how much you'll need to tack on to an item's ending price for shipping before you even bid. If you come across an item you really must own, but the item listing contains no information about shipping, then e-mail the seller to find out.

If a seller quotes a shipping rate that seems inflated, first consult the United States Postal Service's online calculator (http://www.usps.com) to determine whether it's reasonable. If not, consider contacting the seller to negotiate more reasonable terms. One way to do this is to ask the seller whether he or she would be willing to send items by first class mail instead of Priority Mail. Unless it's sent during a holiday rush, first class mail arrives in about the same amount of time as Priority Mail packages, but the cost is considerably less. Some sellers will bend over backwards to make you happy, and others will be insulted by your request. But if you know something should cost $2 to ship, and the seller is quoting $6, you should speak up. I do.

Freeze Frame: Assessing Photos

Back in the old days, eBay listings that didn't include photos to support the item description were much more common. That's because at the time, digital cameras were just coming on the market. Many sellers didn't own them yet (and the ones who did didn't always know how to use them correctly). In fact, when my husband and I started selling online, we used a video camera to capture still frames; that was our best option for getting clear images of small items.

Things have changed—which is good for both buyers and sellers. Heck, bidders rarely even *look* at eBay auctions without photos these days, even for very common objects. Why? It's reassuring to actually see what you're thinking about buying on a number of levels. Not only does the presence of a photograph suggest that the seller actually has the merchandise in his or her possession, but you can examine the photo for the same types of buying clues you would look for if you were holding the piece in your hand.

Of course, it goes without saying you'll want to see a clear photo that reveals the overall look of the piece. Beyond that, you'll also want to look for photos that enable you to assess the piece's condition. In particular, look for evidence of wear and damage in spots you know to be problem areas, and then question the seller appropriately.

Note

Sometimes, digital photos can be shadowy or have flash glare that impedes your ability to gauge a piece's condition. Hopefully, though, the seller will recognize this fact and mention condition issues in a description. If you're not sure whether what you're seeing in a photo is damage to the piece or just a problem with the picture, go ahead and ask.

In addition, more and more sellers are providing photos of marks in auction listings. Being able to view a mark can prove invaluable when assessing age or investigating a possible reproduction. If the person selling a piece that piques your interest notes in the item's description that the item is signed, but *doesn't* include a photo of the mark in the listing, consider asking him or her to provide a photo of the mark so you can better evaluate the piece.

Note

Conversely, if a seller doesn't mention a mark in the item description, it may indeed be an unsigned piece, or the seller may simply have missed the mark. You can always ask the seller to take a closer look at the piece, but be aware that doing so may backfire on you. That is, if the seller discovers that the piece is indeed marked, he or she will be able to better assess its value and revise the listing accordingly—which means the odds of you winning the piece at a bargain are greatly diminished.

Caution

It's true that inexperienced sellers sometimes use out of focus photos on eBay because they just aren't equipped to do any better. But would a seasoned seller purposely post a bad photo to hide a flaw? You bet. It doesn't happen all the time, but it can be a problem; be aware of this while you're browsing listings on eBay.

As I mentioned earlier, any photos that appear with a listing should be clear and bright and should show any damage or other condition issues in detail, as shown in Figure 4.3. But in the interest of full disclosure, I feel I should tell you that every now and then I buy a piece with a fuzzy, out-of-focus, too-dark, all around crummy photo. When I do, it's usually because I suspect that the item is a sleeper because of the way the title and description are worded. As you really get into eBay buying, you'll learn to recognize these as well. The seller usually doesn't supply much information about the piece, and if the price remains really low, I don't ask questions. Of course, operating in this manner is a gamble, and occasionally I live to regret rolling the dice. But, as you know, taking a gamble pays off sometimes. I've bought some fantastic pieces of vintage costume jewelry using this tactic. I've also gotten stuck with some funky pieces that I've simply turned around and unloaded at a deep discount.

Note

Some sellers are ill equipped to photograph the items they're selling. Really small pieces usually fall into this category. Without a decent camera, the seller is never going to get a good enough shot to really tell the piece's story. The seller would be better off holding on to that item until he or she has made enough profit to buy a better camera, but that doesn't usually happen.

Figure 4.3

Unless you want to take a gamble, look for a clear photo like this when browsing to bid.

For me, the key determinant with regard to taking a chance on a fuzzy photo is the price of the item. If I pay less than $15 for an item, I figure I'm not out much if my gamble goes bust. Rather than deal with the hassle of packing the piece back up and returning it, I send the seller a polite e-mail that points out the mistake in an effort to help him or her learn for the next time around. If I feel it was an honest mistake, I'll also forego leaving feedback on the seller; besides, I share the blame for bidding on a listing with a fuzzy photo. If the seller is offended by my actions—sending a polite e-mail and opting out of leaving feedback—I probably won't do business with him or her again.

Caution

Never trust a photo to tell you the story about a piece. When you see an item whose description merely says "see photo" or "the photo says it all," you've got three choices: gamble on the photo actually saying it all, move along to a similar listing with an adequate description, or ask the seller enough questions to feel confident in bidding. Frankly, moving on is often the best choice. After all, if a seller doesn't care enough about the auction to write an adequate description, that may signal that he or she is too lazy to follow through with adequate customer service. Then again, if it's a rare piece that you've been dying to add to your collection, letting it go so easily won't sit well with you. That's when posing a list of questions to the seller will help to set your mind at ease before you place a bid.

Questions, Questions, and Yet More Questions

Unfortunately, sellers on eBay often overlook important details in item descriptions and photos. These particulars can range from shipping charges you'll be expected to pay to details about the size of the piece to condition issues. If reviewing an item's description and photo doesn't answer each and every question you have about the piece, don't hesitate to e-mail the seller to find out more.

For instance, if I were contemplating a bid on a Depression glass pitcher for my collection, I would ask about specific condition issues I know are problematic with pitchers. Did the seller hold the pitcher to the light to examine the base of the handle for cracks? Did she run her finger along the lip and rim to make sure it isn't chipped? Was the base examined for excessive wear and chunky chips? If the pitcher's exact dimensions were omitted, I'd verify the size. I'd also address any issues relating to reproductions that I'm aware of. Lastly, if shipping costs weren't specified upfront, I would also ask how much it will cost to ship the pitcher, because they can be somewhat heavy.

You should never feel bad about questioning a seller when you deem it necessary, and the seller should provide the information you're requesting readily and freely. If she doesn't know an answer, it's fine for her to say so. If you're asking about age or provenance, which is basically the background on the piece, the seller may well be clueless. But any seller should be able to answer direct questions about condition, size, shipping, payment methods, and other issues that may affect the outcome of the deal. If the seller ignores you, or provides evasive or unclear answers to your questions, move along to another auction.

Tip

While you're at it, you might as well ask whether the seller accepts returns. Some sellers state in their auction descriptions that returns are never accepted, others accept returns only if the item is misrepresented in the description, and still others accept all returns, no questions asked. Many sellers, however, don't say anything at all, assuming that in the auction arena, no returns are implied. If it's not spelled out for you in the item description, you'll serve yourself well to ask ahead of time just to be sure.

Conducting Completed Listings Searches:
Is It Really a Bargain on eBay?

People often ask me about the value of an antique, and it's always a hard question to answer—especially because reference guides on antiques and collectibles can be off kilter when you consider that prices tend to fluctuate depending on where you are. As a general rule, prices for antiques are higher on the East Coast, especially when you're shopping in New York City, and also in California. If the author of a reference guide resides in one of those locations, his or her assessment of the market using price points obtained from shows, malls, and live auctions would be different from one I might compile based on what I find in Texas. Some things would be higher in price here, but many would be lower. Depending on where you reside and the location you're shopping, you can find what you perceive to be bargains in different parts of the country.

That's sort of the way it is on eBay, too. Sometimes when I'm browsing the vintage costume jewelry listings, as I'm prone to do any given day, I see people paying a pretty penny for something I could find in my own neighborhood for a song. And I often think to myself, "If they'd just shop around a bit, they could find the same thing for much less in an antique mall." But that's the beauty of eBay; if you don't feel like shopping around to get what you want, you don't have to. Or perhaps you live in a remote area where antiques and collectibles are sparse, or you just don't have the time or energy to spend hours combing flea markets to unearth a decorative item for your home. In all these situations, eBay's a good alternative for shoppers.

If you do have time to shop around a bit, however, it's a good idea. For example, I was at an antiques show recently and spotted a couple of Barbie dolls I might like for my collection. The price seemed reasonable, but I just wasn't sure, so I decided to call home and ask my husband to perform a completed listings search on eBay to make sure they were really bargains. It turned out that both the dolls I had my eye on had recently sold on eBay for $15–20 less than the show seller's asking price. Even with a 10 to 20 percent discount, once sales tax is added back on, the dolls at the show didn't seem like such a good deal anymore. In this case, eBay came out on top. A few booths down at that same show, however, I spotted a pair of nice 1950s earrings designed by Miriam Haskell for $10. I knew from experience that I wouldn't find a similar pair on eBay for that price, so I snatched them up. The same thing happened with a long-stemmed Victorian hatpin for $20 and with several 1950s handbags for $8 each. I walked away from the show very pleased with my purchases, and I waited until I got home to shop online for Barbie dolls.

Even when you choose to buy exclusively on eBay, it's wise to perform completed listings searches for comparison purposes simply because it's so easy. A search like this will help you determine the median price for the item that interests you. By extension, you can determine whether the item you're contemplating has been bid up beyond the usual selling point on eBay, which can happen when inexperienced or uninformed buyers overbid on an item, or when a bidding war occurs. If so, it might be better to back off on that lot and wait for another one with similar contents to be listed. It can also give you an idea of how high the prices for that item have been going *before* you enter your bid. If it's a piece you just have to have, you'll want to know exactly how high you're probably going to have to bid to get it.

Note

Because it's up to each individual seller to set opening bids and reserves as he or she lists items on eBay, starting amounts can vary widely. If you're shopping for items within your area of expertise, you'll be able to identify unreasonable starting bids immediately. For instance, it's pretty easy for me to recognize a vintage Barbie doll dress with a starting price of $50 as unreasonable when I know it regularly sells for $15. When I notice prices aren't competitive on eBay, it's usually a pretty good indicator that the seller hasn't done his or her homework—or that the seller is trying to see just how much he can get away with charging. Either way, that particular listing is probably worth avoiding.

Alternatively, conducting a completed listings search can help you determine whether the item you're considering is *underpriced*. If that's the case, you may simply be lucking into a great deal, or it could be that the item has condition issues that have turned other bidders off. (A third possibility is that the seller has questionable feedback, which has driven potential bidders away. You'll learn more about interpreting the seller's feedback later in this chapter.)

Completed item searches can also help you determine how frequently similar items are listed—and, by extension, whether you can afford to let the item you're considering slip away. For example, if a completed listings search yields

50 listings whose descriptions are similar to the one you're considering, you can safely assume you'll have another crack at finding the item if the one currently on the block costs more than you're willing to pay. Then again, if the completed listings search yields, say, three results, that means the odds of finding the item at a later date are considerably slimmer. If you let it get away today, how long are you going to have to wait to have a chance at another one? In my case, I get really excited when an older piece of Napier vintage costume jewelry surfaces on eBay. The pieces from the 1950s are hard to come by, and when they do crop up on eBay, which happens from time to time, I don't want to miss the opportunity to add new pieces to my collection. I'll go after these items a little more aggressively, keeping a closer eye on them throughout the duration of the auction, than I will a run-of-the-mill piece that pops up for auction on a regular basis.

To conduct a completed listings search, do the following:

1. Click the Search button at the top of the eBay home page (next to the Browse button).

2. Type your search keyword(s) in the space indicated, as shown in Figure 4.4.

Figure 4.4

Click on the Completed listings only check box to begin a completed listings search.

3. Check the Completed listings only check box.

4. Click on the Search button to the right of the keyword text box.

5. Enter your user ID and password, if prompted to do so (you must be a registered member of eBay to use this feature).

6. Review the list of items that comes up on the screen, as shown in Figure 4.5.

7. If needed, revise your keywords in the box below the All Items tab and search again.

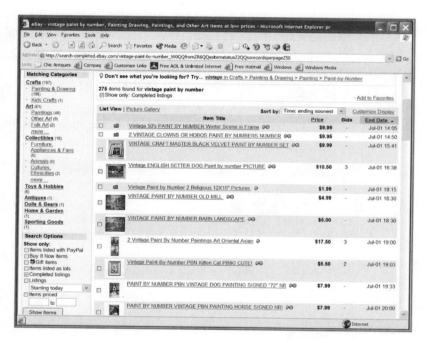

Figure 4.5

Review the results.

When you perform a completed listings search, you may notice that the prices can vary widely on items that look virtually the same, as shown in Figure 4.6. I've heard it said that an antique's worth lies in how much someone is willing to pay for it at any given moment; that assessment is so very true, especially on eBay. A bargain item this week might be the hottest thing going next week, selling for remarkable prices, only to return to bargain status a few weeks later.

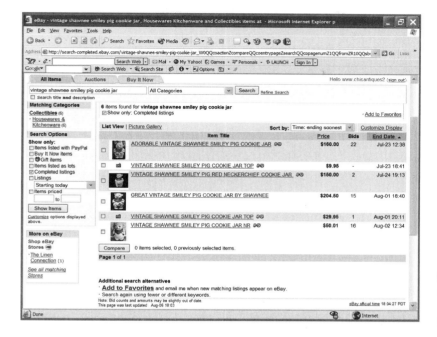

Figure 4.6

Completed listings searches can reveal wide variations in price on very similar items.

Assessing the Seller

You've read the listing, studied photos of the item, asked—and received answers to—any questions you had about the item, hammered out any shipping issues, and have run a completed listings search to make sure it's priced appropriately. You're ready to place your bid, right? Wrong. Before you submit a bid, it's wise to take some steps to ensure that the person selling the item you want is trustworthy.

If you're at all nervous about joining the fray on eBay, the preceding paragraph probably set off some alarms in your head. Before you decide to chuck the whole venture, let me assuage your fears by telling you that in all the years I've been trading on eBay, I've had only one instance of non-delivery of goods. Fortunately, the item in question was a mere $3 piece of vintage sheet music that never showed up. I tried—unsuccessfully—to get in touch with the seller via e-mail, phone, and even snail mail, but to no avail. Finally, realizing that something unfortunate may have happened to the seller, and figuring that the seller probably hadn't made it his life's work to bilk me out of $3, I decided to let it go and move on. And even though other buyers haven't been so lucky—some losing large sums to unscrupulous sellers who set up eBay accounts for the sole purpose of swindling unsuspecting buyers—most of my online friends agree that the threat is minimal when their quarry consists of antiques and collectibles valued at a few hundred dollars or less. The fact is, most transactions go off without a hitch.

Even so, it's an unfortunate fact that although the vast majority of sellers you'll encounter on eBay are decent, upright people, a few bad apples do exist. That's why eBay has given you a few tools to assess whether a seller is credible and trustworthy. Among the techniques that eBay singles out for ensuring that a seller is on the up and up are checking the seller's feedback and verifying his or her user ID.

Using Feedback to Gauge a Seller's Integrity

While reviewing a seller's feedback page won't buy you any guarantees, it's a good place to start when you're trying to evaluate a seller's trustworthiness. It only takes a few minutes, and it's well worth the effort. To access any seller's feedback page, simply click on the number in parentheses located after her user ID on any one of her listings, as shown in Figure 4.7.

First and foremost, as shown in Figure 4.8, which details my own feedback record, you can see whether the seller has received negative feedback, and how long ago that feedback was logged. eBay also enables you to read a seller's response to feedback, so you can get a better idea about the circumstances surrounding the red mark. Sometimes the tone of the remarks can be very telling. For example, if the initial feedback seems irrationally worded, that hint of rage can tell you something about the buyer's disposition. Should he or she really be getting that worked up over a chip in a piece of antique glass? And you can glean something about the seller by the way he or she responds to being criticized.

You can also review positive feedback about the seller, and see how far those comments outweigh any negatives that might be present. One negative feedback among hundreds of positives does not a bad reputation make. For this reason, looking at the percentage of positive feedback is telling. It should be pretty close to 100 percent, but depending on the number of total feedbacks logged, the 99th percentile isn't bad either.

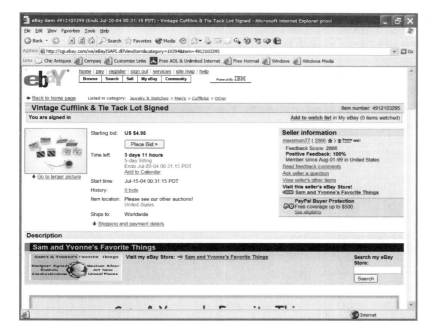

Figure 4.7

This seller has a feedback rating of 2866, as indicated in parentheses after her user ID, maxsmom77.

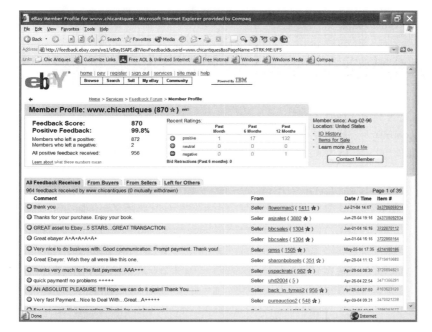

Figure 4.8

A look at a seller's feedback rating can be a very useful buying tool.

eBay's Suggestions for Developing Seller Trust

eBay addresses the topic of developing seller trust in its Buyers Guide. To see eBay's suggestions on the matter, click the Help link at the top of any page on eBay. On the Help page, click the Buying link to open the Buyers Guide, shown in Figure 4.9. Scroll down to the Trusting the Seller link, and click it for more information.

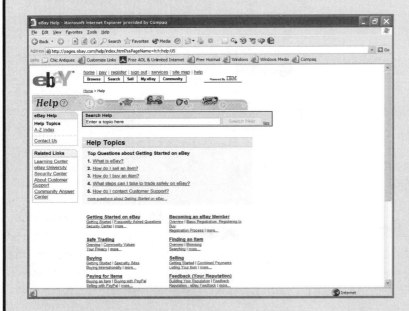

Figure 4.9

Take a look at eBay's Buyers Guide for an overview of some of the topics discussed here.

While I walk you through many of the topics listed in this guide, it's good to know that eBay addresses this important issue. eBay recognizes that bidders who don't feel comfortable on the site not only won't spend much time there, but probably won't venture a bid either. Online sellers depend on bidders to stay in business; in turn, eBay depends on sellers to pay its overhead and turn a decent profit.

Caution

Although eBay's feedback system can give you a sense of a seller's integrity, it is not foolproof. One way in which feedback can be skewed is when sellers use a service called SquareTrade to have negative feedback removed (they must first make a case that the feedback was unwarranted). And of course, a certain percentage of unsatisfied customers will simply opt out of logging any type of feedback at all. I've done this myself from time to time to allow sellers to save face when they make a mistake.

Either way, you'll also want to take note of whether telling feedback—positive or negative—was logged by people who bought from the seller in question or by people who sold to them, since the seller might use the same account for both sales and purchases on eBay. Since you're on the buying side, knowing that the person has enjoyed good feedback as a seller can be comforting. Their buying experiences, however, might be irrelevant, since that's a different kettle of fish.

Viewing the Seller's ID History

While you're on the seller's feedback page, take a minute to see how long his or her user ID has been active. If the individual has been on eBay for many years, he or she probably is not out to defraud anyone; any mistakes the seller has made were probably honest ones. Of course, I'm not suggesting that new sellers aren't honest people; most are. It's just that you just don't have as much information to go on when assessing a new seller's track record. Indeed, I often buy from new sellers; they sometimes list the best bargains around, thanks to the learning curve involved in selling on eBay.

While you're at it, you might want to click the ID History link that appears just below the date that the user registered with eBay to find out how many times that user has changed his or her user ID since registering with eBay. Although name changes are often harmless and don't affect a feedback rating, they can sometimes indicate that a seller is trying to hide from past buyers. If you're dealing with a seller who has numerous negative feedback comments and who has changed IDs a number of times, you may want to move on to another auction.

Getting to Know a Seller: The About Me Page

Sellers who want you to feel confident bidding on their wares often set up an About Me page on eBay so you can learn more about them and their business. You can tell if a seller has taken the initiative to develop an About Me page by looking for a little blue and red "me" icon next to their feedback rating (as shown in Figure 4.10). To access a seller's About Me page, simply click on the "me" icon.

Figure 4.10

To access a seller's About Me page, click on the "me" icon next to their feedback rating.

The About Me page allows sellers to post background information about their business, information about their personal collections, interesting anecdotes, other relevant experience, and also post a photograph, as shown in Figure 4.11. This often adds a personal touch that raises the buyer's comfort level. Even though any registered eBay user can craft an About Me page, most people who take the time to do so are honest.

Figure 4.11

Sellers often include some background about their interests, anecdotes, and photos on an About Me page, along with links to other sites they're associated with, including brick-and-mortar antiques shops and Web-based stores.

In fact, an About Me page can enable bidders to access several of the seller's favorite links. Because eBay no longer allows sellers to post links to their brick-and-mortar antiques shops or even Web shops in their item descriptions, this is the place to look for this type of information. Besides, knowing that a merchant has set up an additional online site to sell their wares is a good indicator that he or she is in business for the long haul.

Note

Many antiques dealers on eBay, including yours truly, have traditional businesses elsewhere. Like me, they see eBay as an extension of their buying and selling activities. Other sellers deal on eBay exclusively, but just because they don't have physical antique shops you can visit when traveling the country (or world) doesn't mean they're less trustworthy.

Resources for Combating Online Fraud

If fraud on eBay is still a concern for you, and you're not alone if it is, you'll be pleased to know that there are several online resources for combating the problem. For example, in the event you're ever a victim of serious online fraud of any type, the Internet Fraud Complaint Center (www.ifccfbi.gov/index.asp), shown in Figure 4.12, and the e-commerce section of the Federal Trade Commission's Web site (www.ftc.gov/bcp/menu-internet.htm) are good spots to log complaints and learn more about Internet trading.

Figure 4.12

The Internet Fraud Complaint Center offers a Web-based center for reporting online fraud issues.

The Internet Fraud Complaint Center (IFCC) is a partnership between the Federal Bureau of Investigation (FBI) and the National White Collar Crime Center. The IFCC's mission deals expressly with addressing fraud committed over the Internet. For victims of Internet fraud, IFCC provides a convenient reporting system to alert authorities of suspected violations. For law enforcement and regulatory agencies, the Web site offers a central location for complaints related to Internet fraud, helps to identify fraud patterns, and provides current statistics relating to fraud trends.

When you visit the Federal Trade Commission's Web site, you'll find a special section devoted to e-commerce. This deals with buying and selling online in many different formats. For eBay buyers, a number of articles on this site provide information on auctions, e-payments, "phishing," and many of the other topics covered in this book. This information is designed to protect you from falling victim to online scammers, so it's worth taking a look. Besides, it never hurts to get another perspective.

chapter 5

Bidding Strategies

Now that you know a good bit about finding items on eBay and assessing whether an item is a good buy, it's time to delve into specific bidding strategies. From understanding the proxy bidding process and sniping alternatives to utilizing eBay's Buy It Now feature to steal a deal, eBay offers a number of ways for you to fulfill your buying objectives with ease. In this chapter, you'll learn the ins and outs of bidding on eBay.

Using the Watch List

Before I get into the details on bidding, I'd like to discuss a very useful eBay tool: the watch list. The fact is, eBay has so many interesting items up for grabs, it's hard to keep track of—let alone bid on—them all. eBay's watch list allows you to track items that interest you without actually bidding on them. That way, if you're on the fence about an item, or you want to track several auctions featuring identical items to make sure you get the best deal, or you just run across a fabulous item that you know will sell high and you want to see how it ends just for fun, you can easily do so—without wasting time tracking down the same items over and over again using eBay's Search and Browse functions. No matter how you end up using the watch list, you've got 30 slots to fill with auctions that tickle your fancy.

You can even use your watch list to monitor items you already have in your collection to see what they're currently selling for on eBay. This is especially useful if you're thinking about selling those pieces.

To add an item to your watch list, simply pull up its auction listing and click the Add to watch list link located right under the item number at the top right of the screen. Then, the next time you access your My eBay page, a list of items you've added to your watch list will be waiting for you to review. From there, you can delete the items that no longer interest you, view the listings again, or even bid on the item. (You'll learn more about using the My eBay page later in this chapter, in the section "Tracking Your Auctions with the My eBay Page.")

Placing the Traditional Proxy Bid

Now that you've thoroughly researched an item you've found up for auction, and have determined the seller to be trustworthy, and maybe even let it sit a few days on your watch list while you mulled it over, you're ready to place your bid. Here's how it's done:

Before you place a bid, be certain you're absolutely committed to buying the item. If you win the auction, you'll be expected to honor your bid by both the seller and eBay. That's a given.

1. Click the Place Bid button found on the listing page, shown in Figure 5.1.

2. In the space provided, type the *maximum amount* you're willing to pay for the item, as shown in Figure 5.2.

3. Click the Continue button.

If you're not currently logged on to the site, eBay will prompt you to do so. Simply enter your user name and password in the spaces provided and click on the Submit button.

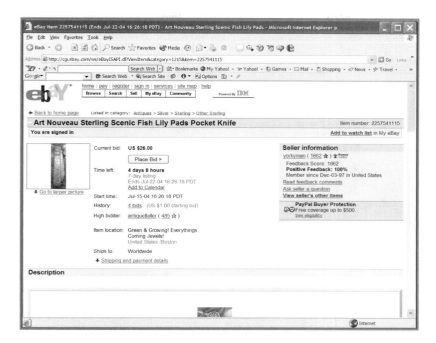

Figure 5.1

This sample listing page shows the Place Bid button you will click on to begin the bidding process.

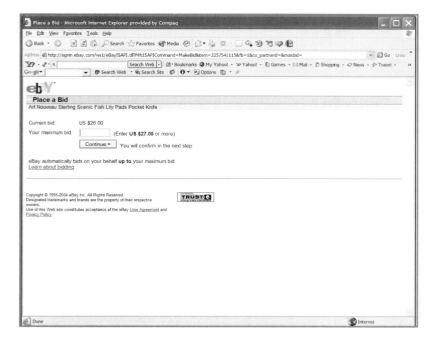

Figure 5.2

Enter the maximum amount you're willing to pay for an item in the blank provided.

4. eBay displays a Submit Your Bid page, where you can ensure you've entered the proper amount. If so, click the Submit button; if not, click your Web browser's Back button and repeat steps 2 and 3.

5. eBay informs you as to whether you are the high bidder. If not, you have the option to bid again, this time upping the maximum amount you're willing to pay for the item.

Notice in step 3 that you enter the maximum amount you're willing to pay for the item. That's because eBay employs a *proxy bidding system*. That is, rather than requiring you to sit by your computer for the duration of the auction to keep track of the bidding, the way you would with a live auction, eBay requires you to bid just once. It then compares your bid—that is, the maximum amount you're willing to pay for the item—to any other bids that have been placed for the listing to determine the new high bid.

Note

The number you enter as your maximum bid is kept confidential; other bidders don't know how much you've bid. In fact, even the seller won't know how much you've bid until after the auction ends. The only number displayed in conjunction with the auction is the current high bid.

Confused? Here's an example. Suppose you're dying to own a vintage Capodi-monte lamp you've found on eBay and one other person has bid on it. The current high bid on the lamp is $21.50, but you'd gladly shell out $100 to make it yours. You place your maximum bid, $100, and click the Submit button. In turn, eBay compares your maximum bid with that of the other bidder. If your maximum bid is higher, then you'll become the new high bidder. But here's the twist: The new high bid *may or may not* be $100. For example, if the other bidder's maximum bid was only $25, then the new high bid might be, say, $26, depending on that auction's specified bid increment. In other words, eBay uses only as much of your allotted bid as necessary to put you in the top bidding position. If, on the other hand, your maximum bid is less than the other bidder's, eBay will inform you that you've been outbid. At that point, you have the option of placing a second, higher bid to try to take the lead—assuming you're interested in paying that much for the item in question.

Note that just because you're the high bidder doesn't mean you should start clearing a space for your new lamp. You can't officially call it yours until the auction ends—with you as the high bidder. In the interim, you may have to fend off other collectors who are interested in the same piece. If another person bids on the item but his or her maximum bid is lower than yours—say, $35— then the price of the lamp will rise accordingly (to $36 in this example), but you'll remain the high bidder. If, however, the other person's maximum bid is higher than your top bid, he or she will be come the high bidder. When eBay e-mails you to inform you that your status as high bidder has been usurped, it will be up to you to decide whether you want to engage in a bidding war for the lamp by placing a new bid. Whoever is the high bidder at the moment the auction closes gets the lamp.

Note

If you're interested in seeing what eBay has to say about bidding, take a moment to check out your My eBay page, which you access by clicking the My eBay button at the top of eBay's main page. On this page, scroll down to the Buying Links area and click More. Available links include Learning Center, which offers quick courses on how eBay operates; Buyers Guide, which covers how to buy on eBay and how to contact sellers; Tips for Buyers, which includes a buyer's checklist with a helpful overview of pre-bidding considerations; Bidding Basics, which offers detailed instructions on placing bids; and Bidding Frequently Asked Questions, where you can find answers on numerous common questions people ask about eBay.

Reserve-Price Auctions

Suppose the person selling that vintage lamp you're salivating over isn't willing to part with it unless it fetches at least $50. In that case, she can set a *reserve price* for the auction. That way, she's required to sell the lamp only if the bidding surpasses $50. Sounds simple enough, right? Well, almost. There is one small catch. Just as your maximum bid is kept confidential, so, too, is the auction's reserve price. All you know when you peruse the item listing is whether the reserve price has been met.

If you come across a reserve-price auction whose reserve price has been met, you'll approach it just as you would a regular auction. That is, you'll place your maximum bid and hope that you're the high bidder when the auction closes.

But if bidding for the item you're interested in hasn't yet reached the reserve price, one of three things will occur when you enter your maximum bid:

- **You'll become the current high bidder and the reserve price *will* be met.** In this case, eBay will automatically jump the high bid up to meet the reserve price.

- **You'll become the current high bidder, but the reserve price *won't* be met.** In this case, your bid will be advanced just enough to beat the maximum bid of the next highest bidder. If you like, you can place another maximum bid, and hope that it is high enough to meet the reserve price.

- **You won't become the current high bidder, and the reserve price won't be met.** That means that another bidder has a higher maximum bid in place—though not high enough to meet the reserve price. In this case, you have the option of placing another maximum bid and hoping that it is high enough to not only best the other bidder, but to meet the reserve price as well.

Caution

Resist the temptation to try to bid up to the reserve-price level in your quest to satisfy your curiosity about just how high that buying price might be. Why? Because once the reserve price is met, then a contract to buy the item is in place. If no one outbids you after the reserve price is met and you remain the high bidder, you will be obligated to buy the item at auction end. Moral of the story: Never bid more than you're willing to pay for an item in an effort to uncover the reserve price.

Dutch Auctions

In addition to regular proxy-bidding auctions and reserve-price auctions, eBay offers a third type of auction: Dutch auction. In a Dutch auction, the seller offers multiple identical items for sale. Interested buyers bid on the auction, and in the process specify how many of the items they want to buy. The high bid at auction close dictates the price of each individual item. Dutch auctions with antiques and older collectibles are rare because it can be tough to find multiple identical pieces. That said, on occasion, a seller discovers "new old stock" after cleaning out an old store, or finds boxes of identical merchandise in an old warehouse. In that case, a Dutch auction may just do the trick.

Recognizing Shill Bidding

Shill bidding, also known as *bid padding*, is the practice of entering in a false bid to unfairly drive up the price of an auction. Although it's not common, a seller can shill bid by setting up a fake eBay account and bidding on his or her own items, or by soliciting a friend to bid on an item without obligating him or her to purchase the item in the event he or she wins. eBay prohibits shill bidding, and sellers found guilty of this tactic can face account suspension.

Shill bidding usually comes to light when a buyer reviews the final bids after an auction has ended, and then reviews the seller's history. If the seller's history reveals that several of the seller's auctions have been won by the same user ID, and if that user ID has a zero or very low feedback rating, then this might be cause for suspicion. To review a seller's history, do the following:

1. Click on the Search button located at the top of any eBay page.

2. Click on the Items By Seller link.

3. Enter the seller's user ID and, in the Include completed listings field, select the All option button.

4. Click the Search button.

5. Review the list that comes up, noting that closed auctions are indicated by an asterisk in parentheses next to the high bidder's user ID.

If you have good reason to believe a seller has employed shill bidding to drive up the price on an auction, then by all means report the seller to eBay. (I urge you to resolve the matter in this way rather than e-mailing the seller directly; eBay has more means at its disposal to investigate the matter than you do.) Keep in mind, however, that this is a serious accusation that places a seller's reputation at stake, and if your accusations prove unfounded, you may be accused of libel.

To Snipe or Not to Snipe

Suppose you're still the high bidder on that vintage lamp, and there's just a minute to go in the auction. You rub your hands eagerly as the countdown begins, certain that victory is yours, when suddenly, with just seconds remaining, you get outbid, and there's no time on the clock to counter.

So what happened?

I'll tell you what happened. You've been sniped.

Basically, *sniping* is the practice of waiting until the final seconds of an auction to place a bid in the hopes that the current high bidder will be knocked out of the running with no time to place a counter bid. Although sniping does sound sort of sneaky, it's widely practiced on eBay, and is perfectly acceptable. In fact, most advanced bidders regularly employ this tactic. Quite simply, they've found that they win more auctions by sniping than they would otherwise.

Should you consider jumping on the snipe bandwagon? That's up to you. That said, sniping does offer some real advantages:

- **Time to think**. If you find an item that intrigues you, but the auction won't be ending for a few days, you can place it on your watch list and mull it over instead of bidding right away. If you decide you'd like to buy it, you can wait until the last few seconds of the auction to bid. You'll learn how to place an item on your watch list later in this chapter.

- **Better prices**. By sniping, you avoid getting caught up in bidding wars, which often result in higher prices. Other "warring" bidders may still outbid you, but you won't be one of the parties driving up the price when you snipe. You simply bid the highest amount you're willing to pay during the last few seconds of the auction, and let the chips fall where they may.

- **Avoidance of bid stalkers**. Bid stalkers—people who track the activities of knowledgeable, more experienced bidders on eBay and attempt to outbid them—are quickly foiled when you employ the sniping tactic.

- **Minimizing of shill bids**. Because sniping occurs at the last second, doing so thwarts shill-bidding sellers. They simply don't have time to counter in order to drive up the price of an auction.

Note

All eBayers are free to snipe, so there's really no unfair advantage at play. Even so, in spite of all the benefits of sniping, some tried-and-true antiquers see it as unfair and downright ruthless, and they refuse to participate. These buyers prefer to put in the highest amount they're willing to pay when they place their proxy bid and let the deal end where it may.

More on Thwarting Bid Stalkers

If you're trying to foil a bid stalker, employing the snipe works extremely well because your user ID isn't on display for other bidders to view. You bid during the last few seconds, so there's no time to stalk. But if you don't want to snipe or pay a service to do it for you, however, you also have the option of using dual IDs. Many people (including myself) have one eBay account for selling and another for buying. They don't let slip their buying ID to others in their collecting groups; they reveal it only to sellers when they pay for their auctions. In the event someone catches on to their buying ID, they may decide to change it (eBay allows you to change your ID once a month without setting up a new account).

Even if you have just one eBay ID, you can still change it occasionally for this purpose. Keep in mind, though, that if you also sell on eBay, this may turn potential bidders off. Rather than realizing you're trying to thwart a bid stalker, they might think you've switched names to hide from dissatisfied buyers, and you won't have the opportunity to explain yourself unless they ask you outright. Worse, your regular buyers will no longer be able to find you when they search for your seller ID, which could be even a greater concern.

Manual Sniping at No Cost

All that's required to snipe on eBay is a little time and patience, and the ability to remember to log on to the site a few minutes before the auction you're interested in bidding on is scheduled to end. Once you're logged on, do the following:

1. With about five minutes to go on the auction you want to snipe, open two Web browser windows, each displaying the auction's listing page.

2. In the first browser window, click the Refresh button every 10 seconds or so to monitor the auction clock and determine how quickly the site and your Internet connection are responding (it may be running slow during periods of high traffic). The Time Left clock will count down each time you refresh the browser window.

Note

If you have a high-speed Internet connection through a DSL line or cable modem, then you're one step ahead of the game. It won't be as imperative for you to gauge how quickly pages are reloading on eBay; you can reasonably assume it'll be pretty quick.

3. In the second browser window, click on the Place Bid button and enter your maximum bid in the space shown.

4. Click on the Continue button to view the Bid Confirmation page, but *do not* click the Submit button.

5. Return your attention to the first browser window and continue to refresh it every 10 seconds or so to keep track of the time and to monitor your connection. Also watch the bid price to see if it changes. There's a good chance that someone else out there is also planning a last-minute snipe, and if your rival enters his or her final bid a bit prematurely, you'll be able to see it and adjust your own bid accordingly.

6. If necessary, adjust your maximum bid by clicking the Back button in the second browser window and changing the dollar amount. Click Continue again to return to the Bid Confirmation page, but again, do not click the Submit button.

7. Continue watching the first browser window, refreshing it every few seconds, especially when you have less than one minute left on the clock. The time will pass quickly at this point so it's important to keep a careful watch. When you get down to 10 seconds on the clock (unless your connection is running slowly, in which case you'll want to adjust to 15–20 seconds out), switch to the second browser window—the one displaying the Bid Confirmation page—and count to three. It's time to bid!

8. Click the Submit button and wait for the results to pop up.

If your timing was just right and your bid was high enough to trump the current high bidder and any other snipers lurking in cyberspace, you've just won an auction and experienced your first snipe. Congratulations! If you didn't win, though, don't get too upset about it. Sniping doesn't guarantee that you'll always come out on top, although it does give you an opportunity to improve your odds. That's why it's worth considering.

Using a Sniping Service

When you get really serious about sniping, it's time to consider using a sniping service. I do, and I'm pleased as punch with my results. Since I buy frequently on eBay, it just makes sense for me to pay a sniping service a small fee to process bids on my behalf. In fact, I rarely place traditional proxy bids anymore!

When you use a sniping service, you're no longer tied to your computer, waiting for auctions to end. Instead, when you find an item on eBay that interests you, you simply enter the auction's incidentals on the sniping service's Web site, adding your maximum bid and how much time you want left on the clock when your bid is placed. Then, the sniping service logs on to eBay at the very end of the auction and places the bid on your behalf. Nothing shady happens; it's just a last-second bid. If your bid is the highest, you'll come out on top.

There are several choices when it comes to sniping services. I prefer eSnipe (http://www.esnipe.com), shown in Figure 5.3, which I find to be easy to navigate and use. It's a very reliable service with very little downtime, and more importantly, it's reasonably priced. Other eBayers like Amhurst Robots (http://www.vrane.com), which looks to be a rather unsophisticated free service; and Auction Sniper (http://www.auctionsniper.com), which offers a free trial period. If you think you've reached a point in your eBay career where a sniping service would be helpful, you can compare auction services on Auction Bytes (http://www.auctionbytes.com), which offers a helpful Sniping Chart, shown in Figure 5.4. The chart is accessible from the site's home page. As more and more people start utilizing sniping services, these services can continue to grow, offering more sniping options to online consumers.

Figure 5.3

Utilizing a service like eSnipe can help you win more auctions at better prices by avoiding competitive bidding and bidding wars that can take place during the course of an auction to drive up the ending price.

Figure 5.4

AuctionBytes.com offers bidders a comparative chart to evaluate which sniping services may serve them the best.

No matter which sniping service you sign on with, there are some definite advantages to doing so. These include the following:

- Your bids are placed on your behalf even if you're away from the computer, whether you're working, spending time with your family, or enjoying a vacation.

- You need not stay up half the night or wake up at the crack of dawn to manually snipe an auction you really want the opportunity to win.

- You can get your bid in a few seconds later with a sniping service than a manual snipe usually affords, which can make a big difference when you're bidding against another sniper.

- You can use your snipe list like a watch list, adding and deleting items as you've had the opportunity to mull them over prior to auction end.

- You no longer forget about auctions you wanted the opportunity to snipe.

Of course, you'll no longer enjoy the thrill of the manual snipe when you switch to a service, but I don't think you'll miss it when you discover the convenience these services present. Working more efficiently to accomplish an objective always feels great.

Retracting a Bid

As you know, you're expected to honor any bid you place on eBay. But the people who run eBay do realize it's possible to make a mistake or to come across additional information about an auction that warrants a bid retraction. Bid retractions are acceptable in the following circumstances:

■ You made a typographical error when you placed your bid. Suppose you type $99.50 when you mean to type $9.95. If this happens to you, you'll need to retract your bid and enter the correct one straight away. Failing to do so violates eBay's policies and may result in suspension of your account.

■ The description of an item you've bid on has changed considerably. With antiques and collectibles, this can happen when bidders contact the seller to ask questions about the item. If issues dealing with condition, authenticity, or another significant oversight in the description arise during this information exchange, a seller will often modify the item's description. If changes to the description indicate that the item is worth significantly less than you originally thought, then you have the option of retracting your bid.

■ You've tried to reach the seller, to no avail. This means you've tried to e-mail and phone the seller with no success. eBay provides detailed contact information to bidders who request it, so there should be no reason that you can't contact a seller should the need arise. If you can't reach a seller, and important questions are going unanswered, retracting a bid is acceptable.

■ Someone else using your user ID and password has bid on an item without your knowledge. Of course, I know you'll never, ever intentionally share your password with others. But in the event someone gets hold of this information, you'll not only want to retract the bids, but also promptly change your password (and possibly your ID, depending on how concerned you are).

Although you are free to retract a bid for any of the reasons cited here, be warned that you should not abuse this privilege. To discourage you from doing so, eBay records each bid retraction in your feedback record. In addition, other factors, such as time constraints, should be considered. For instance, if you bid within 12 hours of the end of an auction, you can only retract your bid within one hour of when your bid was placed. And, regardless of when you bid during the auction period, you can't retract a bid during the last 12 hours of the auction unless the seller agrees to allow you to do so.

Before you fill in the bid retraction form, it's sensible to review eBay's current policies on bid retractions. To access this information, click the Services button at the top of any page on eBay, scroll down to Bidding and Buying Services, and click on the Retracting your bid link. If you're satisfied that your circumstances meet eBay's bid-retraction criteria, retract your bid from the same page by doing the following:

1. Enter the item number.

2. Choose a reason for your retraction from the pull-down menu.

3. Click the Retract bid button.

Shopping with Buy It Now

I mentioned eBay's Buy It Now feature in Chapter 3, "Finding Antiques and Collectibles on eBay." Auctions with a Buy It Now option enable buyers to forego the bidding process and buy the item at a fixed price. When it comes to items that offer the Buy It Now option, the trick is deciding whether the fixed price is a bargain, or whether the item might go more cheaply at auction. If the fixed price is low, and the item is one you really want, you're better off using the Buy It Now feature. But if you're willing to gamble a bit, placing a maximum bid that's lower than the Buy It Now price is the way to go. You may get the item more cheaply—or you may lose the auction altogether. And of course, once you place your bid, the Buy It Now option disappears; when that happens, in many cases, the item's ending price ends up being higher than its Buy It Now price was.

Note

As I mentioned in Chapter 3, I find that searching for Buy It Now items makes sense when you're under the gun to find a particular item—for example, if the item is a gift and the recipient's birthday is just a week away. By focusing on items with a Buy It Now option, you avoid having to wait for an auction's end date to buy, which means you get a jump on receiving the item.

You won't always find reason to use Buy It Now, and many times taking a chance on bidding is the better way to go. But when you recognize an item you're interested in to be undervalued at the Buy It Now price, or even within your budget, why risk bidding and paying a higher price, or losing out to another bidder altogether? In that situation, taking advantage of the fixed price makes good sense.

Note

Some sellers don't even give buyers the opportunity to bid on their wares, offering eBay's Buy It Now feature as an item's only buying option. Other sellers allow you to place a bid on the item, but jack up the starting bid such that it very nearly matches the Buy It Now price. In that case, bidding rather than buying outright just doesn't make sense.

In any case, Buy It Now auctions offer buyers the opportunity to swoop in just after an item is listed and pick it off before anyone else has a chance to place a bid. The best strategy, then, is to search for newly listed Buy It Now auctions. As mentioned in Chapter 3, to find the most newly listed items in one convenient spot, click on the Site Map link at the top of any eBay page. Under the Browse category, click the New Today link to view all auctions listed within the past 24 hours in any category on eBay, and drill down to the category that interests you. In the left column on the category page, check Buy It Now items check box in the Search Options section. Click the Show Items button to narrow the list. Of course, if you prefer to search for a particular item that features the Buy It Now option rather than viewing all new Buy It Now listings, you can easily do so by following the instructions outlined in the section "When You Just Need to Buy It Now" in Chapter 3. You can even just scroll through listings as you normally do; all items available through Buy It Now are marked with an icon on the search result and category pages under the Bids column.

If the item that interests you features the Buy It Now option, and if you'd like to take advantage of using it, do the following:

1. Click the Buy It Now button on the item listing page.

2. Enter your user name and password, if prompted to do so.

3. eBay displays a screen that enables you to review your purchase. Click the Submit button to complete the Buy It Now transaction.

4. To pay using PayPal (assuming the seller accepts it), click the Pay Now button and complete the payment process. Alternatively, you can wait and pay when the seller contacts you by e-mail.

Note

For details on PayPal's payment process, see the section "Paying with PayPal" in Chapter 6, "I Won an Auction! Now What?"

Enjoying eBay Live Auctions

Since eBay has enjoyed such phenomenal success and has carefully built its reputation as a major player in the auction business, the company has started teaming up with some of the world's best-known live auction houses to run live auctions online (http://www.ebayliveauctions.com), as shown in Figure 5.5. These real-time live auctions allow you to bid as items are sold on the floor of an actual action house. Opening up live auctions to bidders in this way provides a boon to both eBay and to the auction houses. More bidders than ever can participate, meaning higher ending values (with many of them being high-dollar pieces) and more items sold in the long run. The auction houses do well, and eBay gets a cut as the facilitator.

When it comes to these live options, you have several options: You can place an absentee bid, bid live against the floor (that is, bid against people who are present at a live auction), or just watch the auction for fun—all through your computer. This is great news for high-end bidders who once had to travel to New York or San Francisco to bid at these auctions. The drawback is that bidders can't inspect the merchandise, which is divided into lots, prior to sale. That said, larger auction houses usually inspect and appraise their wares more thoroughly than the little country auctions frequented by most antiquers, which means that the odds of a major flaw being overlooked or an item being misrepresented are slim. Besides, all items are covered by traditional guarantees offered by the auction houses on all their sales, which should ease your fears somewhat.

To participate in Live Auctions, you must be a registered eBay user (as outlined in Chapter 1, "Getting Started"). Assuming you are, simply log on to http://www. ebayliveauctions.com to access *catalogs*—listings of items to be offered for sale—

Figure 5.5

eBay now offers live
auctions in conjunction
with some of the world's
best-known auction houses.

to upcoming live events. You can browse through the catalogs and search for specific lots to prepare your bidding strategy before entering the real-time competition against bidders actually present at the auction and Internet bidders from around the globe. If you click one of the auction items in a catalog, you'll see a screen similar to a traditional eBay bidding screen; the main differences are the pre-auction estimate of where the auction house believes bidding will end and a Place Absentee Bid button, as shown in Figure 5.6. You may also notice a note under the bidding button denoting that a buyer's premium will be added to the ending price; this buyer's premium can vary, but usually falls between 10 and 20 percent of the ending price.

If you decide to place an absentee bid, it will be collected online, compared to other absentee bids, and then reported to the auction house prior to the start of the live auction. The highest absentee bid is conveyed to the bidding audience, and that's the price at which the live bidding begins. If your absentee bid falls in the range of the pre-auction estimate, there's a chance you may win the auction. If, however, you stick with the opening bid—that is, the lowest permissible absentee bid, which is still high on many of these lots because of their prized nature—don't count on too many victories. You'll be bidding against advanced collectors in highly specialized fields who are often prepared to pay big bucks to add an item to a collection.

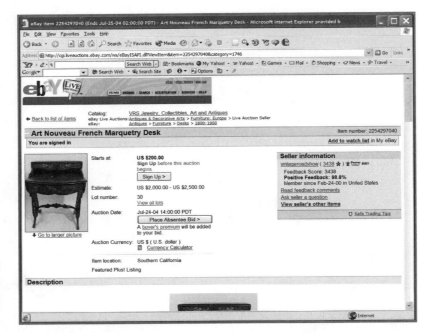

Figure 5.6

An example of an eBay Live Auctions listing, which allows you to place an absentee bid prior to the actual live auction.

When the auction actually begins, you can enjoy the thrill of bidding against live bidders if you like, or just watch the action take place. Even if you don't bid, it's really interesting to browse through the Live Auction catalogs to conduct research (the Search feature on www.eBay.com sometimes includes Live Auction listings in the mix of results as well; they're denoted with a little cartoon-like bidding paddle next to the listing title) or just for fun. A number of items in the Live Auction catalogs are so rare and valuable that they seldom come up for auction on eBay proper.

Tracking Your Auctions with the My eBay Page

One of the most useful tools on eBay is the My eBay page, and one of the great things about it is that you don't have to do anything extra to set it up. Just registering on the site gives you access to this page any time you'd like to view it. To access your own My eBay page, just log on to eBay and click on the My eBay button at the top of the site's main page. As shown in Figure 5.7, from this single page, you can do the following:

■ **Review items you've added to your watch list.** In addition to keeping track of where things stand, you can delete items that no longer interest you or bid on ones that do.

■ **Monitor the items you're bidding on.** This list will include both auctions for which you are currently the high bidder and those for which you have been outbid. (In the case of the latter, you have the option of placing a new, higher bid if you wish.)

■ **View the items you've recently won.** This is handy because in addition to enabling you to keep track of which items you're waiting to receive from sellers, it also enables you to leave feedback on completed transactions.

■ **See all the items you didn't win.** Monitoring this might lead you to place a bid on a similar piece on your watch list. Or you might go back to the drawing board, performing a search for that item all over again. Chances are, another one will be listed at some point in time, so don't fret if you miss something good on occasion.

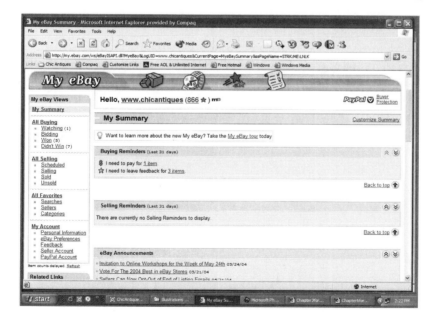

Figure 5.7

Your My eBay page can be a valuable tool for auction management.

Tracking Your Auctions with an Items by Bidder Search

You can also see the items you've bid on by searching by bidder, using your own user ID as the search parameter. To do so, follow these steps:

1. Click the Search button at the top of eBay's main page.

2. Click the Items By Bidder link.

3. Enter your own user ID and click the Search button.

eBay returns a list of all active auctions on which you've bid. If you want to include completed listings, check the Include completed listings check box before you search to bring up all the auctions you've bid on that ended within the past month. If you only want to see the auctions for which you are high bidder, select the As high bidder only option before searching to further refine your results.

chapter 6

I Won an Auction!
Now What?

Winning an auction on eBay can be quite exciting, especially when it involves garnering a wonderful new antique or collectible to add to a burgeoning collection. The excitement only increases when you think you've snagged a really great bargain. But winning an auction is merely the beginning of the procurement process, rather than the end. Most of the time, when you win an auction, eBay will notify you via an end-of-auction e-mail. And of course, whether you won the item through the traditional bidding process or clicked on the Buy It Now button to indicate your interest, you're expected to honor your intention to buy.

Note

If for some reason you don't receive notice about an auction ending, log in to your My eBay page or your sniping service for a quick review. This is particularly important if you have recently experienced e-mail outages.

Stepping through the Buy

After an auction ends, the seller and buyer should communicate to complete the sale. The basic process for concluding a deal remains fairly consistent, although you may experience some variations with regard to how and when you are contacted by the seller with pertinent details and what method you choose to use for payment. In simple terms, after you win an auction, the following occurs:

- You receive payment information from the seller.
- You make your payment.
- You receive your merchandise (this may take a few days).
- You leave feedback for the seller.

Things don't always go quite this smoothly (you'll find out what to do when a deal turns sour in Chapter 7, "Working Through the Bad Buy"), but the majority of the time, this is what happens.

Buyer/Seller Communication

While eBay's policy states that buyers and sellers should contact one another within three days after an auction ends, with equal responsibility being placed on both parties, most auction winners rely on the seller to make contact with them to provide payment details. If the seller provided a shipping amount and payment options when they first listed the item you've just won (which turns on eBay's checkout system), then you'll be able to click on the Pay Now button included in the automatically generated end of auction e-mail to communicate with the seller about your payment preferences and to review your shipping address. You can even access PayPal at that point, if that's an option for your latest win. (I'll go into more detail about that later in the chapter.) That may be the only communication you need to complete your transaction.

Note

eBay's automated checkout system is turned on when a seller enters a shipping amount and payment instructions up front (that is, when he or she first lists an item for sale). Some sellers opt out of eBay's checkout system because they feel it's impersonal, preferring to communicate with buyers directly through e-mail they generate. Other sellers use auction-management programs that offer alternatives to eBay's checkout system. When a seller chooses not to utilize eBay's checkout system, he or she will often note how you should expect to receive payment instructions within the item description.

When payment information is not complete in the automated end-of-auction e-mail, you may need to e-mail the seller to obtain further payment instructions—unless he or she e-mails you first. Most of the time, sellers who've opted out of using eBay's checkout system will get in touch with you pretty quickly, but if you don't hear from him or her within a day or so, feel free to initiate contact to ask for a shipping amount and further payment instructions. (You'll definitely want to do so within three days if you don't hear from the seller first.) In the event you need the seller's e-mail address, you can find it in the end-of-auction e-mail you receive from eBay.

If you do need to e-mail a seller after the sale in order to obtain payment information, do so cordially; don't assume that he or she is some sort of charlatan who is trying to avoid you. Odds are, the seller just isn't adept at handling the many details involved in running an online auction business, or is a bit scatterbrained. Although this may be annoying if you're the extremely organized type, you'll have to be patient and take up the slack in cases such as these in order to close the deal. Of course, if you really feel like the seller is sloppy in his or her business practices, you can always opt to avoid doing business with that seller in the future. Then again, scoring a great buy on an antique or collectible is often enough reward for putting up with a little inconvenience.

Note

You'll find that some sellers e-mail you when they receive your payment, when they mail your package, and again after the package is due to arrive to make sure you're happy with the item. This is great customer service, but not all sellers will take the time to communicate with you so frequently. Honestly, I don't expect that much communication from a seller these days, especially when I pay through PayPal. Most sellers ship within a day or two after receiving a PayPal payment, so I often have my package before I can even begin to wonder if there's a problem. When paying by personal check, however, there may be more of a delay due to a hold period while the check clears the bank. In these cases, it's nice to get that confirmation that your payment was received along with an approximate date of delivery. If you feel like a fair amount of time has passed and you haven't heard anything from a seller about some merchandise you're expecting to receive, it's acceptable to e-mail him or her for more details. On more than one occasion, I've worked with sellers who thought my package had already been shipped; once I notified them otherwise, I had the goods within a few days.

Payment Details

Sellers have loads of payment options at their disposal. There are the old stand-bys, of course: checks and money orders. Some sellers accept credit cards, including MasterCard and Visa. Others allow for the use of PayPal, which, as discussed in Chapter 1, "Getting Started," enables you to quickly and easily send and receive money online. It's up to a seller to decide what type of payment he or she will accept. For example, some accept only money orders; some accept only PayPal; some accept every payment option under the sun. As a buyer, you must accede to the seller's wishes with regard to payment. If a seller clearly states that he or she does not accept checks, then don't send one and expect to receive your goods without some friction from the seller. Of course, as a buyer, I really appreciate it when sellers make things convenient for me by offering as many payment options as possible.

Caution

Sellers who have their own merchant accounts may be able to accept credit cards without utilizing the PayPal system. This isn't uncommon, especially when an eBay seller also has a brick-and-mortar shop. If you decide to pay by credit card outside a secure system like PayPal or a Web shopping cart service, it's wise to either phone in your number and expiration date or send it to the seller in several separate e-mails. For instance, break the card number up into two segments and then send the expiration date separately. Even then, you need to be aware that the way you're communicating sensitive information isn't completely secure.

Clicking the Pay Now Button

When a seller accepts PayPal or supports eBay's checkout system, a Pay Now button automatically appears on the auction listing page when the bidding concludes. This Pay Now button can also be found on your My eBay page and in the end-of-auction e-mail you receive from eBay, as shown in Figure 6.1. All you have to do is click this button to begin the payment process. Assuming that the seller has entered a shipping amount, the total you're expected to pay is shown for you along with the payment options dictated by the seller. (Personal checks, money orders, and PayPal are the most common payment methods listed.)

Purchasing Shipping Insurance

Should you purchase shipping insurance when you're settling the bill with a seller? Some say yes, definitely, no matter what. Others, like yours truly, believe it depends on how fragile the item is and how much it is worth. (Note that how much an item is worth is not necessarily how much you paid for it. If you get a steal of a deal, ask the seller to insure the item for its full value to cover yourself completely.) And when you're dealing with shipments from overseas, the availability of insurance depends on where the mailing originates as to whether insurance is even available to you.

When you do purchase shipping insurance, (some sellers require you to pay for insurance on every buy, others allow you to choose), the United States Postal Service (USPS), currently the most widely used venue for transporting eBay purchases, employs an electronic system that records the item and tracks it through to delivery. If your package goes AWOL, the seller can file a claim to be reimbursed for the merchandise and in turn refund your payment to you. Claims for damage sustained during shipping can be filed on the same type of insurance, but only if the shipper packaged the goods properly. If the seller didn't wrap and pack the merchandise to ensure safe delivery, the postal inspector evaluating the claim may very well deny it. (You'll learn how to submit a claim later in this chapter, in the section "After the Merchandise Arrives.")

Although purchasing shipping insurance won't protect you in the event you buy an item that an unscrupulous seller has no intention of delivering, it can protect you if the item gets lost or broken in transit. When deciding whether it's worth your while to purchase shipping insurance, do take into consideration that very few packages actually get lost in transit, and decide whether you trust the seller to package the item correctly. (Don't be afraid to give the seller a few pointers on proper packaging if it will ease your mind.) If you still have doubts, go for the insurance. If you feel confident, however, save those dollars (which can add up to a hefty sum over time) and buy yourself something nice for your collection instead.

Paying with PayPal

If you have the option of paying through PayPal, after you click the Pay Now button, do the following:

1. Enter your eBay user ID and password.

2. Verify that your shipping address and item total—including shipping amount—are correct, as shown in Figure 6.2.

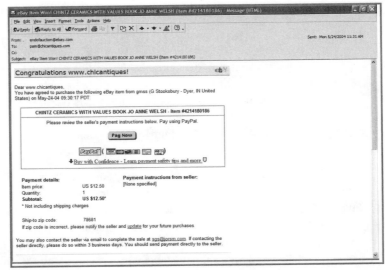

Figure 6.1

Clicking the Pay Now button shown in an end-of-auction e-mail is a convenient way to conclude a transaction.

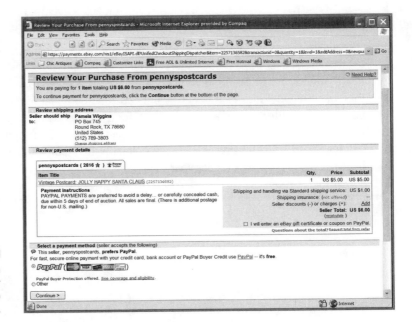

Figure 6.2

The Review Your Purchase page allows you to verify your shipping information and to access PayPal's system.

3. Scroll down and click the PayPal option button at the bottom of the Review Your Purchase page, and then click the Continue button.

4. Enter your PayPal user ID and password, as shown in Figure 6.3, and click the Continue button.

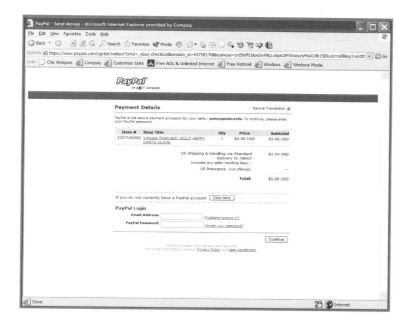

Figure 6.3

Enter your PayPal user ID and password, and then click on the Continue button to move on to the next page where your specific bank account and credit card options are shown.

5. PayPal displays the Confirm Your Payment page. By default, PayPal draws your payment from your PayPal balance. If you prefer to pay through another method, choose the bank or credit-card account you have on file here.

6. Scroll down to click the Pay button at the bottom of the Confirm Your Payment page. PayPal will send both you and the seller a payment-confirmation e-mail.

Note

PayPal offers a type of additional buyer-protection insurance, which you can purchase for qualified transactions when you make your payment. If this coverage is offered, it will be noted on the Confirm Your Payment screen (refer to step 5). As for me, I tend to opt out of buying this additional coverage; instead, I usually purchase shipping insurance on items valued at more than $50. If you feel uneasy about a transaction for some reason, however, consider buying this additional coverage if it's offered to you.

When you pay using PayPal, your payment will be credited to the seller's account and he or she will be notified of the deposit. Unless the seller contacts you via e-mail with additional questions regarding shipping methods or delivery addresses, you can consider your obligation met once payment is made.

Using a Personal Check or Money Order

If you're paying by personal check or using a money order, click the appropriate payment method option button at the bottom of the Review Your Purchase screen before clicking the Continue button. eBay will send your reply to the seller so he or she knows what to expect. The screen that comes up next will show the address where you should send your payment. Printing out a copy of this page to send with your check or money order will help the seller match up your item to your payment once it is received. At the very least, you'll want to note the item number on your check or money order in the memo field to help the seller along. No one wants to receive the wrong item by mistake, and sellers appreciate your help in this respect.

If you plan to pay for your purchase via a personal check or money order, you must follow through promptly to complete the deal. In fact, many sellers impose a payment deadline, which usually falls somewhere between seven and 14 days after the auction ends. Whether or not a seller has imposed a deadline, do yourself a favor and get your auction payments in early. You'll avoid irritating the seller and possibly having them relist the item out from under you. If a seller is prone to relist items that aren't paid for quickly, they usually note this in the item description. And, you'll get your merchandise that much sooner when you pay promptly, which benefits you and makes the entire transaction go more smoothly.

Note

In the old days, before eBay really took off, sellers rarely imposed payment deadlines. As time has passed, however, sellers learned that if they didn't post deadlines, even well-meaning buyers put off paying or simply forgot. Deadlines tend to spur buyers into action, enabling the people who sell antiques and collectibles to spend more time collecting *objects* to sell and less time collecting *payments*.

After the Merchandise Arrives

After you've made your payment and your merchandise arrives, open your packages promptly to inspect them for damage sustained in shipping and condition issues you need to address with the seller. If the item was insured and has been broken in transit or if its condition doesn't measure up to the seller's description, you'll need to take action.

Filing a Claim with the USPS

In the case of damage sustained in shipping, you'll want to file any necessary claims with the shipper as soon as possible. Different shipping companies have different policies with regard to damage sustained in transit; for example, if the item was shipped via the USPS, you file a claim only if the item was insured. (Look for an "insured" stamp on the outside of the package for items valued at under $50 or a blue and white bar-coded sticker for items valued at $50 and up.)

Caution

If you paid the seller to purchase shipping insurance and he or she failed to do so, it's going to be up to the seller to refund your money on the deal. Contact the seller as soon as possible after you discover the damage. Be aware that if he or she requests that you return the broken item, you are prohibited from doing so via the USPS if the pieces are sharp—glass, for example. Packages containing these items are considered to be hazardous by the USPS.

To file a claim with the USPS, surrender the container in which the item was sent, all packing materials, and the damaged item itself to the post office and fill out a claim form. You will also need to take a copy of the auction listing with you to prove that the item was not damaged when you purchased it. If the item is valued at significantly more than you paid for it, bring supporting documentation in the form of copies of the cover and applicable pages from antique and collectible reference guides as proof. The USPS may only refund the amount you paid, but it never hurts to try for full value, especially when you were buying the item with the intention of reselling it for more. I was once reimbursed full value for a Depression glass item that arrived in pieces by providing the necessary proof of value.

Note

You'll have to leave the merchandise at the post office so a postal inspector can evaluate the claim; be aware that it will not be returned to you. If the item is a collectible that you can salvage for parts, you may decide you're better off keeping it and forgoing the insurance claim rather than surrendering it to the postal inspector.

Addressing Condition Issues

Any condition issues you notice when you unpack your purchases not adequately described in the auction listing should be communicated to the seller as soon as possible. These include cracks, chips, crazing, missing stones, missing parts, broken components, excessive wear, and any other issues that would make an antique or collectible less valuable than you expected or, in some cases, worthless. See what the seller offers you in the way of return, refund, or replacement, and negotiate with him or her from there. Many times a partial refund can be negotiated when a piece is damaged but you either can't or don't want to return it for one reason or another. If the seller won't budge on an "all auction sales are final" stance (many old-school dealers have this attitude) or refuses to acknowledge your request, proceed to Chapter 7 to learn how to handle an auction dispute.

Leaving Feedback

If, after you've received your merchandise and inspected it carefully, you consider your buying experience on eBay to have been satisfactory (and most of the time it will be), you can let the seller know you're happy by leaving positive feedback. Doing so is optional, but it can go far in building goodwill between a buyer and a seller. Besides, if you're trying to build your own feedback record, you increase the odds of the seller writing favorable comments about you if you leave positive feedback about him or her. Indeed, some sellers will actually wait until they hear that you're happy with your purchase (like I do) until they conclude the transaction with positive feedback. When you post positive feedback, consider adding a comment that expresses your satisfaction and communicates something useful about the seller to other buyers. That's essentially the purpose of feedback, after all.

Some sellers will post positive feedback immediately after you pay for an item, and that's fine. For all practical purposes, you've completed your end of the deal at that point. But as a buyer, you definitely want to wait until you're sure you're pleased with the merchandise to post positive feedback about the seller.

You may even decide to post positive feedback when a seller has been very cooperative about owning up to a mistake. For example, you might post a comment describing the seller as reputable and fair, and note that the seller backs up his or her merchandise. Don't go into detail about the fact that your merchandise was damaged, as that might turn off potential customers for the seller. Give the seller the benefit of the doubt that it won't happen again, and let him or her save face. This is the kind of evenhanded treatment I like to receive in the event I make an honest mistake, so I operate accordingly on the buying end as well.

By and large, most eBay sellers go beyond what is expected of them to ensure that you're not disappointed in your purchase. But if you genuinely feel that other buyers on eBay need to know about problems you've encountered with a seller, posting neutral or negative feedback can be appropriate. That said, posting neutral or negative feedback should be a last resort, undertaken only after every other avenue toward resolution, as outlined in Chapter 7, has failed. Some buyers (and, for that matter, sellers) fly off the handle, prematurely issuing negative feedback when they're unhappy with an auction's turn of events. This isn't a good practice, and it shouldn't be taken lightly. Once negative feedback has been left, it's difficult to get it removed—in some cases, doing so will cost you money (for example, if you go through SquareTrade, discussed in Chapter 7). Even if you agree to have feedback mutually removed with a seller, a note of this action still shows up in your feedback record.

Never use the threat of negative feedback to make unreasonable demands on a seller. Solving problems with reason and diplomacy is always the best way to go, and it's as important for buyers to be honest as it is for sellers.

Thinking your actions through before posting neutral or negative feedback about a seller is a must. After all, you'll certainly want the same consideration as a buyer. Generally speaking, it's appropriate to leave neutral or negative feedback only in the following circumstances:

- If every other avenue toward resolution of a problem with the transaction has failed or if your differences with a seller are irreconcilable—for example, if you feel your case for a return was completely justified and the seller simply won't cooperate.

- If you believe the seller is dishonest or habitually misrepresents merchandise (check the seller's other feedback to decide whether this is the case).

- If you never received the item in question, and your appeals to the seller have gone unanswered.

Caution

Be aware that if you leave neutral or negative feedback about a seller, that seller will almost always leave negative feedback about you in return—even if you haven't done a single thing to tarnish your good name. It's tit for tat. So before you issue this type of feedback about a seller, decide whether doing so is worth tarnishing your own feedback rating.

Note

There may be times when you feel that leaving neutral feedback is more appropriate than leaving negative feedback. It's not quite as harsh, and it doesn't count against a seller's total feedback rating. If you weren't completely satisfied with some aspect of your buy, but not totally steamed about a seller's actions or item assessment, you can opt for neutral feedback. Be aware, though, that some sellers find neutral feedback to be just as insulting as negative feedback. As a matter of fact, I once had a seller post false statements about my motives in the form of negative feedback because I posted neutral feedback about a vintage handbag in poor condition that the seller would not accept as a return. I thought I was doing the seller a favor by not posting a negative, but ended up being punished anyway—and left wishing I had bit the bullet and issued a negative to begin with.

To view the auctions for which you need to leave feedback, do the following:

1. Click the My eBay button at the top of any page on the site to open your My eBay page, as shown in Figure 6.4.

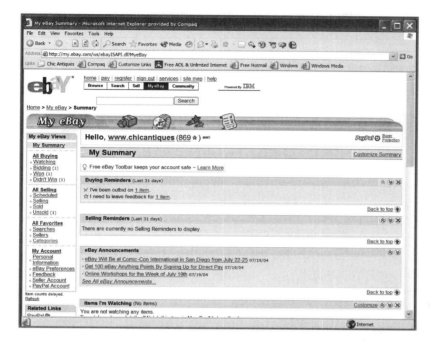

Figure 6.4

Leaving feedback is simple
through your My eBay page.

2. The Buying Reminders section displays the number of listings for which you need to leave feedback. Click on the number to display the listings.

3. Under Items I've Won, any merchandise that has been shipped by the seller will contain a Leave Feedback link in the Action column, as shown in Figure 6.5. To leave feedback on that seller, simply click the link.

4. Click the Positive, Neutral, or Negative option button and enter your comments in the space provided (see Figure 6.6).

5. Click the Leave Feedback button.

Alternatively, you can access a complete list of all auctions for which you need to leave feedback by clicking the Show All Transactions link, shown in Figure 6.6. This is a great way to make sure you don't overlook leaving feedback for sellers who don't use eBay's checkout system (those won't register on your My eBay page). It's also a good way to leave feedback for multiple sellers with one click of the Leave Feedback button, as shown in Figure 6.7.

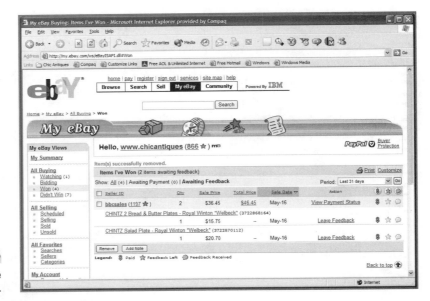

Figure 6.5

Click on the Leave
Feedback link to continue.

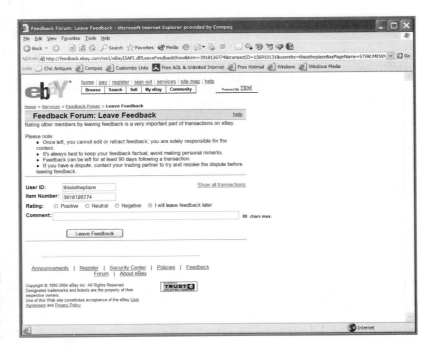

Figure 6.6

Choose the appropriate option
button, enter your comments,
and click on the Leave
Feedback button.

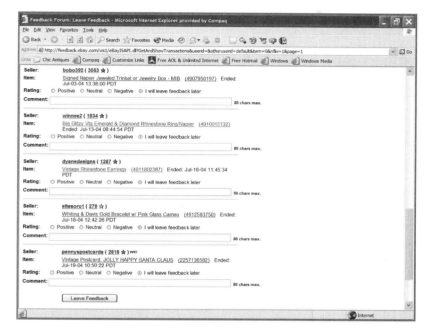

Figure 6.7

Accessing a complete list of auctions for which you need to leave feedback enables you to leave feedback for multiple sellers with one click of the Leave Feedback button.

Note

You can leave feedback in place of sending a closing e-mail or in addition to a final e-mail communication. If you're using your feedback as a final communication with a seller, then take the time to post your remarks as quickly as possible after you receive the merchandise. If you prefer to send a closing e-mail and wait to post feedback, just remember that you have up to 90 days leave your comments on a seller.

Note

If a seller fails to leave positive feedback for you even though the transaction was favorable on both ends, you may want to e-mail him or her with a feedback reminder. Note, though, that leaving feedback is optional; some sellers (and buyers) don't take it as seriously as others. As long as you received the merchandise you expected in a timely manner, you can safely consider the deal done.

Managing Your Buys

If you're a power buyer like I am, then you'll need to come up with a way to make sure that you actually receive all the items you've purchased. As I mentioned earlier, sellers can overlook shipping a package. Maybe they forgot to record your payment as received, or maybe they're just disorganized. In any case, it's not unheard of for packages to slip through the cracks.

I like to manage my eBay purchases by setting up a Waiting for Delivery folder in my e-mail client. I move the End of Auction notices, PayPal confirmations, and any communications from the seller that I want to save into this folder. Every time I pick up a batch of packages from the post office (I use a P.O. box to avoid giving out my home address to strangers, but I've had many items delivered to my home address without issue), I scan these saved messages and delete ones pertaining to any packages I've received. If I receive an item that doesn't quite match what I was expecting, I can use the end-of-auction notice sent out by eBay to link to the auction listing and review the seller's description. If I decide I need to contact the seller about any problems I have with the merchandise, I can also do so easily via the end-of-auction e-mail, since the seller's email address is listed there.

If any messages languish in my Waiting for Delivery folder for an extended period of time, indicating that I have not yet received the merchandise, the first thing I do is verify that I've actually paid for the item. If so, I then determine whether I used PayPal or sent a personal check at the seller's request. If I paid through PayPal, then my e-mail receipt should be right there in the Waiting for Delivery folder to review. If I paid by personal check, I'll confer with the bank to see if it has cleared. Once I know how to proceed, I'll contact the seller to see what's up or to explain myself if I'm the one who has made a mistake.

Note

Even though I try to stay organized, I have, of course, experienced a couple of transactions in which an oversight of my own held up the deal. It can happen. That's why you should be considerate of sellers. Sooner or later, someone, somewhere is going to make a mistake—and when it's you, you'll be grateful for an understanding seller.

Of course, that's just my system for keeping track of things. Some buyers print out copies of auction notices and put them in a paper file, and others simply log on to their My eBay page to keep track of auctions they've won. Indeed, your My eBay page is an excellent resource for auction management because you can simply delete items from your Won list as you receive them (see Figure 6.8). But no matter how you accomplish the task of managing your buys, do it frequently and address issues that crop up in a timely manner. You'll find that there are some time limitations for filing complaints (see Chapter 7), and the sooner you acknowledge a problem, the easier it will be to deal with it to the satisfaction of all parties involved.

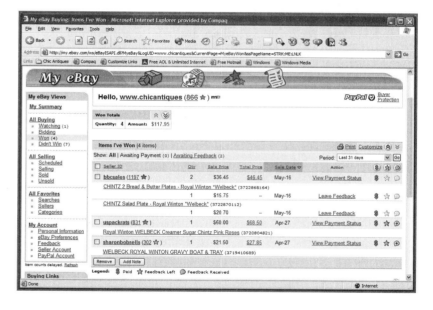

Figure 6.8

Deleting items from your Won list as they are received is an excellent way to manage your buys.

Managing Your eBay and PayPal Accounts

In addition to managing your buys, you'll want to make sure you manage your eBay and PayPal accounts—that is, keep them up to date. In addition to keeping your account information such as your shipping address, credit-card number, and e-mail address updated, you can also specify various buying and selling preferences and notify eBay about what types of e-mail communication you want to receive about your account. One of the easiest ways to change your information on eBay is to log into your My eBay page. In the left hand corner, you'll find a section titled "My Account." From there, you can do the following:

- **Update Personal Information.** Change your user ID, password, e-mail address, physical address for billing and shipping purposes, and update your credit-card information.

- **Change eBay Preferences.** Review and update the types of e-mail communications you receive from eBay regarding your account; change the way you sign in to your account; and change your shipping preferences, your payment address, and the way features are displayed in your listings (that's if you also sell wares on eBay).

- **Leave Feedback.** Leave feedback for others and review the comments others leave for you from a handy list.

- **Review Seller Account.** Assuming you've set up a seller account (covered in Chapter 8, "Setting Up Shop on eBay: Getting Started Selling"), you can use this page to review the outstanding balance in your seller account (that is, fees owed eBay for your prior month's listings), change or update your automatic payment method, or use PayPal to pay your eBay bill.

- **Access PayPal Account.** Follow the links provided to access the PayPal site, where you can view an account overview, review your account history, and update your financial information, account information, and selling preferences. You can also review and update your PayPal user preferences on eBay from this screen.

chapter 7

Working Through the Bad Buy

Some days, I pick up a bundle of packages from the post office, and I'm thrilled with each one I open. Other times, quite frankly, I'm left wondering what the seller was thinking when he or she wrote the item's listing description. The merchandise is so far from how it's described in the listing that I'm truly taken aback. The fact is, most transactions involving antiques and collectibles on eBay end favorably, but disputes do arise. Packages don't get shipped. Merchandise doesn't live up to the seller's description. Whatever problem may arise, you'll be glad to know you have some options for resolving them. The fear of running into trouble on eBay shouldn't keep you from using the venue to add pieces to your collection.

What If Your Package Never Arrives?

Recently, I sent my mother a gift, a gravy boat in her favorite chintz china pattern, and it never arrived. But just because she never got it doesn't mean I didn't send it. Maybe it got lifted from her porch. Perhaps it got delivered to the wrong address. Or the label could have been damaged in shipment and now the package is sitting in an undeliverable mail bin somewhere. Likewise, if you've paid for merchandise from eBay but don't receive it, don't automatically conclude that the seller's a charlatan. If a seller swears he has shipped your item but your mailbox says otherwise, there's a slight possibility that the seller is lying to you (I say *slight* because the overwhelming majority of people who sell antiques and collectibles aren't out to defraud you), but it's also possible that the package actually did get lost in transit (although this happens only rarely). Unfortunately, though, all too often, honest sellers get blamed for delivery SNAFUs.

If you've been waiting an eternity for a package, first gauge your impatience. Sometimes it just *seems* like forever since you submitted payment for an item—especially if you're dying to get it. If it's only been a few days, keep in mind that Priority Mail shipments within the continental United States typically take three days to deliver (although that three-day timeframe is not guaranteed) and First Class mail may take a bit longer. Truthfully, I've had First Class packages delivered in three days and Priority mail take three weeks, so it can be fairly unpredictable. Transit times only grow during the holiday season or if the item has been sent from abroad. The point is, give a package sufficient time to arrive before you panic that it may be lost, or even worse, nonexistent.

If you've been waiting longer than a week or so to receive your item, don't be afraid to send a friendly e-mail message to the sender to ask when the item was sent. Not all sellers make daily trips to the post office, so there may have been a delay of a few days or so between when you submitted your payment and when the item was actually shipped. That's pretty standard practice on eBay, so try not to get too upset about it. Alternatively, you may discover that your merchandise slipped through the cracks on the seller's end; if that's the case, most sellers will bend over backwards to send your shipment as quickly as possible.

Tip

The United States Postal Service, United Parcel Service, and Federal Express offer online tracking. With USPS, a trackable form of delivery that contains a scannable barcode, such as delivery confirmation or insurance coverage, must be purchased by the seller in order for you to be able to take advantage of this online service. UPS and FedEx packages, however, are automatically trackable on the Web with standard delivery. If the seller doesn't offer the tracking number to you, don't be shy about asking for it so you can track the package yourself.

Caution

If you're dealing with a seller who only recently set up shop on eBay, then you might be wise to be wary a little sooner than if the seller has a longstanding record of good service on eBay.

If three weeks after the package was sent, you *still* haven't received it, it's time to take action. If you paid for shipping insurance, it won't do you much good if the seller had no intention of delivering your goods, but it can offer compensation if the item truly does get lost in transit. In that case, ask the seller, who, presumably, has the insurance receipt in his or her possession, to file a claim for reimbursement so that he or she can, in turn, refund your payment. (If the package was sent via the United States Postal Service, no fewer than 21 days must have passed since the package was mailed in order for the seller to file a claim.)

At the same time, ask the seller to mail you a copy of the insurance receipt (as well as a copy of the insurance claim, after it is filed). If the seller doesn't file the claim in a timely manner—assuming the package was sent via U.S. Mail, he or she has 180 days to do so—try filing the claim yourself at your local post office (or at the office of whatever shipping company the seller employed) using your copy of the receipt. If the package *wasn't* insured, the seller may offer a refund or replacement anyway, depending on the cost of the item.

Note

If the seller can't provide a copy of the insurance receipt or if you have good reason to suspect fraud on an uninsured package, file a Suspicious Activity Report with eBay (as detailed later in this chapter) and proceed through the dispute-resolution process from there. You may be able to receive at least a partial reimbursement for the item through eBay.

Note

In order for an item to qualify for a refund, PayPal requires that it be sent through a trackable method. Your credit-card company, however, may offer recourse as well. Policies vary from card to card, so check with your credit-card company to find out for sure. Although it would not be necessary to file a Suspicious Activity Report to work through your credit-card company, notifying eBay of a possible problem seller is still the right thing to do.

Your Merchandise Arrived, But It's Not Up to Snuff: Stepping through Dispute Resolution

The package you've been dying to receive finally arrives, and you can barely contain your excitement as you carefully pry it open. You sift through the packing peanuts, tear through the bubble wrap, and...with palpable disappointment, cradle the object in your hand. It's not *at all* what you were expecting. Whether you're unhappy with an item's condition or it just doesn't match up with the seller's description, there may be times when a purchase you've made on eBay is more than disappointing—it's a rip-off. If this happens to you, you'll be happy to know there are some steps you can take to try to make things right:

1. Review the item description.
2. E-mail the seller.
3. Phone the seller.
4. File a Suspicious Activity Report.
5. Use SquareTrade to mediate the dispute.
6. Contact your payment provider.
7. Petition eBay's Standard Protection Program.
8. Issue negative or neutral feedback.

In most cases, all you'll need to do is contact the seller. Any seller who's serious about selling on eBay won't allow the dispute to reach the reporting stage—not if they're smart, anyway. After all, they'll find it difficult to continue running a lucrative online business if eBay shuts them down. Besides, building a reputation and feedback record take time, and most reputable sellers don't want to have to start over under an alias.

Note

eBay sees itself as merely a *facilitator* between buyers and sellers. As such, the company expects you to contact the seller to try to work out the problem before pulling the company into the fray.

Step 1: Review the Item Description

If you're unhappy with a piece you've received, review the item description. It may well be that whatever peeve you have about the piece—be it a chip, a crack, a missing mark, or what have you—was clearly articulated in the listing description. If you hurriedly placed your bid before noting important condition-related details disclosed in the description, then your dissatisfaction with a piece may not be the seller's fault. Misreading a description—or failing to read it at all—means that you share the blame for creating a sticky situation. I suggest you chalk your error up to experience, and consider it part of "paying for your education," as my wise mother is wont to say. It's a hard lesson to learn, but odds are you'll be more careful about reading descriptions before you bid in the future. I know of what I speak. If, however, the object you received does not mesh with the merchandise described in the item listing (which you read with a fine-toothed comb before bidding), you'll want to contact the seller about it; proceed to step 2.

Tip

Even if you misread the item's description or bypassed reading it altogether, it doesn't hurt to contact the seller to see if he or she is willing to take the item back. Some sellers accept returns, no matter what. If yours doesn't, though, you can't get up in arms if you failed to act responsibly about bidding.

Step 2: E-mail the Seller

Sometimes you can ask all the right questions beforehand and still end up with a less than desirable piece showing up on your doorstep. This is especially true if the item's description was misleading, omitted important details, or just plain lied, then you should e-mail the seller immediately to give him or her the rundown on the situation. Specifically, you should contact the seller if

■ There are condition issues that were not disclosed in the item listing, such as cracks, chips, crazing, missing stones, missing parts, broken components, excessive wear, and so on. The seller should disclose any condition issue that would make an antique or collectible less valuable than expected or, in some cases, worthless. If the seller didn't describe an item accurately, ask for a refund even if the seller states that all sales are final in the item description.

- The item is a reproduction, and not described as such.

- The piece differs widely from the item description—for instance, the piece was described as sterling silver, but it's actually a silver-tone base metal. Or, the seller described a bangle bracelet as Bakelite when it's another type of plastic.

- The size of the item was stated incorrectly—for example, if you were led to believe the vintage sweater you purchased would fit a modern size 10, but it's actually perfect for your size 0 pre-teen daughter. (The seller's being off a quarter inch when citing the height of a Roseville vase in the item's description does not necessarily qualify you to ask for a return, however. Be reasonable in your expectations.)

When you e-mail the seller, don't use a rude tone or point fingers, no matter how irritated you may be. Give the seller the benefit of the doubt. Politely explain that you're unhappy with your purchase and let him or her know why. Then give the seller an opportunity to make good on the deal. Since we're talking about antiques and collectibles here, the seller may not have another, acceptable piece on hand to replace the item that was sent. More than likely, you'll need to ask the seller to accept a return and to refund your money.

Note

Some sellers will issue a full or partial refund and tell you to keep the merchandise to spare you the hassle of dealing with the return—that is, packaging the item, making a trip to the post office, and paying return shipping. After all, if they've found out that the piece they sold you is of little value, such as a bangle bracelet made of cheap plastic instead of real Bakelite, they no longer have a use for it anyway.

That said, there are a few kooks out there who will never, ever, under any circumstance admit they are wrong, no matter how much proof you have to the contrary—nor will they authorize a return. You'll be able to recognize these people straight away because no matter now much sugar and honey you lay on them, all you'll get is sour grapes and vinegar in return. If you find yourself in a dispute with such a seller, proceed to step 3.

On Catching Flies: The Importance of Being Civil

I cannot adequately convey the importance of being civil in your communications with the seller. My grandfather used to say, "You'll draw more flies with honey than vinegar," and he was right—especially when it comes to e-mail, where you can't assess voice inflection or tone. The way you approach a relative stranger in cyberspace can make all the difference in how you're treated in return.

For instance, if you write "You sold me a piece of junk. You're obviously a crook. I demand my money back!" you'll likely get a reply filled with expletives and a refusal to comply. Instead, say "I received the item today, and while someone else may be able to use it with the back wheel missing, I'm afraid I'm going to have to request a return since this absent part wasn't mentioned in the item description." By asking politely—instead of accusing the seller of impropriety, making demands, or threatening to leave negative feedback—you increase the odds that you'll get what you want: a refund. Even if you're not sure whether the seller is being up front about his or her "mistake," let him save face if you can. You'll avoid a lot of grief and negativity, and your buying experiences will be much more pleasant overall.

Step 3: Phone the Seller

When the time comes to take your communication to the next level, whether it's because your e-mails are being ignored or you're not getting the satisfaction you feel you deserve, then you should try phoning the seller. After all, you can't gauge a seller's tone through e-mail, and he or she can't gauge yours. Speaking with a seller on the phone can remove the ambiguity of e-mail communication from of the equation. Taking the time to hold a rational conversation with a seller will often produce the result you're seeking: a refund or replacement item.

Note

eBay recommends that you take this step within 15 days after the end of the auction in question.

Of course, before you can phone the seller, you need to track down his or her telephone number. Here's how:

1. Click on the Services button at the top of any page on eBay.

2. Scroll down to the Bidding and Buying Services section as shown in Figure 7.1.

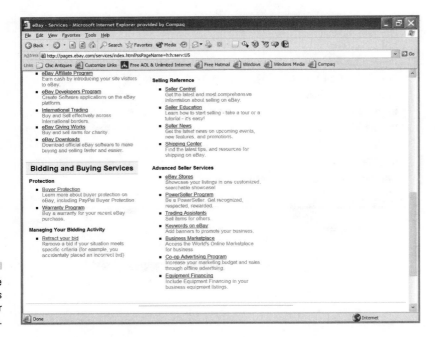

Figure 7.1

After scrolling down to find the Bidding and Buying Services section, click on the Buyer Protection link to proceed.

3. Click the Buyer Protection link.

4. In step 1 of the Buyer Protection page, you'll find instructions for obtaining a seller's contact information. Click the Contact Info link.

5. You'll be prompted to enter the eBay user ID of the person you're trying to contact, and the item number of the auction you're attempting to negotiate. Enter the information, and click the Submit button as shown in Figure 7.2.

After you complete these steps, eBay sends the contact information for that seller, including his or her phone number, to your registered e-mail account; a record of your request is sent to the seller as well.

Figure 7.2

Enter the user ID of the eBay member you're trying to contact and the item number of the auction you're attempting to negotiate and click the Submit button.

If speaking by phone fails to produce the desired results, you may decide you need help handling your dispute. In that case, contacting a mediating service, such as SquareTrade, may help; before you do, though, you should file a Suspicious Activity Report on eBay, discussed next.

Step 4: File a Suspicious Activity Report

If, after you've communicated with the seller via e-mail and phone, you don't feel like you're making any real headway resolving your dispute, and you're beginning to harbor serious concerns about the seller's integrity or even that you're the victim of fraudulent activity by the seller, it's time to file a Suspicious Activity Report on eBay. Here's how:

1. Click on the Services button at the top of any page on eBay.

2. Scroll down to the Bidding and Buying Services section.

3. Click the Buyer Protection link.

4. In step 2 of the Buyer Protection page, you'll find instructions for filing a Suspicious Activity Report. Click the appropriate link (in this case, the one labeled "a significantly misrepresented item" or, if the item you purchased failed to arrive, the link labeled "did not receive an item").

5. eBay displays the screen shown in Figure 7.3. You are prompted to enter the following information:

- Item number

- Date of payment

- Payment method

- Whether you have called the seller

- Whether you have used a dispute-resolution service to mediate this transaction

- Information about the dispute

Do so, and click the Send Email button to submit your Suspicious Activity Report to eBay. A notice that a report has been filed will be sent to the seller as well.

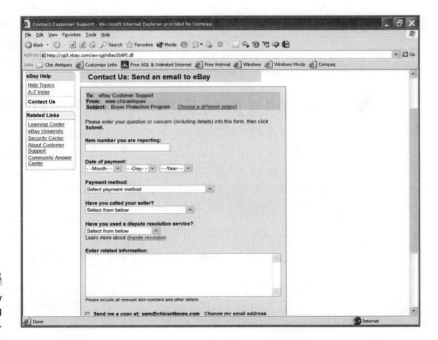

Figure 7.3

Filling out a Suspicious Activity Report is the first step in reporting suspected fraud on eBay.

In truth, you can submit a Suspicious Activity Report sooner—before e-mailing or calling the seller, even—but I urge you to avoid doing so. After all, if the seller made an honest mistake, why alert eBay sooner than you have to? Besides, when you venture into selling on eBay yourself, you'll want others to give you the opportunity to rectify a problem before alerting eBay, so it's just good manners to give others the same consideration.

After you fill out the Suspicious Activity Report, you're ready to proceed to step 5, contacting SquareTrade.

Step 5: Use SquareTrade to Mediate the Dispute

eBay recommends SquareTrade (http://www.squaretrade.com), shown in Figure 7.4, as a mediating service. To access the company's site, simply type its URL in your Web browser; alternatively, you can link directly from eBay by doing the following:

1. Click on the Services button at the top of any page on eBay.

2. Scroll down to the Bidding and Buying Services section.

3. Click the Buyer Protection link.

4. In Step 3 of the Buyer Protection page, you'll find instructions for contacting SquareTrade. Click the SquareTrade link to visit the company's site directly.

eBay recommends that you contact SquareTrade within 30 days after the end of the auction in question.

Once you're on the SquareTrade site, you have the option of filing a case free of charge. After you do, SquareTrade contacts the seller (or vice versa, if a seller lodges a complaint against a buyer) to give him or her the opportunity to reply. If the seller refuses to answer, that's as far as the mediation goes. If the seller does answer, then SquareTrade may make a recommendation for resolving the dispute.

Figure 7.4

eBay recommends SquareTrade as a mediation service to help resolve bidding disputes.

To file a case, do the following:

Note

If you do decide to file a case with SquareTrade, be aware that you will be required to allow eBay to transfer some of your personal information to SquareTrade in order to log your initial complaint.

1. Log in to the SquareTrade site at http://www.squaretrade.com.

2. Click on the eBay button on the home page.

3. Click on the File a Case link.

4. Click on the New User Sign-In link.

5. Click on the Continue button.

6. Enter your eBay password.

7. Read the terms and click on Agree and Continue.

8. Enter your password, confirm the password, and enter in the item number you're requesting help with.

9. Fill in the information on the case questionnaire and click on the Submit button.

Unfortunately, your results may be limited because SquareTrade, while serving as mediator, does not issue a ruling on disputes. That is, although it may offer a recommendation for resolving the dispute, it does not take sides, declaring one party "right" and one party "wrong." And even if it did, SquareTrade lacks the authority to enforce any ruling it might make. Even so, being contacted by a mediator like SquareTrade may indicate to the seller that you're serious about resolving the dispute, and he or she may decide to issue a refund just to put an end to the hassle of dealing with you. If not, proceed to step 6.

Note

Fortunately, I've never had to use SquareTrade; every beef I've ever had with another eBay user has been resolved before this point in the dispute-resolution process. Several of my online buddies have used the service, however—without much luck. That said, they have successfully used the service to have negative feedback removed for a fee (although eBay advertises this as a free service).

Step 6: Contact Your Payment Provider

If you paid for your item with a credit card or with PayPal, your payment provider may be able to reimburse you for deals that fall short on eBay. When you pay for a qualified listing with PayPal, the site's buyer-protection program provides coverage up to $500 at no additional charge, other than a small processing fee to file your claim. This service covers items not delivered as well as those received that are significantly different from the listing description. To see if your item is covered, look for the PayPal Buyer Protection Offered logo in the listing's seller information section.

If your item is covered, file a claim with PayPal by doing the following:

1. Click on the Services button at the top of any page on eBay.

2. Scroll down to the Bidding and Buying Services section.

3. Click the Buyer Protection link.

4. In step 4 of the Buyer Protection page, you'll find instructions for submitting a claim to PayPal. Click the PayPal Buyer Protection link to visit the company's site directly.

Note

All claims of this nature must be filed within 30 days subsequent to when your PayPal payment was made.

Once you're on the PayPal site, do the following:

Caution

You must be willing to provide information about the transaction during the investigation process. If PayPal cannot obtain the necessary information required to successfully evaluate a case, it may cancel the claim without reimbursing you and without refunding your filing fee.

1. Log in to your PayPal account.

2. Click on the Auction Tools tab at the top of the screen, as shown in Figure 7.5.

3. Scroll down and click on the PayPal Buyer Protection link.

4. Review PayPal's Buyer Protection policy. Then, scroll down and click the File a Claim link at the bottom of the page.

5. Click on the Continue button, as shown in Figure 7.6

6. Enter the PayPal transaction ID in the blank provided, as shown in Figure 7.7. (Click on the Get PayPal Transaction ID link to access your payment history and easily access the required number.) Then, click on the Continue button.

7. Review the transaction details to make sure you've accessed the correct transaction. Click on the Continue button after verification is complete.

8. Enter in the particulars relating to your claim including pertinent details in the Additional Information box as shown in Figure 7.8.

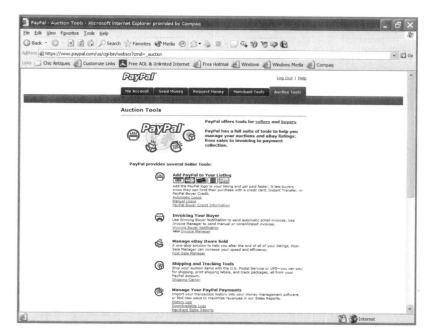

Figure 7.5

After logging in to your PayPal account, click on the Auction Tools tab at the top of the screen

Figure 7.6

Click on the Continue button to begin the claim process.

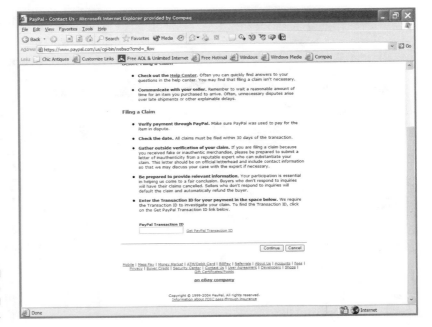

Figure 7.7

Enter the PayPal transaction ID in the space provided and Click on the Continue button.

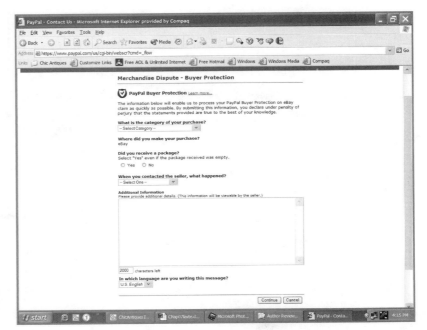

Figure 7.8

Fill in the details of the claim and click the Continue button.

9. Check the appropriate boxes to indicate the condition of the item on which you're filing a claim, as shown in Figure 7.9, and then click on the Continue button.

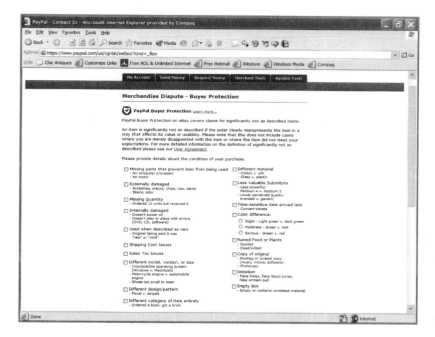

Figure 7.9

Check the appropriate boxes to indicate the condition of the item on which you're filing a claim, and then click the Continue button.

10. Indicate whether you would be willing to accept a partial refund from PayPal by entering a satisfactory amount in the space provided, as shown in Figure 7.10. If you are not willing to accept a partial refund, leave the space blank and click the Continue button.

11. The last screen indicates that a PayPal representative will contact you for more details about the claim, and that if you do not respond to these requests your claim will be cancelled.

Caution

Be aware that you are limited to two PayPal Buyer Protection refunds per calendar year. You might not want to waste them on items of little value.

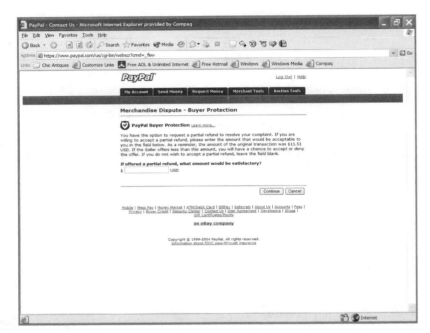

Many credit-card companies also recognize the importance of protecting online buyers and offer 100-percent protection to stay competitive. If you paid for your eBay purchase using a credit card by giving the card number and expiration date directly to the seller, you can contact your credit-card company directly to see if they offer buyer protection relating to your specific circumstance.

Note

Some sellers maintain merchant accounts to accept credit cards, such as those who, in addition to selling on eBay, run brick-and-mortar antiques shops or other Web stores. It's perfectly acceptable to provide your credit-card number and expiration date to these individuals. If you have concerns about giving your credit-card number to an individual you don't know, however, you may decide that operating through PayPal is the best way to go.

If you paid for an item using some other form of payment, or if the item wasn't eligible for reimbursement by PayPal or your credit-card company, you have one last resort: petitioning eBay's Standard Protection Program.

Step 7: Petition eBay's Standard Protection Program

Filing a claim with eBay is a last resort, meant to be done after you've exhausted all other options. It's your last recourse in matters of gross misrepresentation or non-delivery. The eBay Standard Protection Program provides partial reimbursement on qualifying items up to $200 minus a $25 processing fee.

The first step in collecting on a claim is to file a Fraud Alert with eBay. According to eBay, the Fraud Alert acts as

- An online forum for buyers and sellers to resolve transaction disputes.

- A formal complaint with eBay regarding a seller's activities.

- The initial step to file for reimbursement through eBay's Buyer Protection Program.

To file a Fraud Alert, follow the steps outlined on the Buyer Protection Program page. To access this page, do the following:

1. Click on the Services button at the top of any page on eBay.

2. Scroll down to the Bidding and Buying Services section.

3. Click the Buyer Protection link.

4. In step 1 of section 2 of the Buyer Protection page, you'll find instructions for submitting a claim to eBay's Standard Protection Program, which begins by submitting a Fraud Alert.

Tip

Section 2 of the Buyer Protection page includes several clickable links that you can use to answer your questions about coverage and exclusions from the Standard Protection Program.

Note

Buyers are advised to make Standard Protection Program claims from 30 to 60 days after an auction ends.

Once on the Buyer Protection page, do the following to file a Fraud Alert:

1. In section 2, click on the File a fraud link, shown in Figure 7.11.

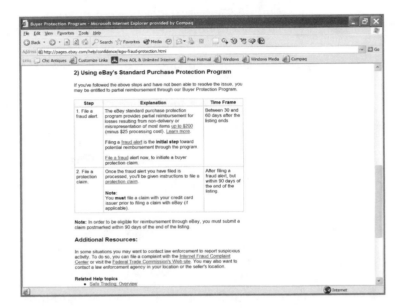

Figure 7.11

Click on the File a fraud alert link to initiate eBay's Standard Purchase Protection Program.

2. Review the information in the Online Fraud Complaint Reporting Form, and then click the Submit a new complaint button shown in Figure 7.12.

3. Answer the question "Do you feel that another eBay member has defrauded you?" by clicking either the Yes or No option button. For the sake of example, I've clicked Yes here.)

4. Review the Online Fraud Complaint Reporting Form information once again and click the Continue button to proceed.

5. Read the information that indicates that an Online Fraud Complaint Form is used solely by eBay to investigate fraudulent and questionable activity and click the Continue button to proceed.

6. Verify that your eBay contact information is correct (change it if needed), and enter the item number in question in the space provided.

7. Click the I was bidder button, shown in Figure 7.13, to file your complaint.

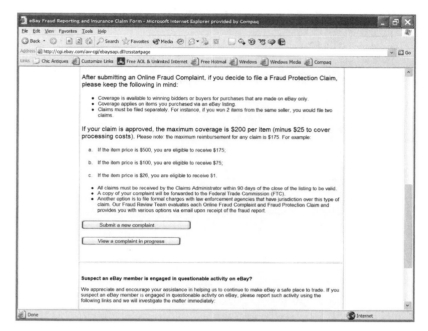

Figure 7.12

Review the Online Fraud Complaint Reporting Form, and then click the Submit a new complaint button.

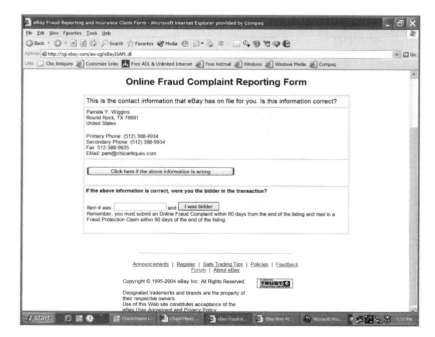

Figure 7.13

Enter the item number in the space provided and click the I was bidder button to file the report.

After the Fraud Alert is filed, assuming your claim is eligible, eBay will send you a form to complete in order to file a Standard Protection claim. In addition to completing the form, you must provide documentation that payment was made in the form of a cancelled check, a PayPal payment notice, or a credit-card receipt.

Note

Because eBay charges a $25 processing fee when you submit a Standard Protection claim, it simply doesn't make sense to file the claim on low-cost items.

If you feel you need to file a Standard Protection claim but eBay did not send you the appropriate form after you filed your Fraud Alert, do the following:

1. In section 2 of the Buyer Protection page, click the protection claim link.

2. Read the information on how to file a claim, as shown in Figure 7.14, to make sure you are eligible (as mentioned previously, in some cases, eBay will notify you to file a protection claim after you file your Fraud Alert). Scroll down and click the Contact eBay link.

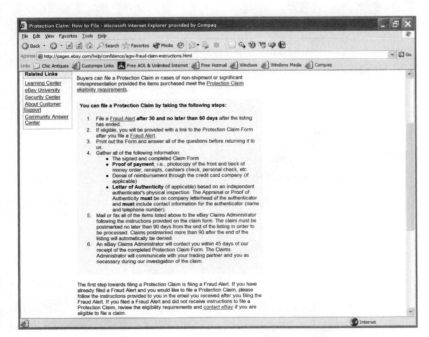

Figure 7.14

Scroll down to click the Contact eBay link to file your protection claim.

3. Enter the item number and articulate your concerns in the spaces shown in Figure 7.15. Click on the Send Email button to submit the claim.

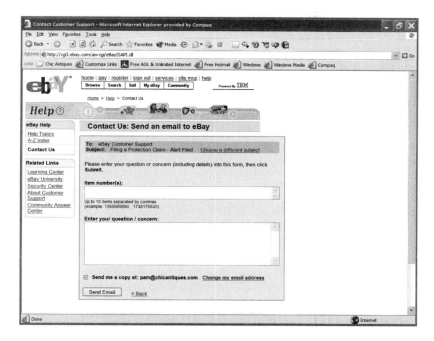

Figure 7.15

Fill in the item number and details before clicking on the Send Email button to submit your protection claim.

When a protection claim is filed, eBay takes appropriate disciplinary action against the seller you reported. For this reason, it is important not to take this action lightly and think through the consequences to the seller of your claim before filing. Make sure you've exhausted all the other resources at your disposal beforehand.

Caution

Items paid for with cash or picked up directly from the buyer are not eligible for the Standard Protection Program. Also, you cannot file more than three claims in a six-month period.

Step 8: Issue Negative or Neutral Feedback

If, after you've exhausted all other avenues toward resolution with the seller—you've worked through the dispute-resolution process and still feel like it's important for you to warn others about the seller—then it's appropriate to issue neutral or negative feedback about the seller, as outlined in Chapter 6, "I Won an Auction! Now What?" As I mentioned in that chapter, though, be prepared for that seller to retaliate by posting negative feedback on you in return, even if you've done nothing to merit it.

Tip

See the sidebar "Resources for Combating Online Fraud" in Chapter 4, "Buyer We Aware: What to Know Before You Bid," for more information about dealing with shady characters on the Internet. There you'll find links to sites that can help you log complaints.

When the Mistake Is Yours...

That model train part you've been stalking for years emerged on eBay, and you bid high without a second thought. The next day, in an incredible coincidence, you found an identical piece at your local antique mall for less money, and snatched that one up, too. "No big deal," you thought. "I only *bid* on the piece on eBay. I can always back out if I win the auction."

Guess again, my friend. eBay views a bid on a traditional auction or Buy It Now purchase as a contract that obligates a buyer (that's you) to complete a purchase. In other words, don't even think about bidding on or purchasing an item on eBay if you're not absolutely certain that you really want to buy it. And although it's disheartening to discover the item for less money elsewhere, that doesn't nullify your obligation as a buyer who's placed a bid on eBay to fulfill your end of the deal. That's why eBay encourages bidders to always use their best judgment when placing a bid on an item or clicking the Buy It Now button; it's also why I tell antiquers and collectors to do their research *before* bidding.

Note

PayPal's buyer dispute service does not cover cases of buyer regret or when you are simply disappointed in the item. In order to submit a claim using this service, there must be a significant difference between the way the auction listing described the item and the item you received. Similar limitations apply to eBay's Standard Protection Program.

That said, mistakes do happen, and many sellers will go out of their way to work with you if you communicate with them openly and honestly right from the beginning. Sometimes requesting the seller's contact information through eBay and giving him or her a call will help you smooth out this type of faux pas. Let the seller know what's going on with you, and see if you can come to a satisfactory agreement; just remember that they are not obligated to overlook your gaffe.

If the seller refuses to recuse you from the deal, you might consider just not paying for the item—but don't. Failing to purchase an item you have won may result in negative feedback from the seller, as well as a Non-Paying Buyer Warning against your account—which could result in the account's suspension. That's a major inconvenience if you want to continue shopping eBay, and one you'll certainly want to avoid. Besides, when you weasel out of a deal, you do a disservice to the honest sellers on eBay. And when sellers get cranky and start listing tons of conditions and disclaimers in their auction listings because of bad buyers they've dealt with in the past, that sours the atmosphere in the marketplace before a deal even takes place for future bidders. That's the bottom line. So when you end up with two identical vintage model train pieces, don't penalize the seller. Instead, just do what I do: Turn around and sell one of them on eBay to recoup your losses. You'll find out how in Part III, "Selling Antiques and Collectibles on eBay."

part III

Selling Antiques and Collectibles on eBay

chapter 8

Setting Up Shop on eBay: Getting Started Selling

You've enjoyed collecting German steins for years, but you can't help noticing that your collection has crossed the line from interesting to excessive. The sad fact is, it's time to let some of your pieces go. But how? eBay, that's how. "Yikes," you may be thinking. "I don't have the first clue how to put an item up for auction." That's true; you don't—yet. Fortunately for you, though, I've designed this section to help you get your feet wet as a seller on eBay. Whether you're simply interested in unloading a few pieces that no longer appeal to you or starting your own online antique business on eBay, this chapter tells you everything you need to know to get started selling, while pointing out some avoidable pitfalls.

Note

You may be wondering whether there's another venue for online sales that offers similar results to eBay. The short answer? No. The fact is, although there are several other online auction venues—some, like Yahoo! Auctions, are general auction sites that offer all types of wares; others specialize in certain fields, such as pottery or jewelry—none draw a crowd like eBay or offer the consistent returns you're probably looking for. If you're looking for lots of site traffic and brisk sales, eBay is your best bet.

The Hunt Is On: Finding Items for Resale

Whenever I do a show, at least one person asks me, "Where do you get all this stuff?" My answer? *Everywhere*. I love shopping for antiques and collectibles, so I can't resist stopping by estate sales, and neighborhood garage sales always get my attention. If there's a flea market in town, I'll be there with bells on. When a friend of a friend calls and says "I hear you buy old jewelry," I'm all over it. I attend live auctions. And, even after all these years, I still like wandering around in antique malls and shows. Almost every time I venture out, I find something I think I can resell for a profit, and a number of those items end up on eBay.

Note

In the old days, all kinds of antiques and collectibles were readily available at garage sales and estate sales and sold for a song. My mother, for example, bought some pretty great stuff at tag sales in the 1970s. Unfortunately, however, that rarely happens today. Too many people have seen items appraised on *Antiques Roadshow* to let their knick-knacks go at bargain-basement prices. As such, you'll have to work a little harder to find your goodies. That makes it more challenging, but it can still be very rewarding when your diligence pays off. Just keep in mind that just about every venue holds a potential treasure if you take the time to discover it.

If you plan to make a career out of selling antiques and collectibles on eBay, then you'll need to know where to find merchandise for resale on the site. Here are a few places to look:

- **Estate sales.** The estate sales that hold the most potential are those run by family members, as opposed to estate-liquidation companies. For one thing, these companies know a lot more about the merchandise they're selling. In fact, they tend to price the merchandise higher than most dealers would in a traditional shop. That said, prices do tend to fall as the sale drags on. Although making the effort to stand in line on the first day of an estate sale will ensure that you get first look at the goods, you'll tend to get better deals on the second and third days. (The same goes for garage sales.) Check your local newspaper's estate-sale list in the classified advertising section each Thursday and Friday to locate the sales in your town. Better yet, if the operators of the estate sales you attend offer mailing lists, be they online or of the paper variety, sign up to receive it. That way, you'll learn about local sales even before they're announced in the newspaper.

Note

A couple years ago, I got up early to hit a local sale. To my dismay, I arrived to find at least half a dozen dealers I knew in line in front of me. I was so discouraged, I almost turned around and went back home—except I couldn't face the drive back across town. Boy, was I glad I stayed! Much to my surprise, I walked out of that sale with a Liddle Kiddles Klub carrying case filled with dolls and accessories in really great condition for the bargain price of $5. I sold just one of those dolls, a Sleeping Biddle Kiddle, for more than $100 on eBay! Apparently the other dealers didn't recognize these pieces for the treasures they were.

- **Garage sales.** I rarely find older things at random garage sales, but do well at neighborhood sales, where several households hold garage sales on the same day. To that end, try to get a sense of which neighborhoods in your area are more upscale; that way, you increase your chances of finding nice things.

Tip

If the best merchandise was priced too high on Friday, then odds are it'll still be sitting there when the 50-percent discounts roll around on Sunday. Case in point: One Sunday afternoon, at a family-run garage sale, I scored several paper grocery bags filled with ornate beaded glass necklaces, Victorian long-stemmed hatpins, and other rhinestone pieces too numerous to mention, all for $5 a piece. The items had been priced at book value on Friday, but hadn't sold. By Sunday, the family just wanted them gone.

- **Flea markets.** These days, many flea markets are actually outlets for new and imported goods, which means that finding antiques at flea markets can be challenging—but it's not impossible. One of the best ways to find out what flea markets (not to mention antiques shows, crafts fairs, and the like) are due to stop in your area is to use *Country Living* magazine's online calendar of events (http://magazines.ivillage.com/countryliving/collect/cal/spc/0,,284648_407677,00.html), which is sorted by region, as shown in Figure 8.1. Don't forget to check the calendar when you travel, too, to find out what sales to hit while you're away!

Figure 8.1

Country Living's online calendar of events offers a good place to start when you're looking for flea markets, crafts fairs, and antiques shows to attend.

■ **Live auctions**. Auctions used to hold more potential than they do now, at least in my area. But you can still hit a good one every now and then, especially when they're estate auctions. The trick is to arrive early to inspect the goods you might be interested in bidding on to make sure the pieces are authentic and in good condition. Take notes of lot numbers, and determine how much you can reasonably pay for a piece and still turn a profit. To locate auctions in your area, check your local newspaper.

Caution

Unfortunately, it's all too easy to get caught up in the action at a live auction and buy a piece that isn't on your pre-auction inspection list for more money than it's worth. Practice restraint!

■ **Thrift stores**. I've never had much luck shopping at thrift stores, but I have a friend who swears by them. In fact, she just completely transformed a charming Victorian home into a vintage themed bed and breakfast using thrift-store finds. She says the secret is to find out the day of the week they stock new merchandise and hit them then. It may also pay off to establish a rapport with the employees at your local thrift stores. When you drop in, be friendly, and make sure they have some idea what types of pieces you're looking to find. Then, leave your phone number with them so they can call you in the event items that might interest you are stocked.

■ **Antiques shops and malls.** These days, antiques shops and malls can be hit or miss. Unfortunately, some are filled with garage-sale junk and not much else. But when you do hit a nice one filled with genuine antiques and older collectibles, there's a good chance you can find some resale items to work with if you shop wisely.

Tip

Some people walk every aisle in an antiques mall in one direction, and then turn around and walk in the opposite direction to get a different perspective. Not a bad idea if you have time.

■ **Antiques shows.** Many eBay sellers avoid antiques shows because they assume everything's going to be priced too high for resale. In some instances, this is true. But when sellers run across items outside their area of expertise, they sometimes put them up for sale at fairly reasonable prices, so it never hurts to take a pass through even the high-end shows to see what you can find. The same goes for specialty shows featuring glass, dolls, ephemera, and other collectibles. Plus, antiques shows can be great places to learn from other dealers and see things you won't run across every day. To find the shows in your area, use *Country Living* magazine's online calendar of events (http://magazines.ivillage.com/countryliving/collect/cal/spc/0,,284648_407677,00.html).

■ **Answering and placing newspaper ads.** Although I don't have much luck finding items in my newspaper's classified ads, I usually take a look at the antiques section when looking up the estate sales and neighborhood garage sales for the weekend. Every now and then I spy an ad that pays off, and odds are you will too. You might want to consider placing a "wanted to buy" ad in the paper as well.

Note

A *house buy* is when a potential buyer goes to an individual's home to view items offered for sale. Unfortunately, some people view the house buy scenario as a way to get a free appraisal. That is, they call you over with no real intention of selling, but you don't realize it until you've spent hours poring over their junk. If people admit to you that they don't know what they have and want someone to look at the pieces, you may want to tell them up front that you charge a fee for assessing items but that if you end up purchasing pieces from them, the fee will be waived.

- **Online antiques malls and shops.** I generally buy in online antiques malls and shops for my own collection rather than for resale. Occasionally, though, I'll run across sellers with good prices, so I do browse them for resale pieces on occasion. That said, I *always* have a look when someone in one of my online collecting groups announces they're having a going-out-of-business (or other type of) sale in an online shop, because that usually means items will be marked down 40–60 percent. Try to get first pick, if you can, and always act quickly when you see liquidation announcements. You won't be the only one in the group anxious to see what's up for sale at bargain prices.

Sometimes, people even buy sleepers on eBay and turn around to resell them in a smarter way in the same venue. That's right: You can actually buy on eBay and resell for a profit. It sounds crazy, but it's true. In fact, I know someone who bought a costume jewelry brooch on eBay for $380 and then turned around and sold it—on eBay—for more than $8,800.

Indeed, many dealers buy pieces on eBay and then turn around and sell them for a profit on the site. It usually happens when a seller has misidentified a piece, or when an item is ambiguously described. Some dealers even search eBay using misspelled words to find things other buyers won't notice. Other times, auctions for great items just end at lower-than-expected prices due to the ending date falling on a holiday or at another time when a large number of bidders might be preoccupied. It just happens. At times like these, the seller's misfortune is your gain. I won't pretend this isn't a time-consuming exercise, because it does take some energy and a meticulous nature, but it's not unlike collecting in that respect. It doesn't hurt to be a bit of a risk-taker, too. It's almost like a sport. Sometimes you come back empty handed after a big game, but when you bag the big one, it feels great.

You'll find that the same applies to shopping flea markets, estate sales, and other brick-and-mortar venues. Keep an eye out for valuable unmarked porcelain pieces, misidentified glassware patterns, and other types of valuable-yet-obscure antiques and collectibles that you learn about in the course of your research. And as I mentioned in Chapter 2, "Research: Don't Buy or Sell Without It," developing an eye for quality and classic style doesn't hurt anything either. The more you develop your discernment skills, the better you'll be at ferreting out sleepers with great eBay potential.

Deciding How Much to Pay for Your Wares

In the old days, when we had to pay for shop overhead, antiques dealers used to strive to double or even triple their money when selling a piece (indeed, those of us with dual selling venues still follow this rule). But with eBay, overhead is generally lower; some sellers make a profit turning inventory quickly at a lower profit margin—say, 25 cents on the dollar. They also try to sell more volume-wise, to keep profits up. Either way, you need to feel fairly confident that you can sell a piece for $100 on eBay if you purchased it for $50–75. And if you're spending $5 at an estate sale, make sure it's on an object that will net at least $10; otherwise, it won't be worth the time you invest in it. Besides, although overhead on eBay is reasonable—especially since you can work it full or part time from home—it isn't nonexistent; when deciding how much to pay for a piece, make sure you take into account any fees you'll need to pay in order to sell it on eBay. (See Chapter 10, "Setting Your Starting Price, Understanding eBay's Fees, and Creating a Basic Listing," for more information about eBay's fee schedule.) A nickel here and a dime there add up over time to hurt your bottom line.

Even with this knowledge at hand, many dealers *still* fall into the trap of paying way too much for the pieces they plan to resell on eBay. This is especially easy if it's a piece you like a lot. If you don't mind getting stuck with an overpriced piece in the event your reserve price isn't met (because—trust me on this—you won't risk selling it for too little if you love it), then buy it with the idea in mind that it might end up as part of your own collection. If, however, you absolutely need to make a profit on the piece to pay this month's rent (or you're considering spending your rent money on this "investment"), keep on shopping.

Research Redux

Of course, in order to sell an item on eBay (and actually turn a profit), you'll need a good understanding of eBay's selling tools, a strong sense of what makes for a compelling keyword, the ability to write accurate and lively descriptions, and the know-how to build credibility with buyers, which is why this book examines all these topics in detail. But the effort you put forth before you ever list an item on eBay—learning about antiques in general, becoming an expert in the areas that interest you the most, and making an effort to shop smart—will pay off as much or more than learning technical skills and listing tips.

Advance preparation includes thorough research of every item you sell on eBay (this might be a good time to review Chapter 2 for a refresher). Before you list an item, you should have a pretty good idea how much similar pieces are selling for on eBay and whether the market is glutted with those types of items. It just doesn't make sense to spend your time, money, and energy listing objects with little value in an overextended market—of which there are plenty in the online auction arena. Conversely, you'll want to pay attention to hot trends in decorating, fashion, and current events that might affect your online antiques and collectibles business. For instance, the week Roy Rogers died, vintage collectibles bearing his likeness skyrocketed in value on eBay (and in brick-and-mortar shops as well). A few weeks later, they were back down to a more reasonable level, where they have remained.

Determining Market Value

Take the old license plates shown in Figure 8.2 as an example. If I were to consider listing them on eBay, I'd want to conduct a completed listing search to get a sense of the market for old license plates as well as an idea of how much mine might fetch. Even though they might look like junk to some, it turns out there's quite a brisk market for some of these items on eBay. By doing a little research into past auction results on antique and collectible license plates, you would then know how to set your starting price, whether or not a reserve is appropriate (to protect your investment if you paid quite a bit for them), and how the most successful auction titles and descriptions were written up in the first place. It never hurts to study the auctions of thriving sellers to learn from their expertise.

Figure 8.2

Doing your online homework will give you an idea of how well old license plates like these might sell on eBay. While not everyone's cup of tea, certain vintage license plates do have a market.

Indeed, your research efforts with regard to market value can bridge the difference between a disappointing or mediocre end price and a fabulous result. Years ago, I bought a vintage 1940s German papier-mâché Easter egg candy container at a garage sale for $1 (see Figure 8.3). It was gorgeous, very colorful and whimsical, and I figured it would fetch a high enough price on eBay to make it worth my while to list it. In my rush to sell the piece, however, I neglected to research recent sales of similar items on eBay beforehand. Long story short, the ending price was a mere $10. By the time I'd paid my fees, I netted very little profit. Had I taken the time to research, however, I would have quickly discovered that the piece would have been worth much more to me as a seasonal decorative object to use in my home. Or I could have held on to it until a few weeks before Easter, and possibly sold the piece for significantly more.

Tip

Researching not only enables you to determine your piece's market value, it can also help you when the time comes to write the listing title and description. Having scads of information at your disposal about an antique or collectible means you can reveal more about it in your titles and descriptions in a clear and compelling manner—and thereby better your chances of getting outstanding results with every listing. Adding relevant details to listings also makes you look like a smart seller, and people like buying from knowledgeable dealers they can trust to provide them with accurate information.

Figure 8.3

Much to my dismay, this papier-mâché Easter egg candy
container from the 1940s only brought $10 on eBay,
even though it's a colorful and enticing collectible.

Making a Glutted Market Work for You

While a quality, uncommon, desirable item will *always* be in demand on eBay, it's a sad fact that a good number of auctions featuring antiques and collectibles end without garnering a single bid, as shown in Figure 8.4. Why? It's simple supply-and-demand economics: too many similar or identical pieces, not enough interested buyers. Take vintage postcards, like the ones listed in the figure, as an example. Although they are beautiful and noteworthy ephemera, most aren't extremely valuable—even when they're 100 years old or more. That's because they were produced in quantity, and because those quantities survived over time—in this case, due to the fact that postcards were frequently stored in sturdy albums. (Certain types of coins and stamps, along with lots of other true antiques, also fall into this category.) Learning exactly which postcards are consistently high sellers, like those depicting Santa Claus and examples celebrating Halloween as shown in Figure 8.5, is a form of market research that can serve you well when deciding which items to list on eBay.

So how do you figure out which items are likely to sell, and which are likely to gather dust on a seller's shelves? Although learning what sells best on eBay can be a matter of trial and error, you can conduct some useful research before you

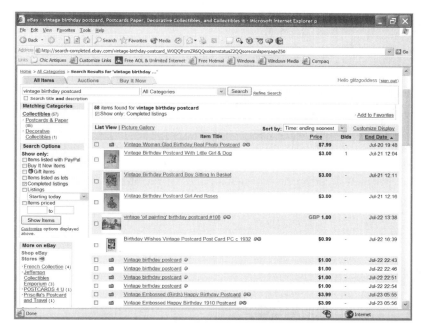

Figure 8.4

Of the 28 vintage birthday postcards listed here, only one has a bid. Unless it's a special case, birthday postcards don't generally do well on eBay.

Figure 8.5

Vintage postcards celebrating Halloween can be among the most desirable and valuable pieces from a collecting standpoint.

begin selling to get a good idea which items on the site tend to stagnate. Odds are, you'll find that the least active categories tend to be the ones with a surplus of "common" items. Put another way, scarcity can make your wares more desirable. Just as people don't want to see the same old stuff in antique mall booths, they don't want to see the same items listed over and over on eBay. As time passes—and as sellers wise up—it's possible that more common items will disappear from eBay listings, thereby rendering them more desirable. But for now, they continue to languish in a bidless existence. You'll find out which items qualify for stagnant status when you do your research prior to listing one of your pieces. If your completed listing search yields pages of unsold or low-bid items similar to your own, it's probably not the right time to sell that item on eBay.

Note

Although sellers might have a hard time dealing with market glut on eBay, buyers absolutely love it. They can find exactly what they're looking for in less time, and often for less money, than they could scavenging acres of booths in an antiques mall.

Of course, one way to avoid falling victim to market glut is to sell only unique, high-quality antiques and collectibles on eBay. Within your area of expertise, you'll be able to assess what types of pieces meet these criteria without much effort. Alternatively, you can try to focus on offering proven sellers—that is, pieces that almost always fetch high prices, such as Roseville pottery, Lalique glassware, vintage mesh purses by Whiting & Davis or Mandalian (see Figure 8.6), and a host of other highly desirable pieces. Of course, that's easier said than done; you must first purchase those prized pieces at low prices in order to turn a profit selling them on eBay, and the fact is, steals on items such as these are few and far between.

Tip

Browse completed listings in your specialty area to review the items selling for good prices on any given day; you'll find it can change from week to week. For example, a few competing buyers can drive up prices unusually high for a short period of time. Once their needs are met, those buyers often move on to something else and prices on those pieces go right back down.

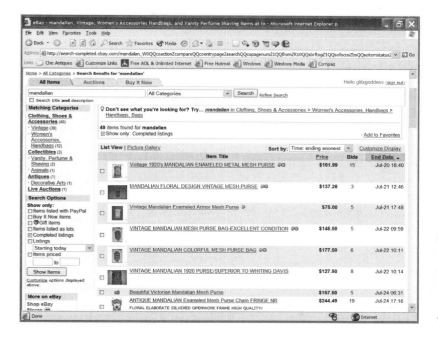

Figure 8.6

Mandalian metal mesh purses almost always do well on eBay, but appear only rarely. Odds are, if you're looking for one in the hopes of reselling it, you won't turn much of a profit.

If it turns out that the market for your pieces is flooded, consider offloading your collection by selling items in groups rather than individually—a pot-sweetening tactic frequently used by live auctioneers as well. For instance, a Depression glass saucer in a common pattern might be hard pressed to get a bid, but add a couple of other pieces to the lot, and suddenly it becomes a bit more intriguing to collectors and other dealers who can make money off the lot in another selling venue.

Tapping into Trends

You could have the rarest antique or collectible around—a truly one-of-a-kind piece. But if nobody out there is interested in buying it, if it hasn't "caught on" with collectors (or its popularity has peaked), it won't fetch much of a price on eBay. If, however, that piece becomes trendy, then suddenly you're in business.

Here's an example: Way back in 1996, I worked at a busy antiques mall. Although several vendors featured Jadeite glassware—specifically, Fire King's wares—the pieces were largely ignored by shoppers...until Martha Stewart put

Has eBay Replaced the Brick-and-Mortar Antiques Shop?

The short answer? No. Although a good deal of focus has been placed by the antiques industry on eBay and online selling in general during the last few years, brick-and-mortar shops can continue to thrive, even faced with the stiff competition that the Internet provides. There will always be those buyers out there who enjoy the instant gratification of buying in a physical shop. Besides, not everything sells as well on eBay as it does live and in person. Take furniture and large decorative items as an example. Because of the high shipping costs associated with delivering these items, they tend to sell better in physical shops or shows. Likewise, items like estate jewelry or a vintage jacket might fetch a better price in person, where a buyer can try the piece on, than they do online. Over time, dealers have gotten a sense of what types of pieces sell more consistently in a brick-and-mortar shop, and what items tend to do better online.

Besides, some merchants just prefer the personal interaction involved in dealing with customers and other collectors face to face. For them, the time required to sell online—researching, photographing their pieces, writing descriptions, communicating with potential buyers, and packaging and shipping purchased items—makes vending on eBay prohibitive; it's more efficient and productive to simply set up shop at a flea market on the weekend.

If you ask me, the advent of eBay has merely forced antiques shop owners and show sellers to be more competitive. After all, savvy buyers can find much of the same merchandise online, and even locate pieces that were once considered hard to find. That means successful sellers must now perform their own brand of market research—which often finds them browsing eBay listings—to determine how much they can mark up a piece. The sellers with staying power seem to be the folks who find a way to balance their business between the selling alternatives.

together a fine vintage-styled kitchen filled with the stuff. The American public went nuts over the look, and suddenly, every reasonably priced piece of Jadeite in the mall flew off the shelves. Influences such as these can spur tremendous fluctuations in the secondary antiques and collectibles market today, including eBay. Not convinced? Here's another example: When Rachel Ashwell began promoting the "Shabby Chic" look a number of years ago, her efforts made a big impact on what shoppers sought from antiques stores and eBay alike. The sellers who tapped into that trend early on made some pretty good money.

Note

When people ask me for advice, or wonder why their merchandise isn't selling, I tell them to look around. If they see what they're offering for sale gathering dust in a dozen different locations, that's not a good sign. It doesn't mean the older items they own aren't nice, just that there isn't a demand for them at the moment. That doesn't mean, though, that those items won't catch on at some point. Trends are fickle, and you just never know when you'll have an opportunity to capitalize on one.

Even so, some dealers just don't bother trying to track the trends. In fact, many people I've talked to about selling on eBay don't feel that market trends really affect them, and to a certain point, I agree. After all, if the powers that be suddenly declare that plastic dishware from the 1950s is "hot," it's not like you can magically summon up pieces among your antiques finds to quickly meet demand. Then again, if you make a point to keep abreast of trends, you just might get lucky selling a piece here or there for much more than you paid for it.

I suppose the main reason so many sellers aren't terribly trend-focused is because tapping these trends is an onerous job. Help does come in the form of a number of "barometers" compiled by one of eBay's public-relations firms, based on searches and sales in several popular antiques-related categories, but the information isn't delivered in what I'd call a timely manner. Indeed, by the time they issue the information so I can post it on my About.com site, it's already a month old. To find more current information, sellers are left to conduct completed listing searches, communicate with other sellers, keep an eye on the newsstand for interesting covers and features related to their business, *and* keep one finger on the pulse of the celebrities, designers, and interior decorators who dictate what's hot and what's not—no small task when, as sellers, we're already swamped pawing through flea markets for items to resell, taking photos, writing descriptions, and loading auction listings.

Note

Some vintage trends are short-lived, like those spurred by celebrities and designers; what's totally hot with today's "it" girl may well be out of style before you can say "next season." Then again, some classics and brand names never seem to go out of style with collectors; I mean, who hasn't heard of Coco Chanel, or for that matter, Coca-Cola? Try performing a bit of market research to determine which trends are of the flash-in-the-pan variety, and what types of antiques and collectibles tend to have more staying power.

That said, you ignore trends at your own peril. If you fail to tap into at least *some* trends, you may miss out on an opportunity for a great sale. Why? Because your description may fail to attract people who are buying solely because of the current trend. You may fail to include a keyword that could spark more interest. Indeed, subtle shifts in the market can even affect how you compose the photos to accompany your item; if you're not aware of these shifts, you could miss out.

Case in point: I once found a Shawnee pottery vase for $5 at an estate sale. It was really pretty, sunshine yellow, and marked U.S.A. on the bottom, but although it was a nice collectible in great condition, there was nothing terribly interesting or unusual about it. I knew it wouldn't sell for much on eBay—demand for this type of vase just wasn't very high at the time—but I bought it anyway. I figured, worst-case scenario, I'd be out $5 and have to find a place for it in my home. Well, imagine my surprise when, a few days later, while standing in the grocery store checkout line, I spotted an entire display of yellow pottery on the cover of *Country Living* magazine. I bought the magazine and, later, as I flipped through its pages, pondered how I could use it to boost the price of my yellow vase.

Tip

It doesn't hurt to visit the magazine stand occasionally to see what you might have in your inventory that's suddenly desirable from a decorating standpoint. Thumbing through a few newly published decorating books doesn't hurt either. Always keep your eye out for the next big trend.

It crossed my mind to simply scan the magazine cover photo showing the yellow pottery, but I knew that doing so might well violate copyright laws—a big no-no. Instead, I photographed my vase alongside the magazine with the *Country Living* title clearly visible. That way, it was clear that this photo was uniquely mine, yet you could plainly tell that similar vases were shown on the cover of the publication.

When I listed the vase on eBay, I selected the Gallery Photo option and wrote the item title so that every person who ran a search for "Shawnee pottery," "vintage yellow vase," "old Shawnee vase" or any combination of those keywords would see my offering lined up next to the latest decorating suggestion from a respected publication. I also worded my description so that potential bidders would know about the type of pottery being shown in the magazine that month, but I was careful not to imply that my vase was *exactly* like the one shown in the photo spread. That's another no-no as far as I'm concerned. My efforts paid off; the vase sold to a bidder in Hawaii for about $30 more than I had expected, increasing my profit substantially.

Setting Up Your Seller's Account

Once you've gotten your hands on a piece you want to sell and determined your selling strategy, you're ready to list it on eBay. Before you can list a single item on eBay for sale, however, you must provide some additional information about yourself and set up a seller's account. Here's how:

1. Click the Sell button at the top of any eBay page. The first time you click this button, eBay directs you to the Sell page (see Figure 8.7). Click on the Sell Your Item button to continue.

Note

After you set up your seller's account, when you click on the Sell Your Item button on the Sell page, you'll be directed to the screen that enables you to begin listing an item.

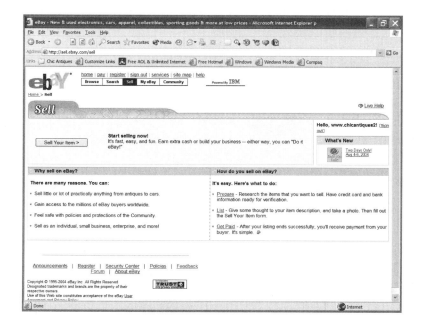

Figure 8.7

When you click on the Sell button at the top of any eBay page for the first time, it will take you to the Sell page.

2. Enter your name, address, phone number, and date of birth in the appropriate fields, and click the Continue button.

3. On the Provide Credit Card Identification page, enter your credit-card number, the card ID number on the back of the card, its expiration date, your name as it appears on the credit card, and your billing address, as shown in Figure 8.8, and click the Continue button.

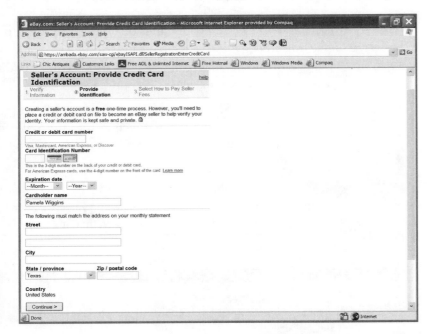

Figure 8.8

Fill in the Provide Credit Card Identification page to place a credit card on file with eBay.

Although as a buyer you can place bids of up to $15,000 in all eBay categories except for Mature Audiences without providing a credit-card number (unless your e-mail provider is Hotmail or Yahoo!, in which case a credit-card number is required whether you're buying or selling), all sellers are required to enter this information.

4. On the Provide Check Identification screen, enter your name, your bank's name, your bank's transit routing number, and your checking account number, as shown in Figure 8.9, and click the Continue button.

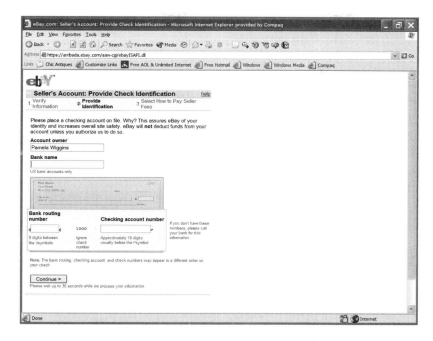

Figure 8.9

You'll be required to place a checking account number on file with eBay by filling in the Provide Check Identification information.

Tip

You'll find your bank's routing number and your checking account number at the bottom of one of your checks (see eBay's sample check on the Provide Check Identification screen for guidance).

5. On the Select How to Pay Seller Fees screen, click either the Checking account or Credit or debit card option button to specify whether you want your monthly seller fees to be automatically paid each month: from your checking account or by credit card. (If necessary, you can change your payment preferences later through your My eBay page as discussed in the section "Managing Your eBay and PayPal Accounts" section later in this chapter.) When you're finished, click the Continue button.

Note

If eBay is unable to access your bank account due to insufficient funds, the credit card on file will be charged by default (and vice versa). If neither of your available payment methods can cover the charge, your account will be suspended until your bill is settled.

After you set up your seller's account, eBay directs you to the Sell Your Item page by default, as shown in Figure 8.10. This is the first screen of the basic listing process, which, from now on, you can access simply by clicking on the Sell button on any eBay page. Rather than entering your first listing now, though, take a moment to explore eBay's selling tools. You'll also want to read Chapters 9, "Titles, Descriptions, Photos, and More," and 10, "Setting Your Starting Price, Understanding eBay's Fees, and Creating a Basic Listing," to learn how to design listing titles and descriptions, and to get a good sense of the fees you'll be required to pay before you really get going.

Figure 8.10

Once you've set up your seller's account, eBay will take you directly to the Sell Your Item page by default.

Setting Up an About Me Page

The handful of times I've sold pieces that went for well over a thousand dollars on eBay, people trusted me to take their payment and then deliver the goods in a safe and secure manner. Why? In part because I have a good feedback rating, established over many years; you'll learn more about establishing your feedback rating in Chapter 11. I suspect, however, that my About Me page, which includes a photo of me and my husband along with some personal tidbits and a link to my personal Web site and my About.com site, also played a role.

Note

In the old days, eBay allowed sellers to list personal Web sites in their auction listings, but did away with that to discourage bidders from buying from the sellers' personal sites instead of through eBay. Indeed, if I were to list my personal antiques site, Chic Antiques (http://www.chicantiques.com), in my auction listings now, eBay would shut those auctions down. I know, however, that giving buyers a chance to click over to another site where I have some impressive items for sale helps prove I'm not just an anonymous blip on the Internet radar. I have a standing Web presence, and I want buyers to know that. That's why I include links to both my Chic Antiques site and to the site where I serve as an antiques expert (http://antiques.about.com) on my About Me page and use www.chicantiques as my eBay user ID.

To set up your own About Me page, do the following:

1. Click the site map link found at the top of any eBay page.

2. Scroll down to the Help section and click the Seller Guide link.

3. Click on the A–Z Index link, shown in Figure 8.11.

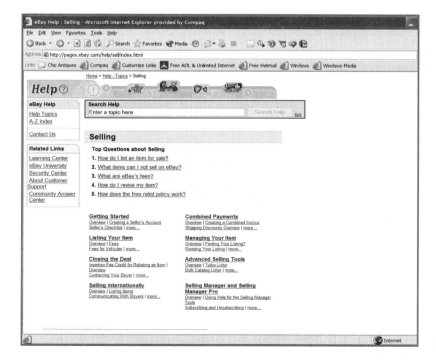

Figure 8.11

Click the A–Z Index link, shown in the upper-left corner.

4. You'll be on the "A" page. Click the About Me Pages link, shown in Figure 8.12.

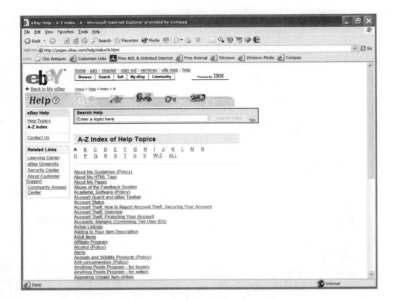

Figure 8.12

From the "A" page of the index, click the About Me Pages link.

5. Scroll down and click the Create your About Me page link, shown in Figure 8.13.

Figure 8.13

Scroll down and click the Create your About Me page link.

6. Click the Create or Edit Your Page button to begin, as shown in Figure 8.14.

Figure 8.14

Click the Create or Edit Your Page button to begin creating your About Me page.

7. Select an option button to choose your page layout, as shown in Figure 8.15.

Figure 8.15

Select an option button to choose your page layout.

8. Fill in the blanks for the title of your page, as shown in Figure 8.16. Including your name or the name of your business is a great way to personalize the page.

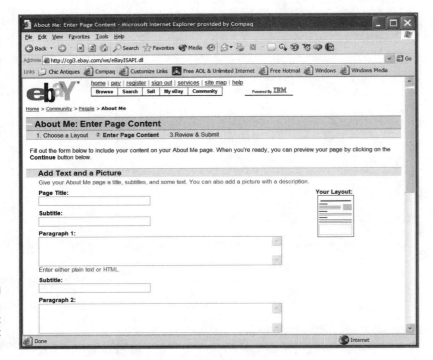

Figure 8.16

Fill in the blanks, adding a title for the page and two short introductory paragraphs about yourself and/or your business.

9. Fill in the title and text for the paragraph sections on the page. This can be used to tell more about your personal collections, experience in the antiques business, or other interests.

Note

Entering plain text works for this task. If you know HTML, however, you can use it to spruce up your About Me page in these sections.

10. Scroll down to add a link to your photo, as shown in Figure 8.17. (If you do not have a Web site where you can host a photo, consider asking a friend or family member to host a photo for you.)

Note

Putting a photo of yourself on the page isn't a bad idea as long as it's a professional shot or related to antiques and collectibles. It puts a face on your online business and establishes a friendly rapport. When a potential buyer can see your smiling face, you no longer seem like a mysterious seller asking him or her to trust you blindly.

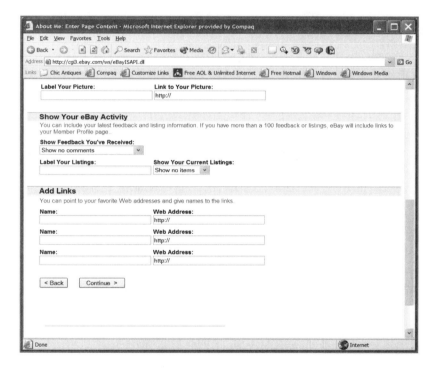

Figure 8.17

Add your photo, decide how you want to display your business activity, and add three Web links.

11. Decide whether you want to display your eBay activity—that is, your feedback information as well as any current listings—on your About Me page. You aren't required to display your feedback or your current listings on your About Me page, but doing so isn't a bad idea.

12. Fill in the names and Web addresses for three of your favorite sites. These sites might be ones you run or that feature you or your wares, or informational sites about your specialty area. When you're finished, click the Continue button.

13. Review the way the page looks, as shown in Figure 8.18. If you'd like to make changes to your content, click the Back button. If you like the way it looks, click the Continue button.

14. If you're satisfied with your About Me page, click the Submit button to make it live on eBay, as shown in Figure 8.19.

Selling Tips and Tools from eBay

I know, I know. You're ready to get to the part where you learn how to turn your collectibles into cash. Before you do, though, I urge you to explore eBay's selling tools, found at Seller Central, and to read through eBay's handy Seller Guide. To access these resources, simply click the Site Map link that appears at the top of any page on eBay. The Site Map enables you to link to many helpful features. In fact, I'd venture to guess that sooner or later, you'll use features in just about every section of the Site Map. For now, though, you'll limit yourself to the Sell and Help categories.

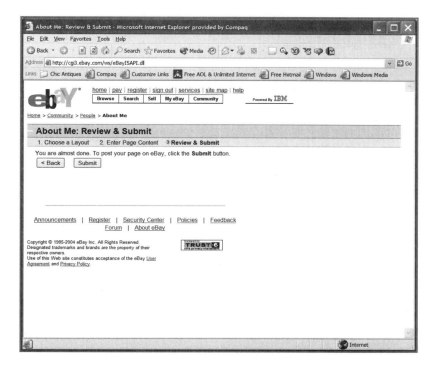

Figure 8.19

Click on the Submit button to make your new page live on eBay.

Exploring Seller Central

eBay's Seller Central, which you can access by clicking the Seller Central link under the Sell category on eBay's Site Map page, features scads of useful information about marketing your wares on the site (see Figure 8.20). Information in Seller Central is categorized as followed:

■ **Getting Started.** Click this link to view information about setting up a seller's account; learn about the basic technical aspects of selling and of accepting online payments; read numerous useful selling tips; discover what other, more experienced sellers have to say about selling on eBay; and even find out how to take an eBay University class in your area or online. (Although I'll cover many of these topics in greater detail, with specifics relating to selling antiques and collectibles, it never hurts to review what eBay has to say on these subjects.)

Note

Knowing dedicated sellers want to learn from and interact with other eBay users, eBay developed a "university" to provide continuing education. To learn more about classes available at locations across the country and online, visit http://pages.ebay.com/university/.

- **Best Practices.** Click this link to read up on researching, pricing, selling formats, merchandising, promotional tools, packing and shipping, customer service, and feedback.

- **Advanced Selling.** Click this link if you've already mastered the basics of eBay merchandising. Topics here include seller tools, eBay stores, the PowerSeller program, the Trading Assistant Program, eBay keywords, the co-op advertising program, international trading, and wholesale lots.

Note

As a person selling antiques and collectibles, you'll find the sections about eBay stores and PowerSellers to be most pertinent. Although most people I've talked to haven't had much luck with eBay Stores, it's good to know they're available just the same. And the PowerSeller program, which rewards sellers for making lots of eBay sales and keeping a high feedback record, may be something you'd like to aspire to in the future. You may also want to read up on Trading Assistants, which are, essentially, experienced eBay sellers for hire. You might opt to use a Trading Assistant if you become too busy to handle your own auctions.

Note

If you get *really* serious about your online auction business, then the section about eBay Keyword may intrigue you. With the eBay Keyword program, you can create banner advertising for a fee. That said, most antiques dealers like to keep overhead low so they have more money to invest in inventory—if that's the case, then the Keyword program may not be for you.

- **Sell by Category.** This is one section in Seller Central where you might want to spend a little extra time. Most notably, each category on eBay is briefly described in the Seller's Edge area; for you, the most pertinent categories will most likely be antiques, art, pottery and glass, coins, collectibles, and stamps—although you may find a few others that pertain to your specialty areas. You won't find what I'd call a wealth of information here, but there are some good tips under each list, as well as information similar to those eBay "barometers" I discussed earlier, in the section "Tapping into Trends." Simply click a category's In Demand link for an assessment—limited though it may be—of what's hot and what's not. Under Sell by Category, you'll also find discussion boards where you can pose questions to other dealers and collectors—a useful way to make some professional connections in the industry or just learn more about a particular piece.

■ **News & Updates.** Click here to sign up for Seller Newsflash, a monthly e-mail newsletter that offers advance notice of promotions and free listing days, along with selling tips and other eBay strategies. (That said, the News & Updates section under the Resources link, discussed next, actually provides a lot more information.)

Note

You'll also find the latest category updates detailed in the News & Updates section. As time passes, eBay adds, eliminates, and changes categories in an effort to better serve both buyers and sellers. Whether or not you agree with what the company does to your favorite categories, this is the place to keep pace with the changes.

■ **Resources.** Click this link to view all the resources you'll need to sell more and grow your business—at least according to eBay. (I'm not sure making such sweeping statements is appropriate when it comes to selling antiques and collectibles; there are just too many variables involved. In any case, this section does contain some resources worth exploring.) Whether your focus is on managing single items or managing your entire eBay account, this information can help familiarize you with eBay's services. You can also access community groups, buy selling supplies, and access other seller services, as well as a News & Updates section that goes beyond reporting category changes to include news releases, community announcements, and system announcements.

Figure 8.20

Seller Central on eBay addresses most of the main questions and issues new sellers may have. Seasoned sellers can pick up a few pointers by reviewing this information as well.

Finding Answers with the Seller Guide

Seller Central isn't the only useful resource eBay provides for sellers about to embark on their maiden listing. The Seller Guide (see Figure 8.21), which you access by clicking the Seller Guide link under the Help category on eBay's Site Map page, can also offer you a good bit of assistance—although you may notice that some of the content in the Seller Guide overlaps with the information in Seller Central. Most notably, the Seller Guide answers the five most-asked questions about selling on eBay. To save you the trouble of looking them up, these questions are as follows:

■ **How do I list an item for sale?** If you've already set up your seller's account, first click the Sell button that appears at the top of every page on eBay, and follow the instructions on each screen that appears. (I'll go over the listing process step by step in Chapter 10.)

■ **What items can I not sell on eBay?** eBay maintains an extensive list of items that cannot be sold on eBay, which you can access through the Seller Guide. The list is broken into three categories: prohibited (items banned from eBay), questionable (items that may be listed under certain conditions), and potentially infringing (items that may be in violation of copyrights, trademarks, and other rights). As a dealer of antiques and collectibles, you probably don't need to worry about your items being prohibited from sale on eBay, but there are sections on artifacts, firearms, used clothing and cosmetics, weapons, and knives worth reviewing if you plan to sell these types of old items.

- **What are eBay's fees?** Any time you list an item on eBay, unless it happens to be a free listing day, you'll be required to pay a fee. For each listing option you choose—for example, adding a gallery photo or scheduling a start time—an additional fee will be tacked onto the total. When an auction ends, yet more fees are assessed based on the ending value of your item. (You'll learn more listing options and their associated fees in Chapter 10.)

- **How do I revise my item?** The basic process for revising a listing that hasn't yet received bids is quite simple. Revising a listing that is currently in play, however, is another matter. eBay restricts when you can revise items based on how much time remains in the auction, whether bids are in place, and whether the listing is offered in an eBay store or as a fixed-price listing. (I'll cover revising listings for auctions with and without bids in place in Chapter 10.)

- **How does the free relist policy work?** If one of your auctions concludes without a winning bidder or results in a non-paying transaction the first time you list it, then you can relist the item free of charge. I'll discuss when it might be appropriate to relist an item and what to do if you run into one of those non-paying bidders in Chapter 11.

Additional Selling Tools on eBay

If, after you learn how to list items on eBay (covered in Chapter 10), you determine that listing your items by hand is simply too time-consuming, you'll be glad to know that eBay offers several tools to help speed things up. For example, Turbo Lister, a free service, enables you to create many listings in one sitting, revise them if needed, and then submit them all at once—or schedule them to start when you specify. You can even use Turbo Lister *templates* to make your listings more appealing and complete. You'll learn more about Turbo Lister in Chapter 10. In addition to the free Turbo Lister, eBay offers a few fee-based auction tools, such as Selling Manager and Selling Assistant. To learn more about them, click the appropriate links under the Sell category on eBay's Site Map page, or flip to Chapter 10, where I discuss them in more detail.

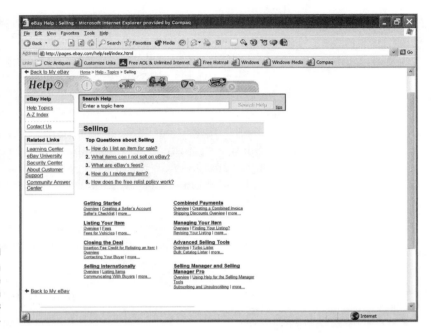

Figure 8.21

The Seller Guide located in the Help section of the Site Map is a good place to learn more about eBay's policies and features for sellers.

In addition to these frequently asked questions, there are a number of links at the bottom of the Seller Guide designed to address other common concerns for beginning eBay marketers. Main topics include the following:

- Getting Started
- Listing Your Item
- Closing the Deal
- Selling Internationally
- Combined Payments
- Managing Your Item
- Advanced Selling Tools
- Selling Manager and Selling Manager Pro

Most of these subjects are covered in detail in this book, with direction pertaining specifically to antiques and collectibles. Should you need additional assistance, however, this area of eBay's Help section will serve you well as a seller.

Managing Your eBay and PayPal Accounts

As mentioned in Chapter 6, in addition to managing your buys, you'll want to make sure you manage your eBay and PayPal accounts—that is, keep them up to date. In addition to keeping your account information such as your shipping address, credit-card number, and e-mail address updated, you can also specify various buying and selling preferences and notify eBay about what types of e-mail communication you want to receive about your account. One of the easiest ways to change your information on eBay is to log into your My eBay page. In the left hand corner, you'll find a section titled "My Account." From there, you can do the following:

■ **Update Personal Information.** Change your user ID, password, e-mail address, physical address for billing and shipping purposes, and update your credit-card information.

■ **Change eBay Preferences.** Review and update the types of e-mail communications you receive from eBay regarding your account; change the way you sign in to your account; and change your shipping preferences, your payment address, and the way features are displayed in your listings.

■ **Leave Feedback.** Leave feedback for others and review the comments others leave for you from a handy list.

■ **Review Seller Account.** You can use this page to review the outstanding balance in your seller account (that is, fees owed eBay for your prior month's listings), change or update your automatic payment method, or use PayPal to pay your eBay bill.

■ **Access PayPal Account.** Follow the links provided to access the PayPal site, where you can view an account overview, review your account history, and update your financial information, account information, and selling preferences. You can also review and update your PayPal user preferences on eBay from this screen.

chapter 9

Titles, Descriptions, Photos, and More

In early 2003, a woman from Michigan listed a blue glass plate she had inherited from her husband's grandmother on eBay. The way she saw it, aside from sentimental value—and the fact that the plate was pretty and old—there was nothing particularly special about it; she didn't expect the plate to fetch much of a price. Imagine her surprise, then, when it sold for more than $16,000! Turns out, it was a Northwood carnival glass plate in a rare color known as "ice blue." When news of this rare offering traveled through carnival glass collecting circles, bidding on the piece went through the roof.

Cinderella stories like this one aren't unheard of on eBay. In fact, a few months before the Northwood carnival glass piece sold, another unlikely treasure made headlines on eBay. This time, it was a fishing lure that reeled in the big bucks. A Canadian seller listed the ultra-rare Heddon lure with a starting bid of only $9.95 and no reserve price, indicating that the seller probably didn't realize what a gem the lure was. Even so, the price quickly rose past the thousand-dollar mark; by the end of the bidding frenzy, it topped out at an unbelievable $31,851.50. Most wooden, brand-name lures aren't particularly rare, but they can still bring several hundred dollars apiece if you've got just the right ones. (If this is news to you, it might be time to take a look at your grandfather's tackle box to see what you can find.)

The point is, if you're lucky enough to list a truly spectacular piece on eBay, interested bidders will probably zero in on it one way or another—with formidable results. Sadly, however, the odds of uncovering such a diamond in the rough are slim. Your items might be of great quality and quite desirable, but chances are they won't be among the rare pieces that generate buzz through the collecting arm of the Internet. That's why you'll need to work harder to get your items noticed by carefully considering keywords, developing compelling descriptions, providing clear photos, and paying attention to details that are important to bidders of all types. In this chapter, you'll learn how to do all this and more; Chapter 10, "Setting Your Starting Price, Understanding eBay's Fees, and Creating a Basic Listing," covers actually creating an auction listing.

Constructing Listing Titles: The Importance of Keywords

Although it's seductively easy to throw an auction title together in a one-size-fits-all fashion, this approach is *not* the best way to snare the maximum number of bidders interested in buying antiques and collectibles on eBay. Why? Because potential bidders for antiques and collectibles aren't a one-size-fits-all group.

On the one hand, you have die-hard collectors who surf eBay looking to buy specific pieces to add to their collection. These people are on a mission, hunting their own personal holy grail. They'll keep searching week after week until they find it—and when they do, they'll pay handsomely to make it theirs. If you sell uncommon or highly desirable items, these people will likely be your best customers. Die-hard collectors perform searches using not only common keywords, but also more specialized terms that knowledgeable dealers would employ. For example, if a dedicated collector is looking for a piece like the one shown in Figure 9.1 to add to her R.S. Prussia plate collection, she won't perform a search using the keywords "porcelain plate." Instead, she'll type `R.S. Prussia portrait plate` or, for even more concise results, `R.S. Prussia Countess Potocka portrait plate`. If the search yields no results, she'll try again tomorrow, and the next day, and the next, until the piece she wants appears.

On the other hand, you have casual shoppers. These people don't know exactly what they're looking to buy. They may not recognize the name "R.S. Prussia" or have a clue that certain portrait plates are highly desirable. They many not even know what a portrait plate is. When they shop for jewelry on eBay, they probably can't tell the difference between a high-quality Eisenberg necklace and a more common Emmons choker (see Figure 9.2). They just want a pretty plate to display on their dining-room buffet, or a rhinestone necklace to wear to a cocktail party. These casual shoppers buy items based primarily on aesthetics—

Figure 9.1

This R.S. Prussia Countess Potocka portrait plate sold on eBay for more than $1,500. Writing the item title so that it showed up in as many searches as possible helped boost the bids.

for example, to match a decorating scheme or clothing—or based on the latest trends, not because a piece holds value as a collectible. In other words, they buy what they like or what they perceive to be fashionable at the moment.

How, then, do you ensure that your listing gets exposure with both groups? The key is using keywords wisely—more specifically, the keywords that appear in the listing title. Why? Because most eBay searches are conducted on this field. If you fail to include a relevant keyword, then you'll miss out on connecting with a potential buyer. Returning to the R.S. Prussia plate example, if you construct your listing's title to read, simply, "porcelain plate," you'll likely fail to snare die-hard collectors who are looking for a specific R.S. Prussia piece. If, on the other hand, you construct the title to read "R.S. Prussia Portrait Plate,"

Figure 9.2

A casual buyer might love this Emmons faux pearl choker, but they won't realize that it doesn't have as much worth as a collectible when compared to other similar pieces of vintage costume jewelry by a manufacturer like Eisenberg.

your listing won't appear when a casual seller searches for the more general "porcelain plate." To attract the most potential bidders, construct the listing title to read "R.S. RS Prussia Porcelain Portrait Plate Potocka."

Tip

You probably noticed in the preceding paragraph that I suggested you include both "R.S." and "RS" in the listing title. That's because the presence or absence of periods can affect the outcome of a potential buyer's search. If a potential bidder enters "RS Prussia" in the Search field but your listing only contains the term "R.S. Prussia" (notice the periods), your listing won't appear in his or her search results. To ensure that your item is seen by all interested buyers, be sure to include in the listing title every popular variation of the item's name or spelling.

To determine which keywords you should use to list *your* item, you must first put yourself in the buyer's shoes. Ask yourself, what terminology will buyers who are looking for this type of item use in their search? Each item will have a unique set of keywords that are best suited to maximize the number of search hits your listing receives.

Note

When you write your listing title, be aware that you are limited to 55 characters. Choose your keywords carefully and use the space allotted to it's fullest potential.

Tip

If a piece is marked, putting the actual name of the manufacturer (even if the mark is a symbol) in the title is imperative. Doing so ensures that experienced collectors will be able to locate your piece. Refer to Chapter 2, "Research: Don't Buy or Sell Without It," for more information on researching makers' marks.

For example, suppose you plan to list a green Depression glass pitcher in the Cameo pattern, sometimes referred to as the "Ballerina" pattern by collectors. Odds are, potential buyers—depending on whether they are experienced collectors or casual shoppers—will use one of the following search phrases:

- Cameo pitcher

- Depression glass pitcher

- Green glass pitcher

- Green Cameo pitcher

- Green Cameo

- Ballerina pitcher

- Green Ballerina pitcher

- Green Ballerina

For this reason, you'll want to ensure that your listing title includes as many of these words as possible in order to maximize your eBay exposure. For this example, a good item title would be "Cameo Ballerina green Depression glass pitcher."

Listing Title Pitfalls

Because each listing will be different, depending on what type of item you intend to sell, it's difficult for me to explain exactly what your listing title should include. But if you've put yourself in your buyer's shoes—and researched the item to determine just what it is—you should be fine. That said, there are a few pitfalls you'll want to avoid when constructing your listing title:

- **Missing terms.** Take advantage of all 55 characters you're allotted for your title to attract as many bids as possible. That is, make sure you've covered all your bases when it comes to keywords, including words that will appeal to both tried-and-true collectors and casual shoppers. Along the same lines, avoid listing titles that are too simplistic. For example, a listing title such as "Rhinestone Necklace Earrings" simply doesn't offer enough information about the listing. How old are the pieces? What color are they? Are they signed? Then again, failing to include the simple terminology alongside more in-depth keywords prevents casual shoppers from finding your piece. For this reason, you'll want to avoid titles like "Kramer Blue and Clear Demi." Why? Because most casual shoppers don't know that "Demi" here refers not to Demi Moore or a demitasse cup, but rather to the collecting term "demi-parure," which is used to indicate two pieces in a set, be they matching pin and earrings or a necklace and bracelet. Instead, the title should read something like "Kramer Blue Vintage Demi Parure Rhinestone Necklace Earrings."

Note

The order of the keywords in your listing title doesn't affect whether eBay's Search feature returns your listing when a potential buyer conducts a search. For example, if your title reads "green pitcher Depression glass," and a potential buyer types green Depression glass pitcher in the Search box, your listing will be among his or her search results. That said, try to present your keywords in some semblance of a logical order. Doing so will make your listing title easier to read for your potential bidders.

- **Meaningless characters.** Many listing titles on eBay are swamped by meaningless characters, such as plus signs, tildes, exclamation points, and the like. Although they are, I suppose, eye-catching, these characters do nothing to educate potential buyers about the piece. Sellers are better off using that space to add relevant keywords, thereby increasing the odds of a potential buyer actually finding the piece.

- **Meaningless phrases.** Using phrases like "very nice" in your listing title does nothing to maximize your exposure; after all, few bidders are going to conduct a search for a "very nice pitcher," a "very nice necklace," or what have you. Leave out this type of language unless you've exhausted your keyword options and still have room in the title. Whether you're selling paintings, portrait plates, pins, or pottery, strive to make every item title address the search requirements of all your potential bidders. After you've done that, you can add "WOW!" if you have room.

- **Incorrect information.** Make sure you've correctly represented the item. For example, if it's a green Depression glass pitcher, don't slip and call it a Vaseline glass pitcher—even though the two types of glass do share some similar qualities. People searching for true Vaseline glass, which is more yellow in appearance (like petroleum jelly, hence the name) and usually older than Depression glass, probably won't be interested in the piece, and people looking for Depression glass won't find your listing at all.

- **Missing the mark.** Leaving the maker's mark out of a title description is never a good idea, no matter what you're listing on eBay. If your item is marked, make sure you say so in the item listing. Don't just say that the piece is "signed," though; go ahead and put the name of the maker in the title. That way, bidders looking for a piece by a particular maker will zero in on your listing.

Be sure you spell your keywords correctly. Doing so enables bidders to find your auctions, and also demonstrates your attention to detail and professionalism. Many bidders feel that sloppy online listings reflect how sellers handle their business overall, and avoid placing bids accordingly. That said, if you have room, using a commonly misspelled word in your listing title alongside a correctly spelled word can work for you—for example, including "Steiff" and "Stieff" or "brooch" and "broach." Just be sure you don't refer to a necklace as a "neckless." That just looks silly.

Adding a Subtitle

If you find that the 55 characters you're allotted for your listing title just doesn't cut it, eBay does allow you to add a subtitle—for a fee. You probably won't want to spend the money to add a subtitle if the item is expected to sell in the low-to-moderate price range. If, however, you're listing a very expensive piece, adding a little more information to the title makes sense. Doing so not only indicates to potential buyers that the listing was important enough to invest in a subtitle, but also reveals additional pertinent information about the piece, thereby attracting more lookers and, perhaps, more bidders.

The information you provide in a subtitle will vary from piece to piece; odds are, research you've conducted prior to listing the piece will dictate what you want the subtitle to address. Performing a completed listing search for similar items may provide some clues with regard to how other sellers have described the piece in similar circumstances to achieve good results. Generally speaking, though, subtitles can

- Add additional pertinent keywords.

- Address condition issues of common concern to buyers.

- Indicate noteworthy publications (for example, a magazine, collectibles reference book, or auction catalog) that have featured this piece or a similar piece, or museums where this exact piece has been on display. You might even want to refer to it as a "book piece," if that's appropriate.

Caution

Use the phrase "book piece" sparingly in your auction listings unless the item you're selling is truly noteworthy. Not all pieces shown in reference guides are rare and valuable. Touting these lesser items as book pieces will be laughable to experienced collectors. And if you're going to use "book piece" in your item title, be sure to back up that assessment in your description so avid collectors can refer to their reference library to confirm the listing.

■ Guarantee authenticity.

■ Add brief information on the provenance (origin and history) of a piece.

■ Provide more information about the maker of the piece.

What Bidders Really Look for in Item Descriptions

If it's happened once, it's happened a million times: I click an item listing on eBay only to find a page filled with disclaimers and perfunctory details, with the actual item description buried somewhere in between. My response? Unless it's a really special item—one that is exceedingly desirable and even more rare—I simply move onto the next listing. The fact is, most eBay buyers want to get in, see what you have to offer, evaluate it quickly, make a bid if desired, and move on to the next listing. If your listings contain volumes of information in a format that is organized poorly and difficult to read, you're almost certainly losing business. By the same token, if you don't add *enough* information, most shoppers will be uncomfortable placing a bid—and you can't count on potential bidders to e-mail you with questions about details you should have included in the first place.

Bells and Whistles: Advantageous or Annoying?

Music, trailing arrows, cute clocks, busy backgrounds, hard-to-read fonts—I've seen more than I care to admit on eBay. Sellers who believe these bells and whistles attract bidders should reevaluate their thinking; after informally surveying many online auction shoppers, I've found that most agree that they do more harm than good. Indeed, many potential bidders are actually driven away by startling music and text that is difficult to decipher. Instead of peppering your listings with extraneous elements, consider focusing your energies on writing articulate descriptions and taking clear photographs.

The bottom line? Buyers don't want to have to hunt for the significant details about an item. If your listing fails to provide adequate information or includes too much detail—or is too busy to be decipherable—you may well lose potential buyers to a seller who takes more care when creating his or her listings. That, in turn, will almost certainly prevent you from fetching the highest possible price for your item. To strike that all-important balance between too-much information and not enough, your listings should include the following details in an easy-to-read format:

- **Maker.** If the piece is signed, potential bidders will want to know exactly how the piece is marked. In addition to describing the mark in your text, you should add a clear photo of the mark to your listing. This is because many makers used different marks during different time periods, so a photo can enable an educated buyer to evaluate the age of the piece.

Note

If you've been unable to identify the maker of an item, it's perfectly fine to admit this and move along to other important aspects of the piece. Be aware, however, that this may affect the price the item fetches. You may decide it's best to perform a bit of additional research to see if you can pin down the piece's maker before listing that particular item on eBay.

- **Size.** An accurate measurement is a critical component of any eBay listing. Avoid using relative terms like "large" or "tiny" to describe a piece without giving exact measurements in inches, feet, or yards. For vintage clothing, be sure to evaluate the item in terms of modern sizing rather than just going by the size on the garment. A modern size 16 can't fit into a vintage size 16; the vintage piece will be much too small.

- **Condition.** Including in your listing description any flaws that might undermine the item's value as a collectible is imperative. When disclosing an item's condition, however, avoid limiting your portrayal of the piece to general terms like "excellent," "good," and "average." Instead, be specific about what you mean. For example, suppose you're selling a piece of pottery that is prone to crazing, but your piece is not damaged in that way. Rather than simply stating that the piece is in excellent condition, say that no crazing is evident on the piece. Or, if it does have crazing, describe the piece as being in good overall condition with light crazing. Likewise, if you're selling glassware, mention that your piece is free of chips, cracks, and scratches (unless, of course, it isn't). No matter what you're selling, if you're claiming that your item is in mint condition, be sure it truly is like new, with no wear whatsoever. For more information about grading a piece's condition, see the section "The Importance of Accurately Grading Condition" later in this chapter.

- **Provenance.** Your potential buyers will appreciate the inclusion of a brief description about the age, history, and any other credible details you can provide about your piece. If you know that a publication has featured the item, mention that fact along with the page number. Hit the high points and avoid getting bogged down in lengthy details that won't have an impact on the desirability of your offering. If you bought the item at an estate sale or auction, a brief mention is okay. Unless the person was a celebrity or other noteworthy individual, including more information about them probably isn't necessary or desirable.

- **Shipping cost.** If you sell the same types of items frequently, you're going to be able to estimate how much a piece will cost to ship, and include that information in your listing. For instance, when I sell jewelry on eBay, I know that I can send a single piece by first class mail to most any location in the United States for about $2. If the buyer wants insurance, it will cost him or her $1.20 for each $50 increment based on the ending price. I put that information in the listing so there's no guesswork involved, and you should too. If you won't know how much shipping will cost until you determine the buyer's location at the end of the auction, state that in your listing so bidders know what to expect.

- **Payment methods.** If you don't accept personal checks, be up front about it. If you require the bidder to purchase a money order, state that in your listing. Don't surprise the buyer after the sale with prohibitive details.

- **To-the-point policies.** If you require auction payments to be received no later than 10 days after the auction ends, say so in your listing. Just avoid the temptation to regale potential buyers with sob stories about non-paying bidders and other details that don't pertain to them. Aside from the fact they probably won't read it anyway, it mucks up your entire listing when people have to scroll down past pages and pages of words to see a photograph of the item you're offering for sale. Also, if you have a return policy, briefly state it in your auction description. Don't wait until a problem arises to tell a bidder that you don't accept auction returns. That's not good business.

Developing Selling Policies

Although your payment policies will more than likely develop as you learn the ropes on eBay and figure out what works best for you, you should still give some thought to what types of policies you want to implement right from the get-go. A great way to start is to put yourself in the buyer's shoes. Odds are you'll find that most buyers want options when it comes to payment and even shipping. For this reason, I tend to accept just about any available form of payment, and to accommodate shipping requests. My default is the least expensive means of delivery available, but if a customer wants to add insurance, priority delivery, or delivery confirmation, I try to oblige.

On the other hand, I don't accept returns on auction items unless I've made an error in the description. In my book, there's no buyer's remorse when it comes to auctions, and if I've described the piece correctly and followed through professionally, then there should be no reason for a return. But that's just my policy. Many sellers do accept unconditional returns. If you feel like that's going to be important to your customers when you're first starting out on eBay, make it your policy as well.

Bottom line: Keep an open mind. Don't set too many limits right off the bat as precautionary measures. Your sales will suffer if you do. See what works best for you and fits your comfort level over time.

If you touch on each of these points in a clear and concise manner, you will have covered all the description areas that are important to most eBay shoppers. I'm not suggesting that you can't tailor your descriptions to make them more interesting or to include information that you deem to be appropriate and necessary, but adding superfluous information will not help your cause.

In the same vein, here are some things buyers *don't* want to see in auction descriptions:

- **Sketchy details.** When you leave out pertinent details, you may be seen by potential buyers as amateurish, as someone who doesn't care enough about his or her business to take the time to write a complete item description, or worse, as shifty, omitting important facts in an attempt to hide something. Indeed, when you provide sketchy details, you can expect experienced bidders to avoid bidding on your auctions. Alternatively, because novice buyers may not ask the correct questions about your piece, they may be disappointed when they receive it from you.

None of these scenarios makes for happy customers, repeat business, and high feedback ratings.

Caution

Never say, "see photo" or "the photo says it all" in place of writing a complete and accurate description. There's no way a buyer can glean all the information necessary to make an educated buying decision simply by looking at a photo or two, no matter how good they happen to be. And besides, it makes you look like you're too lazy or busy to write a complete description. Buyers may wonder, will you be too lazy or busy to answer questions, process a payment, or ship out the merchandise as well?

- **Misleading statements.** Don't oversell your wares by making grandiose statements you can't back up. If a piece isn't in excellent to mint condition, by all means, don't make that claim. If you have other concerns about the condition of a piece, state them in your description in an up-front and easy-to-understand manner rather than burying important facts amid an otherwise glowing review of the piece. Likewise, if you're not sure how old the item is or whether it is a reproduction, don't speculate; instead, simply state that you don't know—or better yet, do some research to find out so you can include that information in your item description in the first place.

- **Claims of ignorance.** Avoid pleading ignorance as an excuse for an inaccurate and/or inarticulate auction listing. As the seller, it's up to you to adequately research and market your goods. Sure, you can tell buyers that Barbie clothes aren't your area of expertise and urge interested buyers to e-mail you with questions. But don't simply write "see photo" or omit the fact that the clothes are soiled when you can plainly see they are in less-than-perfect condition.

- **Long disclaimers.** Most bidders don't much care about problems you've had with buyers in the past. If you write volumes about non-paying bidders, bad checks, and the like, it just comes across as negative. Instead, focus on the good things you have to say about the antiques and collectibles you're offering for sale. Any policies regarding returns, payments, and the like should be brief, informative, to the point, and conveyed in a positive light. No one wants to feel like he or she is being punished for a crime someone else committed.

It should be your goal as an eBay seller to provide bidders with an accurate description so they can make an informed decision about whether to place a bid. Your efforts will almost certainly be reflected by your auctions' ending prices.

The Importance of Accurately Grading Condition

I know, I know, I've discussed condition a number of times already—but that's because getting this aspect of your auction listing right is *so* important, it's worth repeating. Why? Because condition issues are the most common point of contention in disputes with buyers. You can avoid many disputes simply by carefully examining your item and disclosing any flaws you find when you put it up for auction—whether it's a cloudy mirror in a vintage powder compact, a ding in a piece of heirloom silver, or a misplaced clock key. Although many collectors will purchase items with minor condition issues—and for good money, too—they expect to be told *before* they buy that the piece is flawed.

Each category of antiques and collectibles—be it pottery, glass, ephemera, or what have you—has a unique set of commonly found condition-related problems. Here are some common condition issues to scout for, depending on what type of item you're looking to sell:

- **Pottery.** Some pottery is prone to *crazing*, where tiny cracks develop in the surface of the glaze. In some cases, crazing diminishes the value of the piece; in other cases, it's not as much of an issue. Either way, you'll want to disclose any crazing you discover so bidders know what to expect when they get the piece home. You should also inspect pottery for hairline cracks and chips, because both can influence value. Don't overlook a chip on the base or inner rim of a piece of pottery, where it may not be as noticeable.

- **Porcelain and china.** Like pottery, porcelain and china are prone to crazing, hairline cracks, and chips, and through heavy use can also be stained by food or beverages, such as coffee or tea. You should inspect each piece for this type of damage. Run your finger along all edges and rims of the piece; sharp spots can be indicative of chipping. In addition, inspect any hand-painted or decaled decorations for wear. Finally, use a black light to inspect porcelain for signs of repair; the glues used in most repair jobs will fluoresce under a black light. If you do detect a repair, you must disclose that information along with any damage you find to the piece in your listing.

■ **Glass.** Because they are prone to chipping and cracks, all glass pieces should be carefully inspected for damage. As with porcelain, run your finger along the rim and base of all pieces to check for sharp spots that might indicate the presence of a crack (see Figure 9.3). Be aware, too, that glass pitchers are notorious for developing stress cracks where the handles have been applied. Likewise, dishes sometimes show signs of abuse, such as excessive knife scratches. Glass can also develop a cloudiness known by collectors as *sickness*, making diseased pieces virtually worthless. Any of these condition issues should be noted in your description.

Figure 9.3

Running your finger along the rim and base of a piece of vintage glassware will help you to locate sharp spots indicating a chip, which should be disclosed in an item description.

■ **Textiles and clothing.** Improper storage, use, and abuse can really do a number on vintage textiles and clothing. For this reason, you should inspect each item for moth holes, stress to seams, and thin spots in high-wear areas; likewise, embroidered decorations and other embellishments should be inspected for wear or missing elements. All stains, rips, holes, and other signs of wear must be identified in an item description. Likewise, be up front about missing buttons and broken zippers in your item description.

■ **Toys.** Inspect each piece for missing components or wear to existing parts. Anything on a toy that is not "like new" should be described to a potential buyer. Ask yourself, are the rubber tires on a toy truck cracked and dry? Are any of Barbie's fingers missing or chewed? Is the mohair on an old teddy bear worn in spots? Likewise, if the toy is missing any puzzle or game pieces, this should be noted—even if the original box is in mint condition. Mechanical toys should also work—that is, they should do what they were designed to do. If they don't, be sure to include this information in your condition assessment.

■ **Costume jewelry.** Collectors will want to know if any stones in a costume jewelry piece are missing, or if there are obvious replacement stones. They'll also want to know if any of the stones have yellowed or look *dead*—that is, if they've lost their sparkle and have become cloudy or dark. If a piece's finish is worn, that should be noted, along with the degree of the wear. Likewise, any repairs such as soldering or replacement clasps should also be mentioned. If your piece contains faux pearls, be aware that peeling is a common condition issue.

■ **Ephemera.** Many paper collectibles survive quite nicely over time, but others don't fare as well. Make note of any tears, stains, and creases present on vintage valentines, postcards, trade cards, and other types of paper memorabilia. Inspect each piece for fading and discoloration as well as *foxing*, a term used to describe brown spots or discoloring along the edges of vintage art prints.

Tip

Finding a reference guide on specialty areas with which you are not familiar can provide much needed guidance when it comes to noting condition issues. Most large booksellers, such as Barnes & Noble and Borders, offer a selection of these types of guides in their stores, or you can shop for specialty guides online in a number of locations. See Appendix A, "More Helpful Resources," for more information on booksellers offering titles on antiques and collectibles.

Photos: A Valuable Part of Your Item Listing

You know the old saying: "A picture is worth a thousand words." Sure, it's a cliché, but that's because it's true—and nowhere more so than on eBay. You probably guessed that adding photos to your listing is an imperative; it's the best way to convey the beauty of your piece. Be warned, though, that a fuzzy, out-of-focus, too-dark, all-around crummy photo, like the one shown in Figure 9.4, is almost as bad as no photo at all. After all, buyers can't use their expertise to evaluate your piece's condition or to substantiate your claims of its age or authenticity if they can't clearly see what you're offering for sale. And don't count on them to e-mail you for more information if your photo isn't good enough. More often, they'll just move along without bidding. The bottom line? If you're not uploading quality photos to back up your listing descriptions, you stand to lose money every time you list an item.

Of course, taking clear, enticing photographs can be a real challenge until you get the knack of it. As with most things, practice makes perfect. While I don't purport to be an expert photographer, I have picked up a thing or two about photographing antiques and collectibles in my years selling online:

Tip

You don't *need* a digital camera to create digital pictures; if you prefer, you can simply use a regular film camera and use a scanner to digitize your prints. Some people even place small items like jewelry directly on a scanner and capture an image that way (although I've never had admirable results doing so). That said, if you plan to make auctioning items on eBay a regular activity, it can be cost-effective over time to invest in a digital camera instead of paying for photo processing and film. Plus, a digital camera enables you to see your results quickly, so you can decide whether you've obtained an acceptable image.

If you don't yet own a digital camera, you'll be pleased to know that prices have gone down in the last several years, even as technology has improved. While I'm not comfortable recommending a particular camera—the market changes too quickly for my advice to be relevant—I will say that I was once told by a camera expert to purchase a digital camera made by a company that specializes in photography rather than in other types of electronics.

Figure 9.4

Can you imagine trying to discern the desirability of an antique or collectible with a photo of this quality? Incredibly, sellers post photos like this on eBay every day, expecting bidders to do just that.

■ **Backgrounds.** In most cases, using a plain background works better than busy patterns. And although black works well for some items (see Figure 9.5), white is better for others. With regard to texture, some sellers pose their wares on velvet, felt, or other plain fabrics, while others prefer using inexpensive poster paper, available at craft stores. It's wise to have a few different background options at your disposal so you can experiment with your piece to see what looks best.

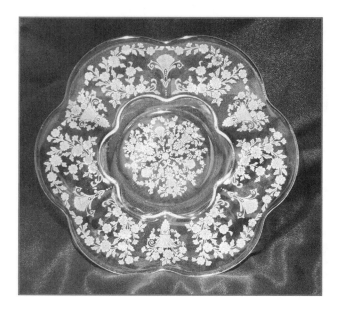

Figure 9.5

This Duncan Miller First Love plate was photographed on a black background to show the pattern detail.

■ **Photo size.** Because not all eBay buyers have access to high-speed Internet connections, it's a good idea to keep the size of your photo small. Resolution should be at 72 dpi for screen viewing, and images should be saved in BMP, JPG, or GIF format. To reduce file size and make the image more pleasing to the viewer, crop excess white space and background areas from your photos (see Figure 9.6 for a comparison). Doing so will bring out more detail in the item you're selling in addition to reducing the file size.

Figure 9.6

The excess background shown in the image on the left detracts from the item being sold and unnecessarily increases the file size. The cropped photo on the right is much more pleasing to the eye and highlights the hatpins and holder.

■ **Multiple photos.** Whenever possible, you should feature multiple photos of your item, including images of the bottom and back of the piece along with close-ups of any marks and/or damage. Why? Because buyers don't always want to rely only on your assessment of condition issues or marks, preferring to evaluate them through photographs before bidding.

Tip

Because eBay hosts only one image per listing free of charge, you may want to consider linking your images to a Web site you maintain for personal use. Alternatively, you can use photo-editing software to combine two or more photos into one image file. Although this may involve a bit of a learning curve on your part, addressing the needs of bidders will usually result in higher prices for your wares.

■ **Lighting.** It's not a bad idea to set up a mini photo studio—in your home, your place of business, or what have you—to help you get the lighting of your photo just right. Doing so can help you minimize shadows, resulting in better photos all the way around. For help in this department, I suggest you check out http://www.tias.com/other/promo4.html. As shown in the TIAS demo, using two lamps on either side of an item can help to reduce shadows during indoor photography. You'll need to experiment to find out whether natural light or artificial light works best with your camera, and when to use a full or partial flash, or even no flash, in different situations.

■ **Learn to use your camera.** If you've never actually read the manual that came with your camera, and you're not getting good photos with it, now's the time for a quick review of that helpful little booklet. Most digital cameras have settings you can employ to greatly improve your image quality if you take the time to learn about them.

Caution

Photos of pets, children, landscapes, and so on that don't relate to the item being listed, though they may be important to you, may *not* be significant to a buyer. In fact, those photos can slow down the loading of your listing for dial-up Internet users, which may prompt them to move to the next item. Being personable doesn't mean you have to get personal. Stick to the minimum amount of information required to adequately represent your antiques and collectibles. Your customers will appreciate your consideration.

chapter 10

Setting Your Starting Price, Understanding eBay's Fees, and Creating a Basic Listing

You've written your listing description and taken some photos of your piece. No doubt you're raring to go, ready to list your item on eBay and watch the bids pour in.

Not so fast.

Before you do, you'll want to carefully consider your item's starting price, which requires a little thought. Set the starting price too high, and you may not get any bids at all. Set it too low, and your ending price may be less than you'd like. Either way, you won't be pleased with your auction's result. Likewise, before you list your item, you need to know how much you'll be spending on eBay fees in order to ensure you sell your piece at a profit. Once you have a handle on your starting price and the fees you'll be paying, then you're ready to actually list your item on eBay; you'll learn how to do all three here.

Setting Your Starting Price

Imagine you're at a live antique auction, and the next item up for bid is a vintage lamp. The auctioneer starts the bidding at $50, but the crowd remains still; there are no takers. When he knocks the opening bid down to $5, however, hands go up all over the house. Incredibly, the lamp sells for much more that $50—so why didn't anybody bite when that was the opening bid? Who knows. There's just some kind of glitch in the bargain-hunter's psyche when it comes to high opening bids—they just don't like 'em. Not surprisingly, the same is true on eBay.

No matter what you're selling, if your starting price is too high, there's a chance that no one will bid on your piece. By the same token, if you start the bidding too low, you may undermine the value of the piece. How, then, do you set a starting price that ensures you not only recoup your investment in the item but also turn a profit?

The fact is, the way you set your starting price has a lot to do with your personality. Are you a risk taker? If so, you'll likely set a relatively low starting price and take your chances on the auction's ending price. For example, if, during the course of your research, you've found that pieces like yours in similar condition routinely sell in the $50 range, then you might list it with a starting price of $9.95 because you can be relatively certain that the price will sufficiently rise by the end of the auction. As an added benefit, in addition to encouraging bidding, this low starting price can help you keep your listing fees low.

If, on the other hand, you tend to be more conservative, you might opt to list your piece with a starting price that equals the minimum price you're willing to accept for the piece. For example, if you aren't willing to part with your item for less than $50, then you'll set the starting price at that amount. That way, even if just one person bids, you'll get the return on your investment that you require. Of course, such a high starting bid may chase off potential buyers, which means you may have to relist the item several times before it sells—or worse, never sell the item, but still owe eBay a listing fee.

Whatever type of personality you have, however, you'll likely adjust your starting fee depending on a few common factors:

- **The type of item.** If the piece you're listing is particularly expensive, then you'll obviously want to adjust your starting price accordingly. For example, bidders willing to pay several thousand dollars for a piece of furniture won't mind a starting price of $199.99. That said, you should still consider starting the bidding at a price much lower than the actual value of the piece to generate some excitement.

- **How much you paid for the piece.** If you got the piece for a song, you might feel more comfortable lowering the starting price a bit. If you paid top dollar, however, you're going to want to protect your investment. Either way, you'll almost certainly do well if you're selling a desirable piece.

■ **How much similar pieces have fetched on eBay.** Always perform a completed listing search to see how similar items have fared. This can help you predict your own piece's ending price and, by extension, set an appropriate starting price.

■ **How fond you are of the piece.** As collectors, we often buy things we like. If the item is something you'd rather keep than sell for less than it's worth to you, set the price accordingly. Again, a completed listing search for similar items will tell you whether your expectations are in line with reality.

Of course, you may decide you just don't have the stomach to risk letting your item go for less than you paid for it—or worse, to not sell it at all, thereby paying eBay a listing fee for nothing. In that case, you might want to consider selling your piece at a fixed price using eBay's Buy It Now feature, or setting a reserve price, or both.

Selling at a Fixed Price with Buy It Now

As you probably know, eBay offers the Buy It Now feature, which enables buyers to forego the auction process and purchase an item immediately at a price set by the seller. Although offering buyers the Buy It Now option does involve an additional fee for sellers, you may decide it's a good way to go. Indeed, some bidders perform searches that exclude auctions that don't offer a Buy It Now option. As an added benefit, when a buyer uses Buy It Now, you may receive payment for the piece sooner than you would if you had to wait for the auction's end date to sell the piece.

Note

Of course, you're still required to pay a listing fee and an ending value fee for fixed-price sales.

You have a couple options when it comes to using eBay's Buy It Now feature to sell your wares:

■ **Listing the item with a starting price *and* the Buy It Now option.** This gives bidders the option of waiting out the auction process to see if they're the high bidder (and possibly obtaining the item for less than the Buy It Now price), or purchasing the item outright before the scheduled end of the auction.

Be aware that on non-reserve auctions, the Buy It Now option disappears when the first bid is placed.

- **Listing the item with a Buy It Now price only.** When you use the Buy It Now feature in this way, your listing becomes an advertisement that runs for a certain time period rather than an auction per se. That way, you ensure that your item sells for exactly the amount you specify, or not at all.

Your best bet may be to list the item as an auction with the price you would have set as the Buy It Now price as the opening bid instead. That way, if two (or more) people decide they want your item, they'll bid it up, and it may end up selling for much more than you expected.

However you choose to use the Buy It Now option, the key for sellers is to set a reasonable Buy It Now price. To do so, simply perform a completed listing search to see what similar items have been selling for on eBay. Alternatively, you can base the Buy It Now price on what you paid for it, calculating your overhead and desired profit.

Setting a Reserve Price

Unlike a Buy It Now listing, where bidders can either buy your piece at a fixed price or, in some cases, take their chances by placing a lower bid, reserve-price auctions *require* bidders to meet the price you've set or the piece will not be sold. If they don't meet your price, you are not obligated to sell the piece to the high bidder. Although listing an item in a reserve-price auction can go a long way toward making sellers feel more comfortable marketing high-value items on eBay, bidders tend to be put off by reserves. The problem is, the reserve price you've set is not revealed to potential buyers until it is reached, so they're left flying blind when they place their bids beforehand. Indeed, some bidders never bother bidding on reserve items—even those with a low starting price—

because they suspect the reserve price is probably higher than they're willing to pay. Other buyers hang back to see of a competing bidder will bid enough to reveal the reserve price so they can bid knowing there's actually a chance they may win the auction.

Caution

If you specialize in a certain area on eBay, regular bidders learn to recognize your seller ID. If you're become known for masking high prices with a reserve, bidders will avoid your auctions—which means you'll end up paying listing fees without making sales.

All in all, I avoid setting reserve prices on my auctions because I feel they deter bidders. (Incidentally, eBay agrees with me, and advises sellers accordingly.) That said, it *does* make sense to use a reserve to protect your investment on certain items. For example, if you own a piece that you'd rather keep if it doesn't fetch a high price, you might consider setting a reserve price. Likewise, if you're selling a piece for someone else, you might set a reasonable reserve to protect his or her interests, as I've done when selling expensive porcelain items for my mother. After all, they weren't my antiques and collectibles to gamble with. If you do decide to set a reserve price, do a completed listing search to see what similar items have sold for on eBay to determine what you can reasonably charge for yours.

Caution

Interestingly enough, you can set a reserve price in conjunction with a Buy It Now listing. If you do, though, be careful not to set the Buy It Now price too high. Bidders who aren't interested in paying the Buy It Now price will assume that it reflects a high reserve (sometimes it does), and they may avoid bidding.

Note

On Buy It Now auctions that also have a reserve, the Buy It Now icon is removed only after the reserve is met.

Fees, Fees, and More Fees

Unlike some live auctions, which charge a buyer's premium for each item won, eBay never charges buyers a fee to purchase an item on the site. As a buyer, all you have to do is honor your bids, pay the applicable shipping costs, and you're all set.

Selling on eBay is another story entirely. On eBay, sellers must pay a fee to list their items based on the starting price of each piece, and yet another fee based on the merchandise's ending price. Beyond those basic fees, which are, essentially, set in stone, eBay charges additional fees in the event the seller wants to

■ **List the same item in more than one category.** In most instances, listing an item in the most popular category for the piece and employing appropriate keywords in the title will be sufficient. But in cases where you have a collectible with great crossover interest, you might want to list it in more than one category. For instance, a souvenir powder compact from the 1933 Chicago World's Fair will interest both collectors of World's Fair memorabilia and compact collectors, which are two entirely different categories on eBay.

■ **Add a subtitle.** As mentioned in Chapter 9, "Titles, Descriptions, Photos, and More," if you find that the 55 characters you're allotted for your listing title just doesn't cut it, eBay does allow you to add a subtitle for a fee. Unless your item is a very expensive piece, you probably won't want to spend the money to add a subtitle.

■ **Set a reserve price.** As I mentioned earlier, if you're ambivalent about selling your piece unless it fetches a certain price, the piece is very expensive, or you're selling it for someone else, avoid setting a reserve price. In general, bidders tend to avoid reserve-price auctions.

Note

eBay does charge you to set a reserve price, but refunds the fee to your account in the event the reserve is met.

■ **List the item using the Buy It Now feature.** As mentioned previously, the Buy It Now feature enables buyers to forego the auction process and purchase an item immediately at a price set by you. Although offering buyers the Buy It Now option does involve an additional fee, you may decide it's a good way to go.

- **Schedule a start time.** If you have time to work on your auctions on Sunday, but don't want to start them until Monday, you can schedule a start time for a small fee. This is convenient when you're going to be out of pocket for a few days, too. Some sellers also swear that certain days of the week and times of day are better than others for ending auctions to get the most notice. It's hard to predict these types of things, but if you feel like you've got it all figured out, then scheduling a start time might be convenient for you.

- **Extend the auction period to 10 days.** Although it's desirable to run most auctions for seven days, sometimes it makes sense to pay a little extra to extend the auction a few more days—most notably for high-end items that may generate a buzz in the collecting community. Having a few extra days to get the word about the rare piece you're offering for sale can pay off.

- **Use a listing designer to spruce up the auction page.** If you opt to use a listing designer when you set up an auction, you can select a template to spruce up your listing. Some sellers feel like it really makes a difference when they coordinate the frame of the page with their wares, and the fee isn't high for this option. This type of decorative technique isn't necessary, however; so unless you feel strongly about it, save the fee eBay charges for something more important to you.

Tip

If you pay for an auction-management service and there's no additional fee involved with using an attractive color scheme or template for your listing, then doing so usually won't hurt. They key word here is *attractive*. Remember that what is pleasing to one person might be off-putting to another. You don't want to turn away bidders because your auction listings are too busy or garish.

- **Add a gallery photo.** In my view, adding a gallery photo is a must. They entice bidders to click through to see your listing more closely, making them well worth the small fee eBay charges to display them. Indeed, some bidders like gallery photos so much, they exclude listings that don't include them when setting their search parameters.

Tip

On occasion, eBay offers one-cent gallery days, when it costs just a penny to add a gallery picture to your listing. Keep an eye out for these promotions!

- **Make the listing boldface.** Making your item title bold is meant to make your listing stand out, in theory, attracting additional bidders. Unfortunately, it just doesn't work very well. This is one area where you can save quite a bit on fees by opting out.

- **Highlight a listing.** Like the boldface option, the highlight option is designed to make your listing noticeable. And like the boldface option, it's just not that effective. Again, you can save on fees by disregarding this service.

- **Buy a Featured Plus! spot.** For a substantial fee, you can make your listing a Featured in Search item, which means that when a potential buyer performs a search that returns your listing, it will be featured at the top of the buyer's search results page. Your listing will also be displayed at the top of each category page. Although some sellers view the high fee associated with this service to be one worth paying, I'm not one of them. Even when selling porcelain items valued at well over $1,000, I've opted out of using this feature; considering that I usually end up paying somewhere between $40 and $50 in listing and final value fees alone on such items, tacking on a high fee to pay for featured-item status seems foolish.

- **Buy a Home Page Featured listing.** This option can get you listed on eBay's home page at http//:www.eBay.com. While that might sound like a great idea, keep in mind that this is a very costly option. If you're not selling an antique or collectible selling for thousands of dollars, it's not going to be anywhere near worth the investment for this promotional feature.

- **Display a gift icon.** Just about anything you can buy on eBay might make for a good gift, depending on the recipient, which is why gift icons don't add much value to a listing. Besides, buyers tend to search for specific items, not for items that display a gift icon. Save yourself some money by omitting gift icons from your listings.

Note

Sadly, eBay's fees have steadily risen over time, and this has some sellers worried. After all, each time fees go up, the cost of doing business from home rises a little more—and profits lower in kind. If you're a concerned seller, you can access discussion boards to chat about fees and related issues with other eBay users by clicking on the Community button at the top of any eBay page. Keep in mind, though, that even though eBay's fees have crept up over time, the overhead costs associated with online auction selling remain very reasonable in the grand scheme of things.

However tempting it might be to load up on services for your auction—listing it in multiple categories, adding a subtitle, highlighting it, and what have you— you must realize that these fees can add up quickly, which can have a profound effect on your profit margin. For example, suppose you have a piece of glassware that you bought for $10 and expect to sell for $50. If you set the starting fee at $9.95 with a reserve price of $50, opt for the Buy It Now feature, schedule a start time, make your title listing boldface, and add a thumbnail gallery photo and a gift icon to the listing, you'll rack up $6.05 (based on eBay's fee schedule at the time this book was published) in fees just to get started (see Figure 10.1)! That sum doesn't even account for the fee eBay will charge you in the event the piece does sell for $50, as expected. Worse, if the item *doesn't* sell, you're still out $6.05—not to mention the $10 you spent to buy the piece in the first place—unless you relist it and try again.

On the other hand, if you list the same item with a starting price of $4.95, nix the reserve price, and add a gallery photo as your only other listing feature, you can bring your listing fee down to 60 cents. If the item sells for $50 as expected, you'll owe an additional fee of $2 based on the ending price for a grand total of $2.60—a significant savings. The fact is, you don't need lots of flash to put together a moneymaking auction listing. On eBay, what you choose to sell is usually more important than any bells and whistles you employ to do it. The bottom line? Choose carefully when listing your item on eBay to keep your fees to a minimum.

Note

You can minimize listing fees even further by taking advantage of eBay's free listing days when they are offered. To keep abreast of news such as this, click on the Community button at the top of any page on the site to access the General Announcements link. You'll also want to keep an eye out for e-mail announcing free listing days. Unfortunately, eBay usually doesn't give much notice of free listing days, so you have to be ready to spring into action at a moment's notice to take advantage of these promotions. If you belong to online collecting groups, other members will sometimes mention free listing days to the group when they come up. Pay attention, and you'll have the opportunity to save a good bit of money on listing fees.

Figure 10.1

Listing fees can add up quickly.

Listing Your Item on eBay

Now that you've established a starting price for your piece (or, alternatively, set on a Buy It Now or reserve price) and familiarized yourself with eBay's fee structure, you're ready to list your piece. As you'll discover later in this chapter, eBay offers several tools to expedite the listing process, some of which are free.

There's no doubt about it: These are great for medium- to high-volume users. If you're just getting started, though, you'll want to stick with eBay's Basic Listing option for the time being.

Note

If you haven't set up your seller's account yet, you'll have to do that before you can list your items. Refer to Chapter 8, "Setting Up Shop on eBay: Getting Started Selling," to learn how.

To set up a basic listing, do the following:

1. Click the Sell button, found near the top of every page on eBay.

2. eBay displays a Sell page, as shown in Figure 10.2. Here, you can learn more about selling on eBay by clicking on the links that pique your interest, or click on the Sell Your Item button to continue to the listing process.

Figure 10.2

The first step in setting up a basic listing is click on the Sell Your Item button on the Sell screen.

3. Specify whether you want to sell your item via an online auction or at a fixed price, choosing the selling format that best suits your needs (I've chosen Sell item at online Auction here), and click the Continue button as shown in Figure 10.3.

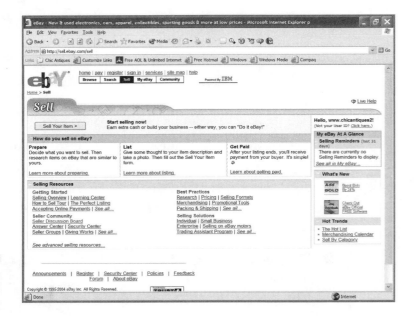

Figure 10.3

Choose whether you'll be selling via auction or listing at a fixed price, and click the Continue button.

Note

If you chose the Sell at a Fixed Price option, you'll follow a slightly different process to set up your listing than what is shown here. Just follow eBay's onscreen instructions, and you'll be fine.

4. eBay instructs you to choose the category that best describes your antique or collectible. Use the scrollbar in the left-hand list box to browse the main categories; when you find the correct one, click it to select it. When you click on a main category, subcategories become available for your selection. In this example, I've categorized my piece, a Bakelite bangle bracelet, under Jewelry & Watches > Vintage, Antique > Costume > Vintage > Bakelite, Plastics, as shown in Figure 10.4. If you like, you can also list your item in a second category for a fee. To do so, click on the link provided. When your category selections are complete, click the Continue button.

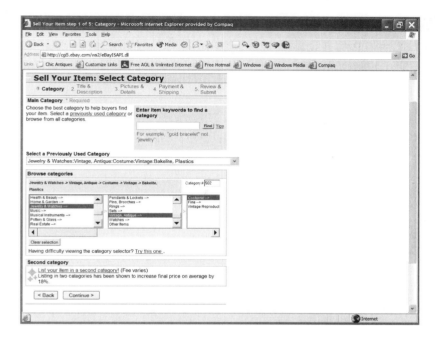

Figure 10.4

Click on the main category
for your listing to display sub
categories.

Note

Although most people won't locate your auction listing by drilling down through eBay's
categories, it's possible that some might. In addition, some people perform searches
based on category, so you'll want to make sure you get yours right. Besides, taking the
time to properly categorize your piece might help you flesh out your item listing. For
example, suppose you're selling a Cameo pitcher. Once you specify it as belonging
under Pottery & Glass, you'll be provided with a series of list boxes that enable you to
provide further categorical information, including the maker of the pitcher (Anchor
Hocking), its dominant color (green), its pattern (Cameo, Ballerina), and the product type
(pitcher). Of course, you'll want to add all this information to your listing description as
well, but by taking the time to categorize the piece, you serve the needs of those bidders
who skim for details in the category description rather than reading whole paragraphs.

5. eBay displays the Describe Your Item page. Consider your keywords
carefully and write an accurate, expressive item title. (Note that I included
the initials "NR," which stand for "No Reserve," because I had room in
my main title.) If you feel that a subtitle can supplement your main title
on high value pieces, add one now. Then, write an item description that

covers all the main points that bidders will look for when browsing your listing, as shown in Figure 10.5. Be sure to include any pertinent keywords relating to the piece for which you didn't have room in your item title. When you're finished, click the Continue button.

Figure 10.5

Your item title and description will be two of the most important aspects of creating an auction listing. Carefully consider your keywords in the title and write a complete description that addresses issues important to buyers.

6. In the Enter Pictures & Item Details screen, shown in Figure 10.6, enter your starting price and, if desired, a reserve price and/or a Buy It Now price.

Note

If you want to change the duration of your auction, you can do so on the screen shown in Figure 10.6. In addition, you use this screen to specify whether you have a single item to sell, or multiple identical items. Since your focus is antiques and collectibles, you'll probably sell multiple identical items only rarely, however.

7. Scroll down to the Item location section of the page (see Figure 10.7) to specify where you are located. This enables local buyers to find your piece, and is especially handy if you're selling furniture or other large items that are costly to ship.

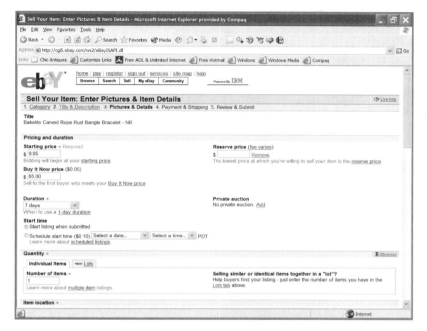

Figure 10.6

The first item details you list are your starting, reserve, and Buy It Now prices, along with the number of items you're selling and the auction duration.

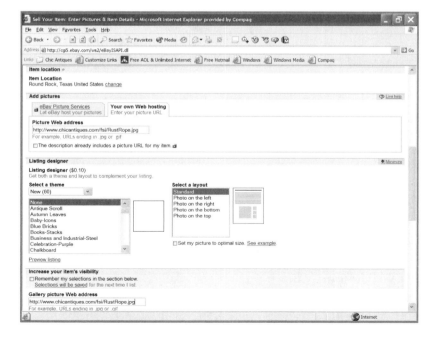

Figure 10.7

Scrolling down to the next screen will allow you to select your item location and add photographs to your listing.

8. In the Add pictures section, you have two choices:

■ **eBay Picture Services.** If you'll be using eBay's photo-hosting service, click on the eBay Picture Services tab, and then click on the first Add Pictures button to upload a photo you have stored on your computer's hard drive (see Figure 10.8). It's a simple process, the first photo is free, and additional photos can be added for a small fee. (Note that this is different from a gallery photo.)

Figure 10.8

If you choose to use eBay's photo-hosting service, the first photo you place in the auction listing is free. Additional photos cost 15 cents each as of this writing.

Note

Back in the old days, eBay didn't offer photo-hosting services. If you didn't have a Web site where you could post your photographs, then you couldn't add a photo to your item listing. With the addition of a photo-hosting service—and other refinements they've made over the last few years—eBay opened up selling opportunities to more people than ever.

■ **Your own Web hosting.** Click this tab if you plan to direct interested buyers to a Web page hosted by your Internet service provider where your photo resides, and then copy and paste the page's URL in the space provided.

Note

Because eBay would rather have sellers use its photo-hosting service for additional pictures (to rack up more fees, obviously), they provide only one space for outside photo URLs. That means if you plan to link to multiple photos on your own Web site, you're going to have to add HTML code in the Item description space to do so—which is beyond the scope of this book. If you'd like to learn more about setting up your own Web page to host photos, and about HTML code you can use to enhance your eBay listings, visit your local bookstore. There are many books on these topics, and browsing through them will enable you to pick the one that best suits your skill level.

Choose the option that best suits your needs.

9. If you want to use a theme and layout template to design your listing, select a theme in the Listing designer section. When you're finished, scroll down to the next section.

Caution

In addition to using templates provided by eBay to design your listing, you also have the option of using an auction-management service to build pages that are loaded with bells and whistles such as scrolling photos, fancy graphics, scrolling marquees, huge fonts, and the like. Be warned, though, that some buyers find these page elements to be annoying—so much so that they click right through to the next auction. On eBay, as in life, moderation is key.

10. In the Increase your item's visibility section, you can choose options such as Gallery picture, Bold, Highlight, gift icon, and so on to help potential buyers locate your auction, as shown in Figure 10.9. (Note that each option involves an additional fee.) I've selected the Gallery option and provided the URL to my own Web site, where the photo file resides. I've used the same URL I used for my main photo because the photo will be adjusted to thumbnail size automatically by eBay. If you're using eBay's Picture Services, simply click on the Gallery button. Choose additional options as desired, and then scroll down and click the Continue button.

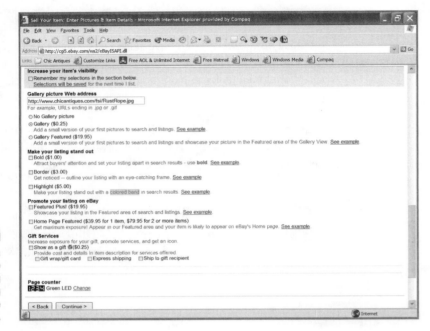

Figure 10.9

Adding a Gallery Photo can be a good way to attract attention to your item listing. Before selecting other visibility enhancing features, be sure to note the fee assessed for each selection.

Tip

If you tend to use the same features time and again, click the Remember my selections box just above the Increase your item's visibility section so you won't have to reenter your preferences every time you set up an auction listing.

Tip

If you would like an alternate type of page-hit counter, click the Change link to make an alternate selection. The default is the Green LED page counter.

11. On the Enter Payment & Shipping page, select the payment methods you will offer bidders, as shown in Figure 10.10. If you are equipped to offer credit-card payments through your own merchant service, be sure to select the cards you accept.

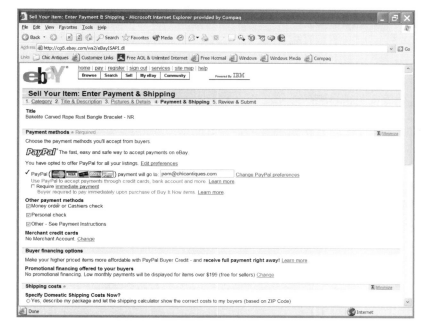

Figure 10.10

Select all the payment methods
you plan to offer bidders,
keeping in mind that refusing
to accept personal checks
may deter shoppers from
bidding on your auction.

12. Scroll down to the Shipping costs section and specify whether you want
buyers to determine their shipping costs using a shipping calculator on
your listing, whether you want to list a flat shipping rate, or whether you
want buyers to contact you after the sale for shipping details, as shown in
Figure 10.11. In addition, use this section to identify a delivery method,
and to disclose whether insurance is offered. Finally, enter the amount of
sales tax you're required to tack onto the ending price, if applicable.

Note

Think twice about leaving out pertinent details regarding shipping and insurance from
your listing descriptions. First, some bidders will not consider auctions where shipping
charges are not stated up front. Second, if you don't include this information, buyers will
not be able to use eBay's Checkout system at auction end. When the Checkout system
is in effect, eBay places an automatic payment button in the end-of-auction notice sent
to buyers via e-mail to let them know they've won an auction. If that button is present,
your high bidder can settle his or her bill with you more quickly, thus getting auction pro-
ceeds into your account in a timely manner.

On Payment Methods

I've noticed a trend of late on eBay: sellers who refuse to accept personal checks. No doubt, these sellers want to avoid the hassle of dealing with bounced checks—in part because eBay offers no assistance with regard to collecting payment from buyers who bounce checks. Other sellers shun credit cards, citing the expense associated with accepting them, not to mention dealing with chargebacks on stolen cards. Still other sellers accept only money orders to avoid paying fees to conduct transactions online. While these strategies may well mitigate some of the risks associated with selling on eBay, it's an unfortunate fact that by limiting your payment options, you may well alienate prospective bidders—which could result in low ending prices or even listings that fail to garner a single bid.

If you're serious about selling, I urge you to accommodate as many payment methods as possible—including personal checks, money orders, credit-card payments, and transactions via PayPal. The bottom line? You don't want a big spender to shy away from your listing just because you don't accept his or her preferred method of payment. Besides, most bidders pay for their merchandise up front in good faith, trusting me to send it to them; I figure I owe them a certain amount of trust in return.

That said, if a buyer does opt to pay via personal check, make sure you hold off on shipping the item until after the check clears—usually about two weeks (unless, say, you're dealing with a trusted customer, such as an individual you've dealt with over and over or someone in your online collecting group). Case in point: I once sold a beautiful portrait chocolate pot on eBay for $1,600 to a buyer whose check bounced. It turned out that money had been fraudulently withdrawn from her bank account; as soon as things were straightened out, she sent me a cashier's check accompanied by a letter from her bank. Needless to say, I was glad I didn't ship the piece as soon as the auction ended! (As an aside, be aware that collection measures for bounced checks and chargebacks vary from state to state; check with your Attorney General's office to see what recourse you have in the event this happens to you. Sadly, you may discover that the cost of recovering the funds overshadows the amount of money you're owed.)

Of course, what payment methods you choose to accept is entirely up to you. If, however, your auctions are ending with low—or no—bids, or if you find yourself in a selling slump, you might want to review your policies and business practices to make sure you're accommodating buyers. The more difficult you are to work with, the more likely bidders are to turn to your competition.

Figure 10.11

Don't skim over the section in your auction listing pertaining to shipping costs. Provide as much information about add-on costs as possible up front.

Note

You can also access a shipping calculator here to help you determine the shipping cost upfront. Information on various delivery options available to sellers is also available here.

13. In the Payment instructions & return policy section, type clear instructions with regard to your policies for payments and returns, as shown in Figure 10.12. For example, if you accept returns only if an item was misrepresented in the listing description—or, conversely, offer a satisfaction guarantee—say so up front.

14. In the Ship-to locations section, indicate the countries to which you are willing to ship. Before you do, however, give some careful consideration to your choices. If you opt out of shipping internationally, you may well exclude foreign bidders willing to pay a pretty penny for your piece, like the Japanese bidder who once beat out a gaggle of American collectors for a hard-to-find Skipper doll—Barbie's little cousin—I once listed on eBay. On the other hand, you should be aware that there are hot spots for fraudulent online activity that you'll want to avoid, one of them being Nigeria. After you make your choice, click the Continue button.

Figure 10.12

Stating your return policies and the countries where you will ship goods is an important part of the listing process.

Tip

Stumped about whether to ship domestically or to accommodate international buyers? If so, consider starting off by offering domestic auctions only, and then branching out to other countries as you become more comfortable over time.

15. On the Review your listing page, take a hard look at your item listing, description, and main photo to ensure that it appears as you want it to and contains no errors. If you find something you need to change, click the appropriate Edit link—Edit title, Edit subtitle, Edit description, or Edit pictures—located to the right of each section, as shown in Figure 10.13. If you click on one of these links, you'll be taken to a prior page where you can make corrections or add more information to your listing in the same manner you did originally. Click on the Review your listing page link when you're finished with your updates.

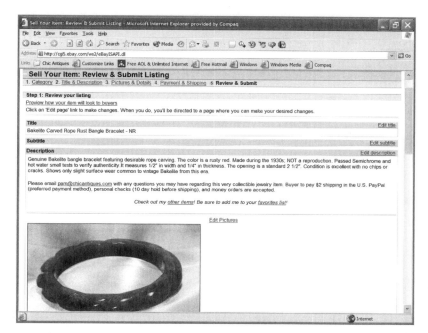

Figure 10.13

Be sure to carefully review
your item title, description, and
photos, and edit any information
as needed.

Note

By clicking on the Preview how your item will look to buyers link, you can see how the
photos, description, and other elements you've selected for your listing page will look to
buyers.

16. Scroll down to view the Pictures & Details and Payment & Shipping
    sections to ensure that your category selection, prices, duration, accepted
    payment methods, and shipping information are as you expected. As
    shown in Figure 10.14, you have the option of changing these details at
    this time if anything is incorrect; simply click the Edit pictures & details
    or Edit payment & shipping link to do so.

17. Scroll down yet farther to the Review your fees and submit your listing
    section, shown in Figure 10.15. If you feel you've gone a bit overboard
    on features, thereby inflating your fees, now's the time to opt out of fea-
    tures to bring the total down. Simply return to the appropriate page and
    deselect those features you now feel you can live without. If you agree
    with the fee list shown, however, click the Submit Listing button to
    begin your auction.

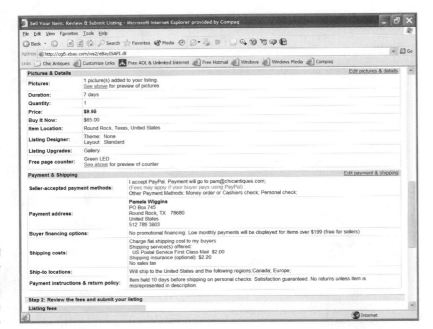

Figure 10.14

Make sure your category selection, pricing, duration, payment methods, and shipping information are correct before proceeding.

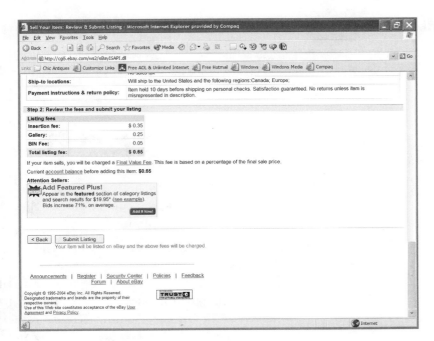

Figure 10.15

Review your fee schedule before clicking the Submit Listing button to begin your auction.

Tip

To get an idea of what you can expect to pay as a final value fee (assuming your item sells), click the Final Value Fee link below the table that outlines your listing fees. You can also view your eBay account balance on this screen.

After you click the Submit Listing button, eBay displays a confirmation screen, as shown in Figure 10.16. This page provides you with the item number assigned to your auction, and with links you can click to learn about revising your auction listing and, if needed, ending your listing early.

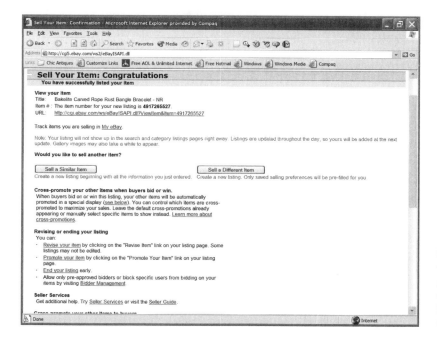

Figure 10.16

Your auction confirmation page provides your item number as well as links you can click to learn about revising your auction or ending it early.

Revising Your Item Listing

Even the most scrupulous seller makes a mistake now and then. Fortunately, eBay enables you to revise your listing to correct any errors or omissions in the title, listing description, or what have you. The process for revising your listing differs slightly depending on whether any bids have been placed for the item.

Monitoring Your Auctions through My eBay

You can easily monitor your current and recently ended auctions simply by clicking on the My eBay link located at the top of any page. There, in addition to being prompted to leave feedback for completed auctions, you can see the progress of all the auctions you currently have listed, as shown in Figure 10.17. In addition, a convenient summary keeps track of the dollar totals of your current auctions as well as auctions that have ended within the last 31 days.

Figure 10.17

Utilizing your My eBay page is a great way to keep track of the progress of your current and recently ended auction listings.

Note

If your item has not yet received bids and does not end within the next 12 hours, you can revise any aspect of the listing except for the selling format. (For example, you can't change it from an auction listing to an eBay Stores listing.) If, however, your item has received bids, you are limited to adding to the item description or adding optional selling features to increase the item's visibility.

To revise a listing that has not yet received a bid, do the following:

1. On your My eBay page under the Items I'm Selling section, click the link to the auction listing you would like to revise.

2. eBay displays the item's listing page, but with a few extra links at the top meant for your eyes alone: Revise your item, Promote your item, and Sell a similar item (see Figure 10.18). Click the Revise your item link.

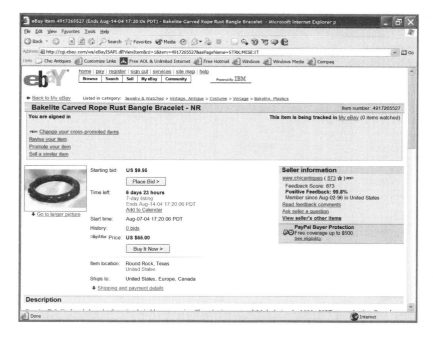

Figure 10.18

The screen to begin the revision process looks similar to a normal bidding screen.

3. The Revise Your Item screen outlines some pertinent details about revising your listing (see Figure 10.19). The item number should be automatically inserted in the field provided; if not, type it in, and then click the Continue button.

4. eBay displays a screen similar to the Review the listing page you saw when you set up the listing, as shown in Figure 10.20. Scroll down to locate the information that needs to be corrected, and click the appropriate Edit link—Edit title, Edit subtitle, Edit description, Edit pictures, Edit pictures & details, or Edit payment & shipping—to make your changes. You'll be taken to a page where you can make the changes you deem appropriate.

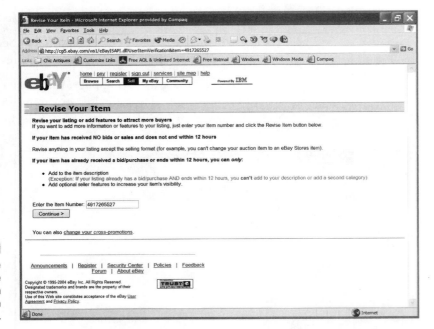

Figure 10.19

The gateway screen to the revision process offers some details about what you can revise in your listing and when you can perform those revisions.

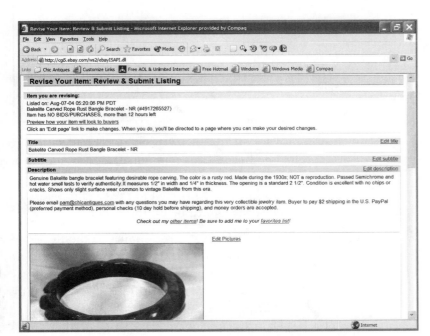

Figure 10.20

The main revision screen looks similar to the one you reviewed when you were setting up your original listing.

5. After you make the required changes, scroll down to the bottom of the page and click the Submit Revisions button (see Figure 10.21).

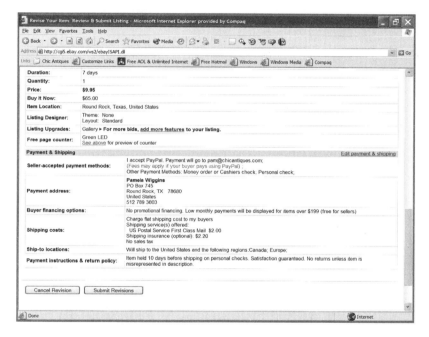

Figure 10.21

Once you've changed everything you're interested in updating on your listing, click on the Submit Revisions button.

After you click the Submit Revisions button, eBay displays a confirmation screen much like the one you saw when you finished setting up the listing to inform you that your corrections have been made, as shown in Figure 10.22.

As mentioned previously, your options are more limited when it comes to revising a listing after one or more bids have been placed:

- You can add a second category for the item.
- You can add details to your item description.
- You can add payment and shipping details.

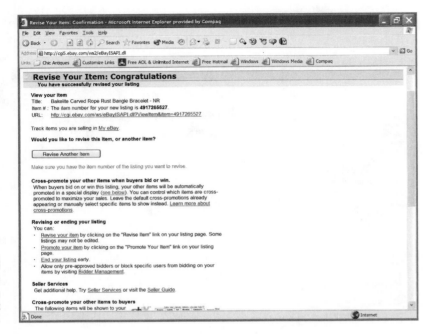

Figure 10.22

The revision confirmation page
looks very similar to the
page you saw when you first
set up the auction listing.

To revise a listing that has received one or more bids, do the following:

1. Access the screen shown in Figure 10.23 by repeating steps 1–3 above.

2. Click the appropriate link, depending on what type of revision you need to make. Chances are, you'll need to supplement the item description to answer questions you've received from potential bidders, so for the sake of example, click the Add to description link.

3. eBay displays the Add to description screen, shown in Figure 10.24. Type your addendum, and then click the Save Changes button.

4. Review your changes, as shown in Figure 10.25.

5. If you're satisfied with your revisions, scroll down to the bottom of the screen and click the Submit Revisions button (see Figure 10.26).

After you click the Submit Revisions button, eBay displays a confirmation screen much like the one you saw when you finished setting up the listing to inform you that your corrections have been made (refer to Figure 10.22).

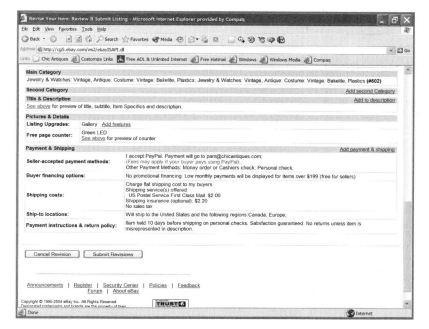

Figure 10.23

After bids are placed on an item, your options for revision are limited.

Figure 10.24

Adding additional details to answer questions about the item listing will be the most common reason to revise a listing after bidding begins.

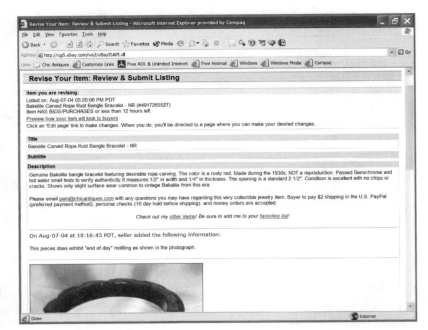

Figure 10.25

Review your changes to
your item description.

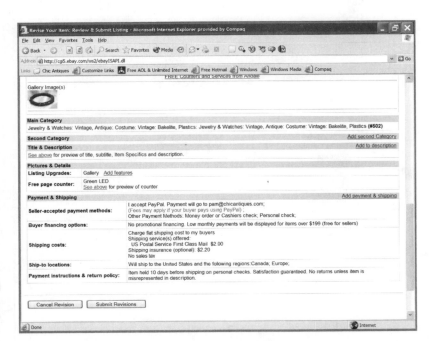

Figure 10.26

Scroll down and click on the
Submit Revisions button to
complete the process.

Ending a Listing Early

If your eBay sales career takes off, odds are someday you'll need to end an auction early. For me, that milestone occurred when I accidentally broke a Depression glass vase—after listing it for auction on eBay. The item was beyond repair, so I was forced to cancel all bids on the auction and end it early. When you end an auction early, eBay displays it among other completed listings. A note at the top of the listing will denote the reason the auction ended early and whether you've relisted the item.

Caution

Be aware that if you end an auction early, you are still required to pay eBay's listing fees, just as you would if the auction had ended naturally with no bids.

eBay enables you to end auctions under the following circumstances:

- The item is no longer available for sale.

- There was an error in the starting price or reserve amount.

- There was an error in the listing.

- The item was lost or broken.

- The seller has decided to let the piece go to the high bidder at the current price.

Note

On occasion, I've had bidders on highly valued items ask me to end an auction early and sell them the piece at my reserve price—usually to avoid end-of-auction scenarios in which prices rise sharply, sometimes doubling or tripling in a matter of seconds. I usually decline to do this, however, because I figure if they want the piece badly enough, they'll stick it out to the end. It also does a disservice to other bidders who were willing to pay more to get the piece but no longer have the opportunity to bid.

To end your item early, do the following:

1. Click the Site Map link that appears at the top of any page on eBay.

2. Under the Site Map's Help category, click the Seller Guide link.

3. In the Managing Your Item section, click the link labeled "End Your Listing Early form," as shown in Figure 10.27.

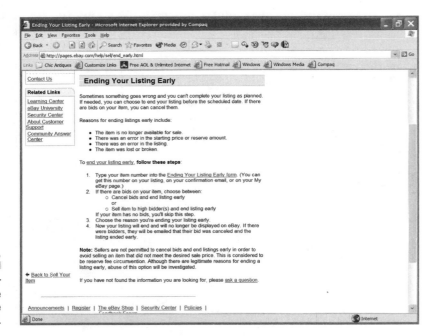

Figure 10.27

Complete instructions for ending an item early are outlined in the Seller Guide under Managing Your Item.

4. Enter the item number of the listing you want to end early and click the Continue button, as shown in Figure 10.28.

5. When you end an auction early, you have two choices:

   ■ Cancel bids and end listing early

   ■ Sell item to high bidder and end listing early

   Odds are, there will be very few occasions when you'll want to end the item early to sell it to a bidder; instead, click the Cancel bids button, as shown in Figure 10.29.

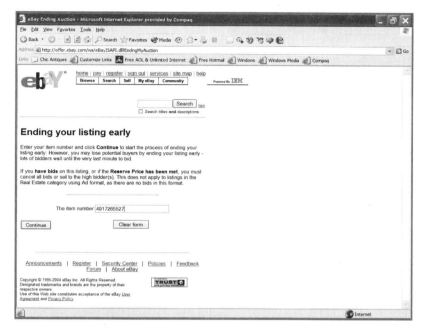

Figure 10.28

Enter the item number of the
listing you want to end early,
and click the Continue button.

Figure 10.29

Most of the times you'll need
to end an auction early, you'll
want to cancel all bids, the first
option shown here.

6. In the screen shown in Figure 10.30, choose the option button that best describes why you want to end your auction early, and finalize the process by clicking the End your listing button.

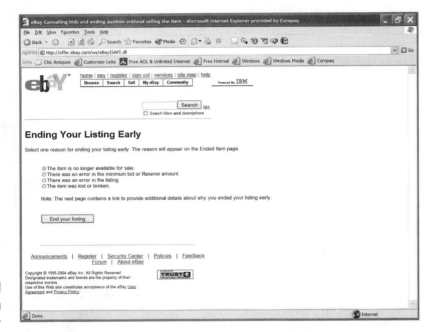

Figure 10.30

Click on the End your listing button to complete the process.

Relisting an Item

If an item you put up for auction fails to sell the first time around, don't get too discouraged. It happens to the best of us. The fact is, when an item doesn't sell, it might be for one of any number of reasons. For example, it might be because your auction ended on a holiday, when most potential bidders were away from their computers. Or maybe it was because you set your opening bid too high. Alternatively, it might have been because bidders were turned off by the fact that you added a reserve. Worst-case scenario, the item simply isn't all that desirable on eBay.

Depending on why you think the item didn't sell, you may decide not to relist it right away. For example, if your piece is a vintage Christmas tin, and it's currently the middle of February, odds are the item isn't terribly desirable just now.

In that case, you might decide to simply hold on to the item until November rolls around. If, however, you think your item failed to attract much interest because you set the starting price too high or because you set a reserve, then you might want to make a few adjustments to the listing to adjust those issues and relist it right away. Here's how:

Note

If you do decide to relist an item, note that you will be assessed additional fees. If your item sells the second time around, however, eBay will credit the amount of the relisting fees back to your account. Note that this applies only if you relist the item within 90 days after the original ending date, and that only one relisting fee credit per item applies. Thus if you relist an item multiple times, the second and third relist fees will affect your profit on that item.

1. Open the listing page of the item that didn't sell (see Figure 10.31) by clicking its link on your My eBay page under the Items I've Sold section. (Even if an item didn't sell, that's where completed auctions are listed.)

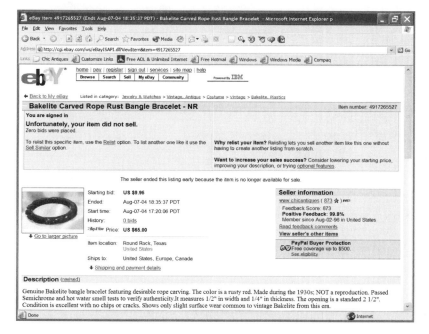

Figure 10.31

To relist an item, simply bring up the listing and click the Relist link.

2. Click the Relist link in the blue shaded area in the top-left area of the screen.

3. Relist your item using the same basic procedure as the one for revising a listing, as outlined in the section "Revising Your Item Listing" earlier in this chapter. Simply make any necessary changes and then begin the auction again. Sometimes a fresh start is all you need!

Listing-Management Tools

Odds are, when you first get your feet wet using eBay, the site's basic listing option will probably be adequate for your needs. Later, however, if you start selling numerous items on eBay, you may find it advantageous to use a listing-management tool. One such tool is Turbo Lister (see Figure 10.32), a free service offered through eBay that enables you to create many listings in one sitting, revise them if needed, and then submit them all at once—or schedule them to start when you specify. You can even use Turbo Lister templates to make your listings more appealing and complete.

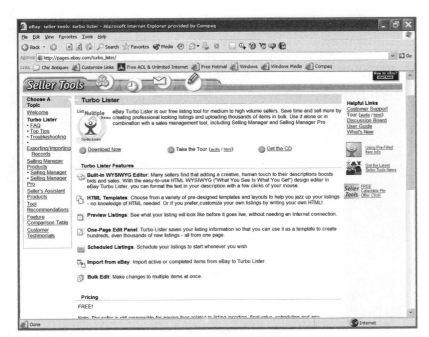

Figure 10.32

Turbo Lister is free through eBay. This product provides medium-to-high volume sellers with tools to make their listing process more efficient.

Note

I read on eBay that one seller used Turbo Lister to list more than 63,000 items in 12 hours on a free listing day. Odds are, as a purveyor of antiques and collectibles, you'll never have the inventory to mount an effort of that magnitude. That said, if your eBay antiques business takes off, you may well find yourself listing anywhere from 25 to 100 items per week, and perhaps more. When you consider how much time and effort go into research, photography, and writing good descriptions, you'll probably conclude that any amount of time you can save during the listing process will prove valuable.

If you decide you'd like to try Turbo Lister, you must first download it directly from eBay. Here's how:

1. Click the Site Map link that appears at the top of any page on eBay.

2. Scroll down to the Sellers section and click on the Turbo Lister link.

3. Click on the Download Now link.

4. Click on the Turbo Lister Web Setup link.

5. A Security Warning dialog box may appear. If so, click on Yes to proceed. (You'll see a Starting Web Setup screen at this point behind the Security Warning dialog box.)

6. When the InstallShield Wizard opens, follow through the process to download the software by clicking on Next.

7. Click Yes to consent to the License Agreement and type your name before clicking Next.

8. Note where the software will be saved on your computer. If desired, change the location. Then click Next.

9. The software will begin to download, a process that may take a few minutes to complete. (The time it takes to download depends on your computer's processor, which must be a Pentium II or better in order to download Turbo Lister.) When the installation is complete, click the Finish button.

Note

If needed, you can cancel the download process by clicking the Cancel button.

Note

If your system requirements don't support the download (they'll come up when you click on the Download button), you can request a copy of Turbo Lister on CD-ROM from eBay free of charge. To obtain the program on CD, simply follow the preceding steps, but click on the Get the CD link instead of the Download Now link in step 3. The free CD will be added to an eBay shopping cart and will be shipped to you via U.S. mail.

Note

Creating a listing using Turbo Lister is beyond the scope of this book. For detailed instructions on completing this task, consult Turbo Lister's Help information.

Not surprisingly, Turbo Lister is not the only listing-management tool available to you, although it is one of the few tools that are offered free of charge. If you're a medium-to-high volume seller who is willing to pay a monthly fee for additional services, eBay offers a few additional tools:

- **eBay's Selling Manager.** This is an online auction-management tool, meaning you'll have to remain constantly connected to the Internet to use it. It allows you to manage your auctions directly through your My eBay page without downloading additional software onto your computer. You do have to subscribe to the service, however, to use this tool. Bulk listings, status reports, and tools for creating shipping labels are just some of the features you can utilize through Selling Manager.

- **eBay's Seller's Assistant.** This tool is loaded onto your computer's desktop so you can work on your auction listings without being connected to the Internet—a definite advantage in households still using dial-up connections. Seller's Assistant enables you create bulk listings, track and manage your sales, send customizable e-mails and process feedback in bulk, print shipping labels, and keep sales records.

Note

You can learn more about eBay's Selling Manager and eBay's Seller's Assistant through links located in the Sell section on the Site Map page. Both tools offer free 30-day trial periods, after which the monthly fee varies depending on which combination of services you choose.

eBay isn't the only company that offers listing-management tools, however. My online antiques dealer buddies recommend the following other sites:

- Andale (www.andale.com)

- Channel Advisor (www.channeladvisor.com)

- Vendio (www.vendio.com)

Although I've not employed these tools, you may decide it's worth your while to investigate these services further. This is especially true if you're considering making a full-time job out of selling antiques and collectibles on eBay. For a review of auction-management services in a helpful side-by-side comparison format (see Figure 10.33), visit AuctionBytes at www.auctionbytes.com (click on Auction Management under the Cool Tools list).

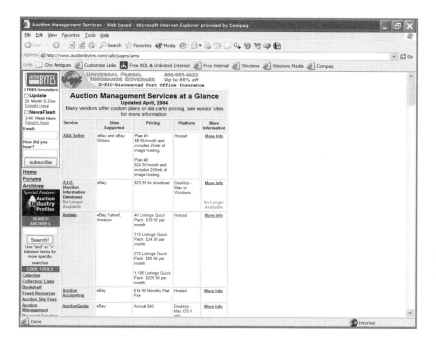

Figure 10.33

AuctionBytes offers a number of features appealing to eBay sellers including a helpful side-by-side comparison of various auction-management tools.

Managing and Completing the Sale

I once won an auction for a Texas Centennial Exposition plate on eBay that I couldn't wait to add to my collection. The photo of this 1930s piece was beautiful, the description just what I expected from a knowledgeable seller, and the shipping charge stated in the auction was reasonable. I thought I had it made on the deal. Boy, was I wrong. Even though I paid promptly, I had to wait weeks and weeks to receive the package. When it finally arrived, I discovered that the fragile plate had been haphazardly packaged in cruddy packing materials. It's a small wonder that it arrived in one piece. In this case, it wasn't the merchandise that disappointed me; the plate was just what I was looking for. But the seller's follow-through on the deal left a lot to be desired. I never bid on one of his items again.

So you see, although it's of utmost importance to represent your goods clearly and professionally when listing antiques and collectibles on eBay, it's often how a seller behaves during and after an auction that leaves an indelible impression on buyers. The way you communicate with buyers, the care you show when packaging items and mailing them in a timely manner, and your willingness to follow up with feedback demonstrate to buyers your integrity as a seller and bolster your reputation as a trustworthy eBay seller.

Answering Bidders' Questions

I once placed a very expensive decorative plate up for auction on eBay. During the course of the auction, a potential bidder e-mailed me to ask whether the plate had wear marks, which can occur when a plate has been stacked under other plates over the years. As it turned out, the plate *did* have wear marks; I just hadn't noticed them amid the piece's complicated pattern. I e-mailed the potential buyer right away and immediately revised the item description to note the wear and added some photos showing the flaw. (Incredibly, the piece still sold for more than $1,500.)

Note

Not all communiqués about auction items come in the form of politely worded questions. If a potential bidder insults you or your merchandise, politely thank them for their input—or, if they're overly rude, ignore them. Either way, try not to get too worked up. You don't even know this person, so it's not worth the rise in blood-pressure levels to get upset about their insensitivity.

My point? Although most auctions won't involve direct communication with bidders until after they're over—especially if you've thoroughly researched your merchandise and detailed its attributes in your listing description—don't be surprised if bidders e-mail you during the course of an auction with questions about the antique or collectible you're selling. In some cases, these questions may indicate that you've left out important details in your auction description, cueing you to update it or to upload additional photos—a process you may need to repeat several times. Indeed, educated buyers contemplating a large bid will likely ask specific questions about issues that may never have crossed your mind, like when my bidder asked me about the wear marks. When this happens, treat it as a learning opportunity. Thanks to my bidder's communication with me, I learned that I needed to check plates for this type of wear in the future, which has subsequently helped me write better listing descriptions for similar pieces. Besides, by answering a potential bidder's questions, you're helping to manage his or her expectations about the piece; the last thing you want is for someone to buy from you and be disappointed with the purchase.

Note

Some eBay browsers take it upon themselves to "police" auctions. They may e-mail you with criticisms of your description or of your assessment of an object. Although this can be irritating—you'd think folks would have something better to do with their time—these communiqués may yield a tip or two that might help you adjust your description such that you net a few extra bucks at auction end.

Not all questions will be about the item's condition, however. Some potential bidders may e-mail you to make specific requests with regard to payment methods or shipping charges. Others may wonder if you have similar items in your stock that you haven't yet listed. Whatever a potential buyer asks, be sure to read the question carefully. Make certain you understand the inquiry, and ask for clarification if necessary. When answering the question, be as honest as possible, and communicate in a clear, polite manner.

Note

If bidders with high feedback ratings make reasonable requests about payment methods or shipping charges, carefully consider amending your policy for them. They're probably worth the risk, and may end up being repeat buyers if you give them outstanding customer service.

Communicating with the High Bidder after the Auction Ends: Using eBay's Checkout System

Although eBay's policy states that the buyer and seller should contact each other within three days after an auction ends, placing equal responsibility on both parties, the fact is most eBay shoppers rely on the seller to make first contact to provide payment details. Fortunately, if you're the seller, eBay does a certain amount of communicating for you automatically at auction end through its checkout system. Specifically, when an auction ends, eBay automatically e-mails the high bidder with the payment and shipping information you provided up front when you created your listing. The high bidder can use this e-mail message to do one of the following:

- The high bidder can link directly to eBay, where he or she can enter the appropriate shipping address and provide you with details about payment. If your high bidder will be paying by personal check or money order, you may want to go ahead to e-mail back acknowledgment that you've gotten word about how they will be paying and thank them for their prompt attention.

- If using PayPal, the high bidder can use the e-mail message from eBay to link to PayPal's site, where he or she can pay you directly in addition to providing his or her shipping address. Some sellers e-mail the buyer after a PayPal payment is received to acknowledge the payment and to let the buyer know when the item will be shipped.

As a buyer, I like using eBay's checkout system. It's much easier and more efficient than exchanging initial e-mails with a seller. The fact is, though, that eBay's checkout system is virtually useless if you, the seller, fail to provide shipping and payment information when you create your listing. That's because eBay culls the information you provide up front to populate the message it sends to the high bidder at auction end. If you fail to include the relevant info, your buyers will be left wondering how to pay, how *much* to pay, and where to send their payment.

That said, some sellers *don't* use eBay's checkout system on purpose (although the only way you can totally disable it is by removing the PayPal payment option from your auction listings, which neither I nor eBay recommends). They prefer to rely on the old-fashioned method of e-mailing their high bidder directly after an auction concludes. Other sellers use tools provided by auction-management services (like those mentioned in Chapter 8, "Setting Up Shop on eBay: Getting Started Selling"), and prefer that buyers bypass eBay's checkout system in favor of some proprietary e-mail–driven payment-submission form to complete the transaction.

I recommend you use eBay's checkout system unless you subscribe to an auction-management service that doesn't support it. If you opt out of using the checkout system simply because you want to keep communication personal, make sure your method of communication is timely and concise so your high bidders will understand your payment instructions and respond accordingly. And in all cases, more communication is better than less. Thanking your buyers at least once personally through e-mail and keeping them informed along the way will go far in building ongoing eBay relationships.

Beyond the initial contact with payment information, the times at which you should consider communicating with buyers include

- When payment has been received
- When an item has been shipped
- After the merchandise is slated to reach the buyer, to ensure that he or she is satisfied
- When you leave feedback for the buyer

Some of these communications can be combined. For instance, you can ask the buyer in a single e-mail whether the package was received and let him or her know that you will be leaving feedback after you hear back that he or she is satisfied with the purchase.

Shipping Tips to Ensure a Smooth Transaction

Once you've received payment for an item, you're ready to ship the piece to the buyer. In a nutshell, you'll want to keep the following points in mind:

- **When it comes to shipping, give your customers what they paid for.** If your buyer paid for Priority Mail delivery, odds are he or she expects to *receive* Priority Mail delivery. Likewise, if your buyer paid for insurance, then it's up to you to purchase it when you ship the piece. Charging for insurance but not actually purchasing the coverage not only cheats your buyers out of a service they paid for, it makes you look really bad—especially if the item is lost or damaged in transit. In such a situation, in order to avoid being accused of dishonesty—or worse, fraud—you'll need to pay for the item out of your own pocket to cover losses.

- **View extra expenses associated with shipping and handling as the cost of doing business.** Jacking up your shipping and handling fees to cover overhead expenses such as packing materials, gas for trips to the post office, and the time it takes you to wrap up a package might seem logical to you at first. After all, if Spiegel can get away with it, why can't you? The fact is, though, that eBay shoppers—especially the bargain hunters who are interested in buying antiques and collectibles—aren't interested in paying much more than the actual shipping charge to get their purchases from point A to point B. Considering that Priority Mail boxes from the post office are free and that most people have clean newspaper lying around at the very least, it's not terribly hard to keep expenses to a minimum—and customers really appreciate it when you do. If you must charge a "handling" fee, keep it to a dollar or less per package, and be sure to disclose it in your auction listing so you won't surprise your buyer at auction end.

- **When customers pay instantly, try to return the favor by shipping instantly—or at least within a few days of payment receipt.** For buyers, part of the appeal of paying for auctions instantly via services such as PayPal is that, in theory, they get their packages sooner than would be possible if mailing a personal check or money order. Most buyers are rubbed the wrong way when the seller delays shipment for a week or more after receiving an instant payment.

Special Packing Considerations for Antiques and Collectibles

I once purchased a very pretty vintage costume jewelry brooch on eBay—a rhinestone flower bouquet with a number of wire stems extending from a base. Although a sturdy box would have been the appropriate shipping container for this piece, the seller put it in a small jewelry box, and then put the box inside a padded envelope. The real problem, though, was that the seller didn't put any packing materials in the jewelry box—no tissue paper, no packing peanuts, not even a couple of pieces of cotton—to prevent the delicate brooch from being jostled across thousands of miles on its way to me. Not surprisingly, when the piece arrived, even though the outer package was unscathed, the brooch—not to mention my spirit—was broken into three pieces. When I politely confronted the seller about her careless packaging, she was offended. "The post office said it would be fine," she curtly replied.

Note

Even when an item is insured, it's still a drag when it arrives damaged. After all, most collectors would rather have the goods than the money they were willing to part with to buy them.

Word to the wise: The folks at the post office may have many wonderful traits—a remarkable adeptness with firearms comes to mind—but antiques experts they ain't. It's *your* job to know how to package each piece you sell to survive the journey to its new home. This is especially crucial for antiques and collectibles, which tend to be unique pieces that can't be easily replaced if damaged during transit. Realize, too, that packages being delivered tend to be handled roughly. In addition to being tossed, dropped, and generally mangled, there's a good chance the box housing your delicate Ming vase will be stacked under a crate of encyclopedias. Even if the merchandise you're shipping doesn't look particularly fragile to you, in the face of these odds, some defensive packing is in order. Keep these suggestions in mind:

- **Ephemera.** Paper goods can be easily—and inexpensively—shipped in an envelope. Don't assume, however, that the shipper won't bend or fold the envelope in transit. Whether you're dealing with a vintage postcard, an entire magazine, or a piece of sheet music, you should always place a piece of cardboard that is the same size as the envelope inside with the merchandise. That's the economy version; you can also buy cardboard envelopes that are a little more costly at office-supply stores that work well with paper collectibles. In addition, it's not a bad idea to put paper goods inside a plastic sleeve or bag to further protect them. Avoid using newspaper when packing ephemera, however, as the ink can rub off on the paper.

- **Pottery and porcelain.** Some trouble spots on pottery and porcelain include handles of all kinds and spouts on teapots and coffee pots. To provide extra protection to these easily damaged areas, I usually wrap them individually with bubble wrap secured with packing tape, and then wrap the entire piece in another sheet of bubble wrap. I place the wrapped item in a box, surround the piece with packing material (foam peanuts, bubble wrap, or plenty of crumpled paper), and seal it. Then, I place that box inside another larger one and surround it with *more* packing materials. If I feel like the piece I'm sending doesn't require quite this much attention, at the very least, I'll put it in the middle of an oversized box and surround it with packing materials, making sure there are at least six inches of packing between the object and the side of the box. I also make sure there's enough packing material in the box to keep the delicate contents from moving even a little bit during shipping.

Tip

It's perfectly acceptable to use recycled packing materials. Clean corrugated boxes, bubble wrap, foam peanuts, and the like are often available free of charge if you ask friends and business associates that frequently receive packages to save reusable materials for you. Note, however, that there's a fine line between "recycled packing materials" and "garbage." While using yesterday's newspaper to pack a piece is perfectly acceptable, you'll want to avoid employing materials like opened TV dinner boxes, diapers (even clean ones), boxes from feminine products, food wrappers, and anything else that is soiled, holds an odor, or might be deemed offensive or inappropriate.

- **Glassware.** Wrap each glass piece in bubble wrap individually. The box-within-a-box packing method described in the preceding bullet also works well with glass, especially when you're shipping more than one piece together. (At the very least, if you're shipping multiple items, make sure to prevent the pieces from touching.) That said, a very heavy piece of glass, such as a single Colonial Block Depression glass footed tumbler, can usually be shipped in a single box, provided you wrap the piece in bubble wrap and use an oversized box to ensure that there are six to eight inches of packing material between the item and each side of the box. Be sure to use enough packing material in the form of foam peanuts, additional bubble wrap, or crumpled paper to secure the item so it won't jostle around during shipment.

- **Jewelry.** I've noticed a trend in the shipment of vintage costume jewelry whereby sellers use a padded envelope. If you wrap the item carefully in tissue paper or place it in a small Ziploc bag and then place it in a sturdy box before inserting it in the envelope, that's generally going to provide enough protection to get the piece from one point to another without damage. Just make sure the piece has enough padding so it can't move around inside the box. That said, I prefer to use the small corrugated software boxes that my husband brings home from work in lieu of a padded envelope. Then, even though I'm using a box, I wrap the item in tissue or place it in a small Ziploc bag. If the piece is particularly fragile or valuable, I may even use the box-within-a-box method. In any case, when shipping fine jewelry, it's wise to invest in some nice jewelry boxes to ship your items in, but do still secure the piece in the box as described here.

- **Textiles and clothing.** Some people use large envelopes to ship vintage clothing and textiles, similar to those employed by mail-order clothing catalogs. For new items that aren't stressed due to age, that's usually sufficient. But old fabrics and the thread holding them together can be more fragile than they look. I prefer to wrap this type of item in tissue, place it in a plastic bag, and then neatly stow it in a in a box that is big enough to contain the item(s), but not so big that the piece is swimming in it. If there's a little room left, I also place additional packing material in the box to keep the textile from sliding around in transit. Avoid using newspaper when packing textiles as the ink can rub off on the cloth and cause stains that are difficult to remove.

See Appendix A, "More Helpful Resources," for ideas on where to buy plastic sleeves sized to fit postcards, magazines, comic books, and other collectibles; shipping materials; and jewelry boxes.

Of course, these are only a few types of antiques and collectibles; no doubt, each subcategory of goodies—from small furniture pieces and clocks to antique firearms and militaria—will have its own set of tips and tricks when it comes to proper packing. Covering the unique shipping issues related to each specialty area would probably merit a book in itself. If you find yourself in the position of selling a piece unlike the types mentioned here, consider seeking advice from a more experienced seller who specializes in that piece's genre.

Tip

If the piece you've sold is particularly unusual, cumbersome, or fragile, you may decide that it's better to let a professional packaging company handle the packaging and shipment of the item. If you've not previously used a packing company in your area, contact a local antiques mall and find out who they use. Most malls ship packages home to traveling customers on occasion, and employ package services for difficult items.

Tip

It's best to investigate these issues before you list your piece. That way, if a bidder asks you how exactly a fragile item will be packaged and delivered—and just how much it will cost—you'll have the information at the ready. This can go a long way toward building a bidder's confidence in you!

Dealing with Non-Paying Bidders

"My dog ate my checkbook."

"The mattress where I keep my money caught fire."

"Aliens hijacked my eBay account and bid on your piece without my knowing."

Sometimes, it seems like there are as many excuses for buyers reneging on an auction as there are items on eBay. From death to taxes and everything in between, bidders can come up with some real doozies to avoid completing a deal, despite the fact that eBay considers non-payment to be a serious infraction. (Indeed, if a buyer is reported for non-payment three times, he or she can be suspended from the site.) Some excuses are undoubtedly true, but more often than not, people simply overextend themselves, winning more items than they expected—which is when they'll try to back out on you.

Note

Some buyers just ignore you altogether, offering no excuse for their failure to pay and leaving you wondering why they bid on your item in the first place.

If you buy the bidder's excuse, and happen to be feeling benevolent, you can just let it go—especially if the value of the item sold is relatively low. After all, if the piece is only worth a few dollars, the Final Value Fee assessed by eBay will be minimal, so it probably isn't worth your while to invest a lot of time in collecting from a deadbeat bidder. In that case, it's probably best to offer the item to the backup bidder, if there is one, or just relist it.

When the value of the item is a little higher, however, chances are you'll be hit with a hefty Final Value Fee. In that case, rather than releasing the hounds on your buyer, your best bet is to request a refund on the fee from eBay. First, though, eBay suggests you do the following:

1. **Contact your buyer.** If your high bidder has disappeared into the void, try contacting him or her by e-mail on several different days, with your first contact occurring no later than three days after the auction ends. If you can't reach your bidder through e-mail, consider calling him or her on the phone; after all, the problem may be as simple as a downed e-mail account.

2. **Send a payment reminder.** This step, which you should perform between three and 30 days after the listing ends, is optional, but it's not a bad idea. A simple e-mail message may do the trick, or you can use eBay's payment-reminder form to make it look more official. (See the section "Sending Payment Reminders" for details.)

3. **File a Non-Paying Bidder Alert.** If you want to file for a Final Value Fee credit, you must first file a Non-Paying Bidder Alert. You'll need to do this at least seven days but not more than 45 days after your listing closes. After you file the alert, you have 10 days to try to coax the buyer into paying. For more information, see the section "Filing Non-Paying Bidder Alerts."

If performing steps 1–3 fails to yield payment from the deadbeat bidder, proceed to filing a request for a Final Value Fee credit. You must make your request no more than 60 days after the auction ends. For details, see the section "Requesting a Final Value Fee Credit."

Sending Payment Reminders and Filing Non-Paying Bidder Alerts

If your frequent-yet-friendly and persistent e-mails—or even telephone calls—have failed to yield an acceptable response from your bidder, it may be time to appear a bit more authoritative by generating a payment reminder through eBay's Unpaid Item Dispute Process. This is actually done at the same time you file a Non-Paying Bidder Alert: at least seven days but no more than 45 days after the auction ends. By filing this report, you don't actually log a black mark against the bidder, but you do alert eBay that you're having a problem and prompt the site to send the bidder a payment-reminder e-mail (you'll be copied on the message). This can be especially useful in getting the attention of those bidders who seem to fall off the face of the earth after an auction ends, totally ignoring your communication efforts.

To file a Non-Paying Bidder Alert and generate a payment reminder, do the following:

1. Click the Site Map link at the top of any eBay page.

2. Scroll down to the Help section, and click the Seller Guide link.

3. Click the Closing the Deal link (see Figure 11.1).

4. Click the Non-Paying Bidder/Buyer Policy link (see Figure 11.2).

5. Click the File a Non-Paying Bidder Alert link, shown in Figure 11.3.

Figure 11.1

After pulling up the Seller Guide through the Help section of the site map, click the Closing the Deal link.

Figure 11.2

Click the Non-Paying Bidder/Buyer Policy link.

Figure 11.3

Click the File a Non-Paying Bidder Alert link.

6. If prompted, enter your user ID and password and click the Sign In button, as shown in Figure 11.4.

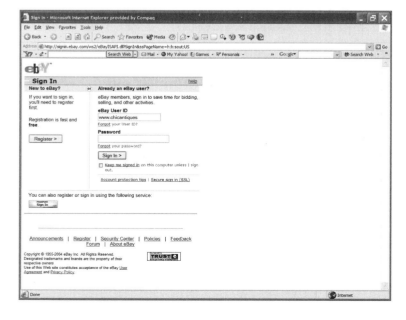

Figure 11.4

Enter your user ID and password and click the Sign In button, if prompted to do so.

7. Read the instructions on the Unpaid Item Process page to make sure you understand what will take place when you file an alert. Then click the File an Unpaid Item Dispute link to continue, as shown in Figure 11.5.

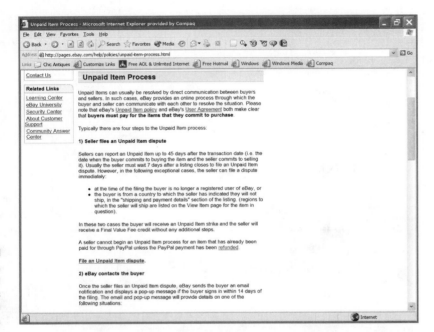

Figure 11.5

Read the instructions to make sure you understand how the Unpaid Item Process works, and then click on the File an Unpaid Item Dispute link.

8. Enter the item number of the completed listing in question and click on the Continue button, as shown in Figure 11.6.

Don't be surprised if, after you submit the alert, the buyer contacts you via eBay to pay for the item before the seven-day grace period lapses. Alternatively, you may end up communicating back and forth through eBay and come to the conclusion that you are not going to hold the buyer to the deal. This action will not result in an Unpaid Item strike against the buyer, and you can still request a Final Value Fee credit in this instance. If the high bidder doesn't follow through after you've filed an alert, however, and you're fed up with dealing with him or her, you'll want to go ahead and request a Final Value Fee credit and have an Unpaid Item strike logged against the bidder.

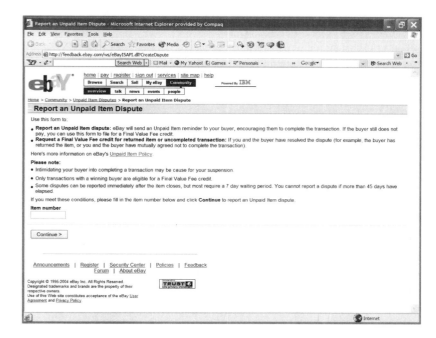

Requesting a Final Value Fee Credit

After you've filed a Non-Paying Bidder Alert and have worked with your buyer for seven days to resolve the problem, you can request a Final Value Fee credit if your efforts were unsuccessful or you decided to let the buyer off the hook. To file a request for a Final Value Fee credit, do the following:

1. Click the Site Map link at the top of any eBay page.

2. Scroll down to the Help section, and click the Seller Guide link.

3. Click the Closing the Deal link.

4. Click the Non-Payer Bidder/Buyer Policy link.

5. Click the Request a Final Value Fee Credit link.

6. Click on the File an Unpaid Item Dispute link.

7. Enter the item number of the auction in question and click Continue. Because you've already filed a Non-Paying Bidder Alert, eBay recognizes this as a Final Value Fee credit request.

The Final Value Fee credit is the only fee credit eBay offers. That is, eBay won't refund any of your other fees, such as the listing fee or any upgrades you may have paid for, such as a gallery photo. eBay will, however, waive the listing fee in the event you relist an item for which you didn't receive payment. You become eligible for a free relist credit when you file an Unpaid Item Dispute.

The Importance of Feedback

As a seller, accruing positive feedback is very important. This is especially so if you're just establishing a business on eBay because feedback is one of the main ways a bidder can gauge your integrity. That is, when a potential bidder pulls up your feedback listing and sees glowing comments with little or no evidence of negative or neutral feedback, this helps him or her feel more secure bidding on your items.

Savvy eBay shoppers know that although eBay's feedback system can give you a sense of a seller's integrity, it is not foolproof. One way in which feedback can be skewed is when sellers use a service called SquareTrade to have negative feedback removed (they must first make a case that the feedback was unwarranted). And of course, a certain percentage of unsatisfied customers will simply opt out of logging any type of feedback at all in an attempt to put a bad experience behind them. That said, buyers of all types do access feedback records at least occasionally, and some deal only with sellers who have an established feedback record, so it does pay to work toward building a high feedback rating.

One way to build up your feedback rating is to enter positive feedback about your buyers. Indeed, many sellers leave feedback on a buyer immediately after the buyer has completed his or her obligation and paid for their merchandise. As for me, I prefer to leave feedback after the buyer receives his or her merchandise and expresses satisfaction with the deal either via e-mail or by leaving positive feedback about me.

To leave feedback for your high bidders, do the following:

1. Click the My eBay button that appears at the top of any page on eBay to view your My eBay page.

2. If prompted, enter your user ID and password.

3. Review the Selling Reminders section. The total number of pending feedback transactions will be shown for auctions that have ended during the last 31 days. Click the number to access the list of ended auctions for which you have not yet issued feedback.

4. On items whose auction has successfully concluded, click the Leave Feedback link to access eBay's feedback system.

5. Select the Positive, Negative, or Neutral option button to choose a rating. Alternatively, choose the I will leave feedback later option button (selected by default), as shown in Figure 11.7.

6. Type your comments about the buyer and the outcome of your transaction.

7. Click the Leave Feedback button to complete the process.

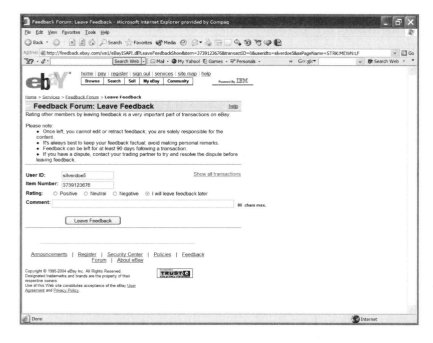

Figure 11.7

Select the Positive, Negative, or Neutral option button to choose a feedback rating.

Remedies for Negative Feedback

I make it a point to try to work out a solution with an unhappy buyer that doesn't involve leaving negative feedback. On occasion, though, I've had to leave neutral or negative feedback for problem bidders, even though doing so put me at risk of receiving similar feedback in return. In those instances, I felt like I needed to warn other sellers about my experiences, so I took my chances. Fortunately, however, this has only happened to me a couple times during my many years as an online seller.

If you find yourself in the position of having received a negative feedback, be it from an unreasonable buyer or from someone with whom you've had a disagreement, you'll be relieved to discover that although there was a time on eBay when a once-a-negative-always-a-negative policy existed, this is no longer the case. These days, sellers have a couple options for removing negative feedback:

- Mutual Feedback Withdrawal
- SquareTrade

Mutual Feedback Withdrawal

Comments left for a particular transaction may be withdrawn through Mutual Feedback Withdrawal. For this to happen, both parties in the transaction must agree that the feedback they left is no longer valid. Then, both parties must withdraw the feedback using the process outlined by eBay. A lengthy discussion of the ins and outs of Mutual Feedback Withdrawal is beyond the scope of this book; suffice it to say that withdrawn feedback remains in both the buyer's and the seller's profile, but is no longer counted in their total feedback score. So, basically, as time goes by, the negative feedback will be buried by the positives you receive afterward; in order to spot that negative feedback, bidders would have to manually page through your feedback.

Note

 To find out more about Mutual Feedback Withdrawal, click the Site Map link on any eBay page and scroll down to the Help section, where you'll find a link to Seller Central. Perform a search for "feedback removal" in Seller Central and click the Policy—Feedback Remove link for details.

Utilizing SquareTrade as a Mediating Service and to Remove Negative Feedback

As mentioned in Chapter 7, "Working through the Bad Buy," eBay enables sellers to use SquareTrade (http://www.squaretrade.com) both as a mediating service to resolve disputes with buyers and also as a tool for completely removing negative feedback from their records. (Although eBay advertises this as a free service, SquareTrade does charge a fee to remove negative feedback.) To access the company's site, simply type its URL in your Web browser; alternatively, you can link directly from eBay by doing the following:

1. Click the Services button at the top of any page on eBay.

2. Scroll down to the Selling Reference section.

3. Click the Seller Central link.

4. Click on the Resources link at the bottom of the Choose a Topic box.

5. Scroll down to Third Party Service, where you'll find a SquareTrade link. Click the SquareTrade link to visit the company's site directly.

Note

eBay recommends that you contact SquareTrade within 30 days after the end of the auction in question.

As mentioned in Chapter 6, "I Won an Auction! Now What?" once you're on the SquareTrade site, you have the option of filing a case. (Unfortunately, the steps involved in filing a case in SquareTrade are beyond the scope of this book; see SquareTrade's Help information for specific details.) After you do, SquareTrade contacts the buyer (or vice versa, if a buyer lodges a complaint against a seller) to give him or her the opportunity to reply. If the buyer refuses to answer, that's as far as the mediation goes. If the buyer does answer, then SquareTrade may make a recommendation for resolving the dispute.

Note

If you do decide to file a case with SquareTrade, be aware that you will be required to allow eBay to transfer some of your personal information to SquareTrade in order to log your initial complaint.

Unfortunately, your results may be limited because SquareTrade, while serving as mediator, does not issue a ruling on disputes. That is, although it may offer a recommendation for resolving the dispute (called a *settlement agreement*), it does not take sides, declaring one party "right" and one party "wrong." And even if it did, SquareTrade lacks the authority to enforce any ruling it might make. Even so, being contacted by a mediator like SquareTrade may indicate to the buyer that you're serious about resolving the dispute.

If your goal is to use SquareTrade to remove negative feedback, then you'll need to file a case first. If the buyer responds to the case within 14 days and accepts the settlement agreement put forth by SquareTrade, then negative feedback will be removed. If the buyer does not respond within 14 days, then the feedback will be automatically removed.

Fraud Information Important to Sellers

When people consider the issue of fraud on eBay, they usually think of sellers who take money and then don't deliver the goods. The fact is, though, that although there are a few rogue sellers on eBay, rogue buyers also crop up from time to time. In particular, sellers must occasionally contend with checks drawn on insufficient funds and chargebacks on stolen credit cards. For this reason, you'll want to be wary in the following situations:

- If a buyer with whom you are unfamiliar wants you to rush a shipment before his or her check has time to clear the bank, think twice about being accommodating. Likewise, if someone who has received little or no feedback wants you to send a shipment out before his or her check clears, that's not a good idea either.

- If the shipping address and the billing address on a credit-card sale don't match up, it could mean that the item is being sent to a third party, or it may indicate a problem. Consider the buyer's feedback record and PayPal rating (if applicable) before shipping. Be aware, however, that if you ship to an address other than the billing address and the transaction turns out to be fraudulent, you'll be charged back for the goods by the issuing credit-card company.

■ If a seller from Nigeria knocks on your cyberdoor, don't open it. Unfortunately, there're just too many fraud reports and e-mail scams coming out of that country (these include stolen credit card rings and bogus business partnership offers) to do online business there right now. You'll also want to pay attention to the buzz on the Internet about other areas of the world where fraud seems rampant at any given time. This is another situation in which belonging to online collecting groups comes in handy, because sellers often share information of this nature when they feel like it could benefit someone else.

My best advice is to follow your instincts. Just as you would when dealing with customers face to face, if something about a situation just doesn't seem right, stick to your guns when it comes to business policies you've put in place to protect yourself, such as holding shipments until checks have cleared or shipping credit-card orders only to billing addresses. There will be times when you'll bend the rules, but only do so if you're completely comfortable with the situation at hand.

Note

Odds are there will come a time when a buyer seems to be operating aboveboard and things go awry anyway. Don't blame yourself for being naïve (unless you failed to heed the warnings outlined here—and any others your online colleagues might report to you!). It's the crooked buyer who's to blame, not you.

chapter 12

Standing Out in a Competitive Market: Building a Good Reputation

On any given day, you can expect to find more than 2.6 million collectibles on eBay. Of those items, 3,700 sell each hour, including more than 600 coins and 240 stamps. In addition, more than 5,700 collectible lunch boxes and 7,100 Pez Dispensers are sold on eBay each month. These numbers refer to collectibles only; imagine if they included antiques as well! I'm not just spewing numbers to impress you here. The real reason I'm pointing this out is that there's a seller behind every single one of those items listed on eBay. These are the people you'll be competing with to get a share of the action, and some of them are doing very well for themselves. With a little effort, you can too.

The best way to stand out among a sea of competitive sellers is to establish a reputation for selling exceptional antiques and collectibles with reasonable starting bids and no reserves. (Of course, it's not always possible to sell without a reserve, but buyers do appreciate it when you do.) Even on eBay, where sellers come and go daily, there are always a few outstanding sellers specializing in any given category. If you can prove yourself as one of these sellers, more bidders will place you on their favorite seller lists and look up your auctions on a regular basis.

Of course, building a good reputation is easier said than done; doing so requires a lot of time and effort. For starters, you must regularly list quality pieces at reasonable prices, find ways to promote your auctions in order to drive interested buyers to those listings, and, to the extent that it's possible, ensure that each transaction concludes with a satisfied buyer. Beyond that, you can nurture your good reputation by doing the following:

- Build a customer mailing list that enables you to communicate to potential buyers when you have pieces that might interest them.

- Chat up other collectors.

Promoting Your Listings

One critical aspect of building a good reputation on eBay is ensuring that as many people as possible see your listings. Driving traffic to your auctions can be tricky, however. Indeed, it's *so* difficult to promote eBay auctions, many sellers don't even bother to do it. After all, by the time they've researched, photographed, and written an item description for a piece, they feel they just don't have time to deal with promoting the auction. Besides, because online auctions run for such a short period of time—from three to 10 days, with most ending in seven—traditional promotional avenues, such as a classified ad for the auction in a collectibles newspaper, simply aren't cost-effective. The way I see it, though, promotion is an oft-neglected area that the wise seller will explore—especially if you're selling a rare and valuable piece. Indeed, tapping into the right resources both on eBay and elsewhere to promote your auctions can generate tremendous buzz, which can pay off in a big way.

Promoting Your Items on eBay

eBay offers several tools for promoting a listing on its site; most result in extra fees being tacked onto your listing total. You choose these promotional options when you create the item listing itself. Promotional options include the following (many of these are discussed in Chapter 10, "Setting Your Starting Price, Understanding eBay's Fees, and Creating a Basic Listing"):

- **Listing the item in two categories.** When your item offers crossover collecting appeal, listing it in more than one category may deliver more exposure. For instance, jewelry made in conjunction with the release of *Gone with the Wind* might appeal to collectors of *Gone with the Wind* memorabilia as well as collectors of vintage costume jewelry.

■ **Listing the item for 10 days.** If your piece is one that is likely to generate tremendous buzz, tacking a few extra days to the end date will allow the news of your auction to travel farther, giving larger numbers of qualified collectors the opportunity to view it.

Note

Although listing an exceptional item for 10 days rather than seven isn't a bad idea, it doesn't pay to list average items for a longer period because of the additional fee involved. For run-of-the-mill pieces, you're better off letting your auction end in the standard seven day time period and getting your profits to the bank a little sooner.

■ **Placing the item in the Gallery.** From a promotional viewpoint, I feel like the most beneficial tool is to choose eBay's Gallery option. When you do, the listing is displayed with a thumbnail photo both in eBay's Gallery and among the regular listings (see Figure 12.1). At first glance, you might think that a thumbnail photo doesn't offer much detail, but if you've ever shopped by skimming through them, you know that you can glean quite a bit of information from those little gems. In fact, they're often more expressive than the auction title.

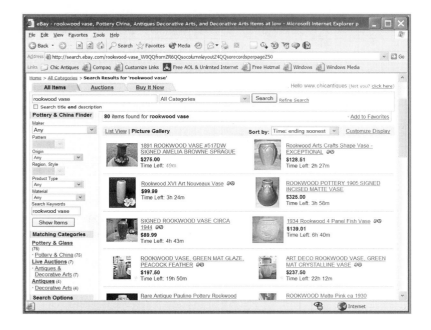

Figure 12.1

When bidders conduct a Gallery search, items listed in the Gallery appear as shown.

■ **Featuring the item in the Gallery.** This promo tool places your gallery photo at the top of the Gallery page. It's not going to be worth the extra expense to do this unless you're selling a hard-to-find item that's apt to bring in a high value.

■ **Having your listing displayed in bold or highlighted text.** Although eBay sells these features, shown in Figure 12.2, as promotional tools designed to make your listings stand out in the crowd, they don't really work all that well. They are also rather pricey when tacked on your listing fees. Personally, I never splurge on them.

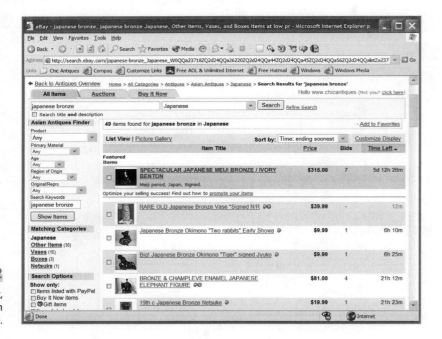

Figure 12.2

When paying for highlighted text, your listing will appear as shown in the top item on this page.

■ **Using Featured Plus.** Paying for Featured Plus to promote an auction moves the auction up to the top of the page when a keyword search is conducted (as shown in Figure 12.3). It also places your auction at the top of the category where your item is listed. This option is expensive, and only makes sense if you're selling an expensive item that will net enough profit to recoup your promotional investment.

Figure 12.3

Featured Plus items are listed at the top of each search results page regardless of the ending date, and also at the top of the category in which the item is listed.

- **Using Home Page Featured.** Promoting your item on eBay's home page might seem like a good idea, but it's such a costly promotional tool that you would have to be selling an item worth thousands of dollars to make it worthwhile. But honestly, most people don't spend a whole lot of time on the home page once they get started on eBay, so it may not get the attention you were hoping for anyway.

Note

The cost of a featured item listing is so prohibitive that it just doesn't make sense unless your piece is a rare, high-value one. For example, if you stand to make thousands of dollars on a listing, it might be worth upgrading it to show up at the top of each search and category page. Otherwise, I'd advise you to keep your bottom line in mind and pass this option by.

- **Using counters.** Having a counter on your auction doesn't provide a ton of promotional value, but some buyers will be interested in seeing just how many other potential bidders have viewed the page. It can generate a little excitement and might encourage someone to go ahead and bid on an item he or she believes to be popular.

■ **Purchasing a gift icon.** Although you probably see a good number of gift icons on eBay, and the site sells them as a promotional tool, I don't think they add much value to a listing. After all, virtually anything on eBay can be a gift under the right circumstances, so it just doesn't make much sense to pay extra money for a gift icon. This is another one of those things that can erode your bottom line without adding much value if you let it.

In addition to using eBay's promotional tools, you can encourage bidders to check out your other auction listings by clicking the View seller's other items link that appears automatically on each eBay listing. Although some bidders will click this link without being prompted, it's not a bad idea to insert into each auction's item description a short list detailing the other related items you currently have available on eBay. (Take care to ensure that this list does not muck up your item description such that it prevents bidders from finding pertinent details about the auction they're perusing at the moment, however.) Also, tell potential bidders in the body of each listing what types of pieces you specialize in; that might motivate them to keep you on their radar.

Note

Some auction-management services, like those mentioned at the end of Chapter 8, "Setting Up Shop on eBay: Getting Started Selling," offer nifty tools that help you display photos of other items you have up for sale within each auction listing you post on eBay. For more information, see your auction-management service's Help information.

Promoting Your Business on Other Venues

eBay isn't the only place where you can promote your listings. Indeed, many online antiques sellers, including myself, maintain personal Web sites to sell our wares directly as well as to point buyers to our eBay auctions. For less than $20 a month—plus a bit of time and expertise to maintain the site—I have a sure-fire way of driving business to my listings on eBay. I usually do this by putting "on eBay" with a link to the auction listing where the price would normally be on my site. I can also net interested buyers by promoting my site among various collector groups online. To drive traffic to Web sites, some owners even provide educational tools for potential buyers and collectors. (Of course, if I want top placement in the major search engines or targeted advertising to promote my site, my cost of doing business can increase dramatically.)

Alternatively, you can set up a site in an online antiques mall to sell your wares. This won't necessarily point interested buyers to all your listings on eBay, but it can help you sell pieces on occasion. When you upload items from your site to eBay, a link denotes this on the mall site so browsing collectors can click through to view the auction. Currently, the two best-known online antiques malls are Ruby Lane (http://www.rubylane.com) and TIAS (http://www.tias.com), short for The Internet Antique Shop. (Dealers also seem to be turning to a third site, Trocadero, located at http://www.trocadero.com, as a selling alternative, but it hasn't yet reached the popularity levels of Ruby Lane and TIAS.) With both Ruby Lane and TIAS, you pay a fee (it differs from site to site); in return, the online mall provides space on its server for your listings and tools for uploading your listings onto a site template. (Realizing that most online sellers are likely to tap the eBay market as well, both sites also offer auction-management tools that help sellers move items from the online mall to eBay.) Although the TIAS site offers a bit more flexibility with regard to look and feel, buyers routinely visit both sites, offering you great exposure by investing in a top listing placement with search engines. Both sites also offer a global search feature, like eBay's, that allows a buyer to browse many shop listings for a particular item. If the item the search results yield is one you have listed on eBay, the shopper can click through to the auction.

And of course, you can always take out an advertisement in a collectibles newspaper or antiques-related magazine—but only if it's a general ad. That is, rather than placing an ad about a particular listing, you might point doll collectors or old-book enthusiasts to your eBay ID, letting them know you consistently offer a great selection of items they'd be interested in viewing. Unless you do a simple classified ad, however, this option is probably too expensive for the average eBay seller, although fancy display advertising will work for high-end dealers who benefit from reaching a very sophisticated market.

Building a Customer Mailing List

Don't assume that your favorite customers will always be on the lookout for your wares. After all, computer users tend to lead very busy lives; a fair amount of time may pass before even the most satisfied customer gets a chance to troll eBay for your auctions again. To keep past buyers attuned to your offerings—especially when you have a particularly special piece on the block—consider building a customer mailing list and contacting them directly.

Note

It's a little harder to build a customer mailing list if you deal in a wide variety of antiques and collectibles, but if you consistently specialize in pottery or glass or any other types of goods, then keeping a list of your customers makes sense. Depending on your selling habits, you may even find it necessary to maintain more than one list, with each one tailored toward certain groups of customers.

Be aware, however, that you must ask people whether they are interested in receiving informational e-mails from you before adding them to your mailing list. Why? Because most computer users wade through daunting batches of spam each and every day, and you don't want to add to their burden by sending even more unsolicited communication. In fact, doing so can actually work against you; some buyers view unsolicited mail as an invasion of their privacy and a waste of their time. Besides, it's against eBay's policy to send unsolicited e-mail to other users.

So what's an honest seller to do? I've found that mentioning my mailing list to customers right after they have commented on how pleased they are with a purchase tends to yield good results. I simply e-mail them back, thanking them once again, and asking whether they want to be added to my list to be notified about future auctions of interest to them. I think you'll find that if you follow this practice, a number of them will give you the thumbs up.

Note

If you don't hear back from the customer—of if he or she declines your offer—don't be offended. Some people just don't like to receive e-mail from sellers, and that's okay.

Of course, simply collecting e-mail addresses of interested buyers isn't enough. You must then make it a point to contact them about auctions that might interest them. In your e-mail notifications, consider including the following types of information:

Don't email your customers more than once a week. Indeed, sending your notifications once every two weeks is probably even better to avoid becoming a nuisance to your customers.

- A quick thank you to your customers for their past patronage

- A short list of items that would be of specific interest to the customers on your list

- Direct links to several of your listings on eBay

- Information on your low-starting-bid, no-reserve auctions, when applicable

If you do paste links to your listings on eBay in your e-mail notifications, consider using a service that shortens the links, like MakeAShorterLink.com, if they're too long to fit in the body of your e-mail. When a long link wraps to a second line, it is no longer "hot"— that is, you can't simply click on it to open the Web page it references. Instead, you must highlight the link, copy it, and then paste it into your Web browser—something you can't rely on potential customers to do.

The most time-consuming aspect of maintaining a mailing list is being diligent about gathering e-mail addresses and promptly adding them to the list. For example, I created my customer-notification list in Outlook, my e-mail client, by setting up a group within my address book; when I get a new name to add to the list, I simply add it to the group. When you get in the habit of doing this, sending a note when you list a new batch of impressive items to eBay is easy.

Make it a point to include very little personal information in your e-mail notifications. Most people just want to get to the information about your auctions, not read about your child's graduation party or your dog's latest ailment. In fact, if you don't get to the point pretty quickly, people will quit reading before they ever get to the crux of your message. Another important aspect of the message is the tone, which can be very professional or casual and newsy, depending on your personal style. Once you set your tone, however, it's best to stick to that style of communication in each e-mail you send out so your customers will learn to recognize your messages. Indeed, some customers will even come to look forward to hearing from you over time, especially if you make them feel like you're doing them a favor by giving them a heads up on some great merchandise.

Note

One thing to keep in mind about sending e-mail to large lists of people is that spam filters sometimes catch them. To bypass them, you may have to set up several small groups amounting to 10 or 15 addresses. It's a little more work, but it does help to ensure that your e-mails will get through.

Chatting It Up with Other Collectors

Getting to know other collectors can be a great way to promote your auctions. That means that in addition to ferreting out collectors in your own area, you'll want to reach out to others in cyberspace as well. Over time, as you interact with these birds of a feather—even if they're scattered throughout the country or even across the globe—you'll find out who collects what; when you list a piece that one of your online buddies covets, you can drop him or her a note. Indeed, you can even keep the tastes of your online community in mind when shopping for items to resell. As an added bonus, you may find after a while that your collecting group begins to feel a little like family.

Just how do you latch onto an online collecting group? The listservs on TIAS.com and the clubs on Yahoo.com (as shown in Figure 12.4) are excellent resources for reaching out to like-minded collectors, and as such make great places to announce your auction listings. And if your item is especially valuable or rare, you can use your online group to generate some buzz about it. Even if none of your fellow collectors are interested, one may pass your info on to a favored customer.

If you do join an online group, make sure you understand the rules of the group and stay within those guidelines to avoid making waves with more established members. For example, some groups allow for sale posts every day, while others

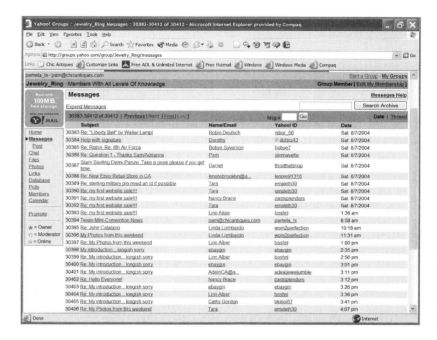

Figure 12.4

Groups like this one on Yahoo! gives collectors the opportunity to share information as well as buy and sell from one another.

limit it to certain days of the week. Even in groups where there is no moderator reading every single post, someone usually "owns" the list or group and sets the parameters for participating there. Indeed, you may even have to wait for the approval of the list owner or group coordinator before you start participating in the conversations.

Note

Why do some groups prohibit members from posting sale information on certain days? Because when a list gets too mucked up with sale information, it impedes the exchange of needed information by members. In fact, you may decide you prefer chatting within the groups that limit sale posts—and learn quite a bit in the meantime—even though your original reason for joining was to hawk your auction listings.

part IV

Appendix

appendix A

More Helpful Resources

Exploring eBay's Help Resources

I've covered the high points of using eBay in this book (and some low ones as well), but there will almost certainly be times when you have an eBay-related question that's beyond the scope of these pages. That's when eBay's Help section will serve you well. To access it, just click on the Help link at the top of any eBay page.

These are the Help features I use most often:

■ **Click on an FAQ.** On the Internet, *FAQ* stands for "frequently asked question(s)." On its FAQ page, eBay provides answers to the five most-commonly asked questions by buyers and sellers. Always look here first for the answer to your question.

■ **Search the Help section.** You can search eBay's Help information. Simply type a keyword such as **fraud** or **checkout** in the space provided, click the Search Help button, and voilá! A list of related topics pops up for you to browse.

■ **Pull up the A–Z Index.** When you click on the A–Z Index link, the list of help topics that start with the letter A appears. Simply click on the other letters to pull up another alphabetized list to peruse for answers.

eBay Live Chat

If you've searched eBay's Help pages for an answer to a question to no avail, the next step is to log on to eBay's Live Chat system and converse online with an eBay technician one on one. To do so, click the Live Help link on eBay's home page. A chat window will open, where you can type your questions and read responses from a member of eBay's tech-support staff. I've used this service several times since it was introduced and walked away with great answers to my questions every time.

Note

Be aware that the Live Chat system does get backed up from time to time, and it can take a while to work your way up in the queue. It's not any worse than waiting on the telephone to talk with tech support, although you will have to supply your own mood music during the lag time.

Other Online Resources

Truth be told, you can probably find a lot of the supplies you need to keep your business running—shipping materials, plastic sleeves, and what have you—on eBay. But in the interest of hunting down the best deal (and most expeditious way to get the supplies you need in hand), I urge you to check out the sites listed here for some comparison shopping. In addition, you'll find several listings for informational sites that concentrate on antiques and collectibles; be sure to check these out.

Collecting Supplies

If you sell the same types of goods over and over, you'll quickly learn the best places to buy supplies for storing and shipping them. But if you only buy batches of old postcards, magazines, photographs, and comic books on occasion, you might need a resource for supplies to organize, store, and ship these goodies. For plastic sleeves, albums, and backing boards, check out these sites:

- Dotpattern.com (http://www.dotpattern.com/supplies/collecting-supplies.html)

- Mary L. Martin, Ltd. (http://www.marylmartin.com/pages/supplies.htm)
- The 2 Buds (http://www.the2buds.com/index.htm)

Jewelry Supplies

Having displays specifically designed for jewelry on hand will help you photograph your items more easily. You'll also find boxes of different shapes and sizes appropriate to hold both costume jewelry and fine jewelry pieces. These are *not* shipping boxes, but rather smaller boxes (often used by jewelers) that will allow you to further protect jewelry and present it nicely within your shipping box.

- Fetpak, Inc. (http://www.fetpak.com)
- Jewelry Display, Inc. (http://www.jewelrydisplay.com/)
- NileCorp.com (http://www.nilecorp.com)

Identifying Materials

When you're doing research to write your eBay item descriptions, it's best to be specific about the materials used in construction. There are a number of tests you can employ to tell, for instance, bone from ivory. Being able to distinguish Bakelite used in jewelry, flatware handles, and radio cases from other types of plastic is also useful. Here are a couple of resources to help you with these tasks:

- "What's It Made Of?" booklet (Order via e-mail at SGShatz@aol.com)
- Bakelite testing squares (http://www.vintagejewelryartsandantiques.com)

Shipping Materials

Although you can often find clean shipping materials to recycle with a little help from your friends and business associates (and that's the best way to go in terms of economy and the environment), there may come a time when you need to purchase packing materials. These are available at your local office-supply store, but ordering in bulk can save you money in the long run. Check eBay first, and then compare what you find there to these resources:

- Brasspack Packing Supply (http://www.brasspack.com/)
- Gator Pack Shipping Supplies (http://www.gatorpack.com/)
- Uline.com (http://www.uline.com)

Magnifiers

Whether you're a casual buyer or a serious seller, chances are you'll run across something you need to examine in closer detail sooner or later. For example, you may require magnification to read poorly stamped marks on pottery and porcelain, not to mention tiny jewelry marks. Likewise, more closely examining what you believe to be damage to a piece may reveal a factory flaw rather than a true condition issue. If you don't have a good magnifying glass and/or jeweler's loop, consider ordering one through these resources:

- Magnify Store and More (http://www.ppgift.com)
- NileCorp.com (http://www.nilecorp.com)

Black Lights

Black-light testing can provide valuable information that you can incorporate into your item listings. Because the glue used to repair ceramic items will fluoresce under ultraviolet light, examining a piece in this way can help you detect the presence or absence of repairs. Green Depression glass and Vaseline glass will also glow under a black light due to the uranium content in the pieces, helping you to distinguish reproductions from originals. The first entry in the following list also offers a great book that covers other aspects of black-light testing that's worth looking into:

- *Antique & Collectors Reproduction News* (http://www.repronews.com/blacklight.html)
- The Black Light Shop (http://www.blacklightshop.com)
- Photon Micro Lights (http://www.photonmicro.com/Qstore)

Booksellers

Having a few good general reference guides on antiques and collectibles in your reference library is a must, but you'll also want to invest in a number of books on your collecting and selling specialties. Barnes & Noble and Amazon.com offer all types of books, including titles that will help you as an eBay antiquer. But for a broader selection of books on these topics through a number of different publishers, checking out L-W Book Sales will serve you well. They also offer a quantity discount if you buy six or more titles in one order. Collector Books, Schiffer Books, and Krause Publications are direct publishers of titles on antiques and collecting topics. Both Collector Books and Schiffer also offer quantity discounts. Visit these booksellers online at

- L-W Book Sales (http://www.lwbooks.com)
- Collector Books (http://www.collectorbooks.com)
- Schiffer Books (http://www.schifferbooks.com)
- Krause Publications (http://www.krause.com)
- Barnes & Noble (http://www.bn.com)
- Amazon.com (http://www.amazon.com)

Magazines and Newsletters

Subscriptions to periodicals that specialize in antiques and collectibles enable you to learn about the items you sell and collect, keep up with reproduction news, and find out about trends that could have an impact on how you buy and sell on eBay. There are many newsletters available on specific collecting topics, usually published by collecting clubs located around the country. You can access an extensive list of collecting clubs I've compiled on my About.com site at http://www.antiques.about.com/od/clubsforcollectors/. For general publications, take a look at the following options:

- *Antique & Collectors Reproduction News* (http://www.repronews.com)
- *Antique Trader* (http://www.collect.com/interest/periodical.asp?Pub=AT)
- *Antique Week* (http://www.antiqueweek.com/subscribe.html)
- *Antiques & Collecting* (email info@acmagazine.com for subscription information)
- *Antiques & the Arts Weekly* (http://www.antiquesandthearts.com/default.asp)
- *New England Antiques Journal* (http://www.antiquesjournal.com)
- *The Magazine Antiques* (http://www.magazineantiques.com)
- *Kovels on Antiques and Collectibles* (http://www.kovels.com)

Other Helpful Web Sites

In addition to the online research resources mentioned in Chapter 2, "Research: Don't Buy or Sell Without It," you'll find many others on the Internet. Here are a few I refer to frequently for information related to information on antiques and collectibles, as well as online auctions, shopping opportunities, patents, and foreign-language translations (which you'll need from time to time as an antiquer):

- Antique Periods and Motifs (http://www.tace.com/reference/periods/index.html)

- Online Price Guides and Appraisals (http://www.antiques.about.com/od/valuingantiquesonline/)

- U.S. Patent and Trademark Office (http://164.195.100.11/netahtml/srchnum.htm)

- U.S. Design Patent Numbers (http://www.goodgator.com/glitter/designpatents.htm)

- Antique Shop Locator (http://www.curioscape.com/curioscape.mapage.cgi?action=brand&page=MallIndex.txt)

- Auction Bytes (http://www.auctionbytes.com)

- Babel Fish Translation (http://babelfish.altavista.com/)

Index

381.   Wiggins, Pamela Y.
177   Buying & Selling
WIG   Antiques and Collect-
         ibles on eBay   2004